Pearls, Arms and Hashish

New York
Coward-McCann, Inc.
1930

Printed in the United States of America

Abd el Hai navigating by sight, crossing the reefs

Contents

List of Illustrations

Foreword

Abd el Hai is great:
he has conquered all men
from the White-Man's country—
English, Italians, French,
peoples like the sea
immense and menacing;
like butter he floats
ever on the surface
of the storm-tossed water.
(Dankali song)

Djibouti in August . . . "The capital of French Somaliland," according to the guidebooks. "Coaling station for eastern- and southern-bound liners. Twelve degrees above the Equator . . . and one of the hottest spots on the globe," adds the experienced colonial.

On that particular August morning, Djibouti gave every sign of living up to its reputation. The *Amboise*, ten days out from Marseilles, dropped anchor at dawn in the outer harbor. We had steamed down the Red Sea with the wind behind us—a constant fiery blast pelting us with sand and showers of locusts, piling up long, even swells that drove us forward in the airless heat, plunging with the dizzy regularity of a seesaw.

Djibouti came as a relief. For the majority of the passengers, government employees en route to Indo-China and the usual sprinkling of missionaries, it promised the air currents of the Indian Ocean, welcome in spite of the tricky monsoon. To the rest of us, it meant the high plateau of Abyssinia and a European climate, a day's journey inland.

The abrupt silence of the engines, and the grinding clank of anchor chains, stirred even the limpest of the pajama-clad from their deck chairs. Damp and hollow-eyed, they hung above the rail, watching the land stream out to them in a bobbing procession propelled by steam, and motor, and paddle. Tugs towing coal barges, launches flying pennants of the *Messageries*, the Customs, and the Quarantine, manned by turbaned Somalis and bearing white-clad, helmeted Frenchmen. Rowboats, dugouts, and last of all a splashing school of swimmers, brown and black, as born to the water as a band of dolphins.

A scuffle on the swinging ladder. Confused cries and splashes. A voice shouting orders in a strange tongue. My neighbor at the rail, an officer of the French Colonial, translated. "No one allowed on board who hasn't a vaccination scar!" A chorus of protesting voices like an echo of the hubbub between decks rose in the passage behind us. Passengers besieged the maître d'hôtel, mustached and affable.

"I am sorry, sorry," he repeated amiably. "Quarantine allows nobody ashore but Djibouti passengers."

"You are going to keep us here all day in the heat and coal-dust?" panted a young Frenchwoman, impeccably rouged in spite of the early hour. "*Monsieur le maître d'hôtel*, you are not *gentil!*"

"*Tais-toi*, Amélie," her husband broke in shortly. "Do you want to catch the smallpox?"

"Smallpox, *O Seigneur!*" the young Frenchwoman lifted terrified plump hands to her powdered cheeks and collapsed heavily in her deck chair.

"When she has lived in the colonies, she will not be so

impressionable," my neighbor commented grimly. "Small-pox, and typhus, and cholera and the plague . . . you live next door to them most of the time. One of them may get you in the end; but chances are they won't." He shrugged his shoulders philosophically. "Quarantine is a necessity no doubt; but just the same, I would be glad for a cool drink on shore!"

The sun shot over the horizon like a pale balloon. A fan-shaped coating of molten brass spread over the surface of the harbor. Above the distant cubes and arches of the town, heat waves quivered, transparent and liquid. The *Amboise*, all portholes shut, rolled gently on its anchor chains, while on either flank a busy army of black men poured coal into the bunkers to the rhythm of an interminable chant. From the barges a column of dust rose like smoke to the promenade deck where it spread and settled in a gritty crust on all things horizontal—planks, rails, deck chairs, sun helmets, pajamas—while the thermometer climbed: 99, 100, 101. . . .

Limp along the rail, the passengers for Saïgon, Hanoi, and Abyssinia (the latter waiting for landing papers) envied the little Somali boys, naked and dripping, who wriggled lizard-like up the ship's side, brandishing straw fans, bracelets of elephant's hair, and bottles of eau de Cologne which they hawked noisily, scattering in a scramble when the burly shape of the maître d'hôtel showed in the passage, their bare feet leaving crescents of black mud in the dust of the deck.

Propped on their elbows, the pajama-clad stared through sun spectacles at the blazing harbor, the town, the tossing barges, hoping dully for a shark, a fight, an accident—anything to help them forget for an instant the vertical sun, the coal-dust, and general boredom.

Like a great tan bird, a sailboat slid in a supple curve about the stern of the liner. On the deck of the *Amboise* the row of sun helmets rotated clockwise towards the apparition. Forty pairs of eyes registered with mild interest the taut canvas, the untidy litter amidships, the bronze bodies of the Somali crew. Then abruptly came a change. A stir of curiosity rippled along the rail. Elbows nudged.

"*Dis, donc,* look at the two at the stern!"

A white man stood at the helm of the sailboat. That is to say, no one could have mistaken him for a Somali. But whether Arab or European it would have been difficult to decide. His body, lean and muscular, bare to the waist, had the color of tobacco or old leather. Under the equatorial sun he was hatless. Feet planted firmly on the deck, he stood braced against the heavy bar—a pose that in its arc-like tensity suggested the nicely adjusted mechanism —or the animal crouched to spring.

Beside the helmsman, on the broad steering bench with its arched rail, sat a slight figure wearing loose trousers and a sleeveless shirt, and crowned by a mass of pale bobbed hair that the *Kamsin* (the desert wind) whipped and tossed.

"*Cristi,* it's a girl!"

Along the rail of the *Amboise,* the passengers jostled for a better view. A sun helmet dropped spinning into space, and was rescued in passing by a steward on the deck below. From the bridge of the liner a gold-braided sleeve waved a greeting, while far below the Somalis on the coal barges ceased for a moment their ant-like labors, hailing the bark in a long cry:

"Abd el Hai! . . . O-o-o-o Abd el Hai!"

At the shout, the helmsman turned. We caught a rapid glimpse of lean, bronzed features barred by the darker

line of a crisp mustache. He lifted a hand to his forehead
in brief acknowledgment of the greetings. (It was not evident whether this was directed towards the gesticulating
figures on the barges or the officer on the bridge.) The
young girl at his elbow flashed a smile through her blowing
hair and the boat swept on towards the distant wharf.

Leaving the rail, my fellow-passengers pressed the
maître d'hôtel with questions. For once that gentleman's
store of knowledge was inadequate. He could tell them
nothing. Their curiosity was destined to remain unsatis-
fied: the bridge being too exalted and the coal barges too
lowly for contact.

To me, chance brought greater luck.

After the sweltering harbor, the town. Djibouti by
night, with the thermometer perched inert somewhere at
the top of the nineties. The glare of a dozen electric lamps
flooded the hotel terrace whose predominating white—the
plaster wall, the tables, the frosted glasses, the linen
clothes of the Europeans—tantalized with the illusion of
coolness. Beyond the border of mimosas, drooping and
gray, bare feet padded past in the dust, and mangy dogs,
close cousins of the jackal, prowled and snarled.

On the terrace, nothing stirred but the Somali boys
carrying trays with bottles and ice pails, and two tame
gazelles with ears and tails twitching who pattered deli-
cately over the cement. A group of men sat about a phonograph heavily digesting the *Clair de Lune* from *Werther*,
Mistinguett's latest, and the visceral melancholy of American jazz. Others were deep in the columns of the *Petit
Marseillais*, ten days old, brought that morning by the
Amboise. A forlorn couple, government employees shunted
from Indo-China to Madagascar, merely sat, heavy-eyed

and speechless, while their baby slept in a go-cart, like a dislocated doll of yellow wax.

Not a sound but the grinding metallic voice of the machine. One had the feeling that a spell lay on the terrace and its white-clad mannequins: the prank of some malicious heat-god, or the revenge of a local jinn, forgotten or ignored. As on the morning of that day, a single event sufficed to break the charm, to send a current vibrating over dead wires, setting the inert figures in motion.

Beyond the mimosas, the lights of an automobile swept the square. With a rush of tires and the flutter of a dying motor, the car drew up beside the terrace. A man in white, brown-skinned and slight, a Basque cap pushed back on his dark hair, sat at the wheel; a blond young girl beside him. This I saw in the flash before a group of dark shapes, sprung apparently from nowhere, closed in about the car. The phonograph ended its musical chatter in a squawk. The cloud of lethargy was lifting; the terrace listened. A chorus of light voices filled the silence, broken by a deeper one speaking rapid words in Arab. The group by the curb parted; the man in the Basque cap stepped out from the knot of Somalis, and strode across the terrace with a light step. A handshake with the hotel keeper, a nod towards the group about the phonograph, and he disappeared beneath an archway. The slight stoop of the shoulders, the vigorous gesture would have sufficed. . . . But already I had recognized the helmsman of the morning.

"That"—at my question, the hotel proprietor settled himself conversationally in the chair beside me,—"that is the most remarkable figure from Suez to Bombay."

He had no opportunity to add more. The clock-work

dolls whom the stranger's passing had set nodding and gesturing, had found their voices.

"From all appearances, the great Abd el Hai keeps to himself as much as ever," remarked a long-nosed man by the wall, folding his newspaper in a neat rectangle.

"Possibly he finds the climate of Djibouti . . . a little too hot. . . ." That, with pompous satisfaction, from an official-looking personage at the next table.

"That last attempt of yours to . . . catch him in the act—not too successful from all I hear," a third speaker put in.

The stout official flushed. "How was I to know he had a band of government geologists on board that boutre of his?" he blustered. "You can be sure they were a blind. Chances are he landed a cargo of arms under the very noses of his scientists! But we watch him now. . . ."

"A little late in the day, don't you think?" a voice— the same one that had provoked the official gentleman's explosion—observed. "Along the docks they say Abd el Hai has given up smuggling for good."

"A new trick of his," snapped the official. "Rest assured, we mean to get him in the end."

"That is what your predecessors, *Monsieur le Commissaire*, have predicted for fifteen years or more," the same cool voice insisted. "And until now, no one . . ."

"The miracle to me . . ." Another *Petit Marseillais* was laid aside as a new speaker joined in the conversation. "I say, I never have understood why the English didn't finish him off properly when they had him in their hands. They're not ordinarily squeamish in matters of that sort."

The group about the phonograph drew closer.

"My dear Garnier, the English like him," drawled an

immaculate person with a pale mustache who might have passed for an Englishman himself. "Quite aside from their official attitude of course. You see he is what they call a good sport and a gentleman besides. . . ."

"You know the story of how he saved his life by playing the piano on a British gunboat," some one recalled.

"They say a lot of things. Personally I never saw a piano on any gunboat," the man by the wall contributed.

The official at the next table snorted his indignation. "I would be merciless if I could catch him red-handed."

"But my dear fellow, you never will. That is the poetry of the situation. When you think that for eighteen years our countryman, Abd el Hai, has cruised up and down the Red Sea, carrying arms, and drugs, and God knows what else besides . . ."

"Slaves," the stout official supplemented.

"Is . . . is it true that every time he met a coast-guard, he threw all the slaves overboard?" A timid young man at a table by the mimosas spoke for the first time.

"Worse than that," he was told gravely. I identified the speaker, the same one who had already taken pleasure in baiting the official. "Haven't you heard that when a British gunboat followed him, he kept them off all day by tossing overboard a slave in a barrel every time they came too near. The tender-hearted English stopped every time to rescue the drowning Soudanese, and that is how he got away."

"Horrible!"

"They believe all this," murmured the hotel proprietor in my ear. The tone quite as much as the words gave me to understand that the mysterious Abd el Hai counted one partisan. The gossip of the terrace rose and fell.

"That affair of the two British sailors . . . it might have cost him dear."

"What affair was that?"

"One of the stories they tell along the coast. A sambuk loaded with hides, running the British blockade of Arabia back in '15 or '16. A gunboat captured it off the Farsan Islands, but the sea was running too high to take it in tow. The English put two marines on board their capture and steamed off with the sambuk following behind. At dusk when they were skirting a coast reef, the Arabs flung themselves on the two sailors, disarmed them, and threw them down a hatch. The sambuk shot through a passage in the reef and away through shallow water to the Arab coast. The British had to pay two thousand pounds ransom. . . ."

"But where does Abd el Hai come in?"

"He was the instigator of the trick. Certainly, left to themselves, no Arab would have dared. . . . But no one could get an Arab to swear that Abd el Hai was aboard the sambuk."

"It has been my experience," the stout official remarked pompously, "that you can always find a native to swear to anything!" He checked his speech abruptly as if he had said too much, or perhaps not precisely what he meant to say. Or it may be that I misunderstood. . . .

"Not to swearing against Abd el Hai. The natives think he has supernatural powers. One of your predecessors, *Monsieur le Chef de Service*, tried shutting up a black of Abd el Hai's, cutting down rations and water for a month or so. The beggar slept twenty-four hours in the day. When they woke him up, all he would say was: 'Dig a hole and when I am dead put me in it.' "

"Sounds like Abdi, that black mate of his," the long-

nosed man by the wall contributed. "He has shipped with
our smuggler friend for fifteen years. I had him up before
me once myself. He had the impudence to shake a finger
in my face and warn me against touching that precious
master of his. 'He will come out on top and you will be the
one to pay,' he kept saying."

"Well, wasn't he right?"

"We held him in jail, at any rate, until the case collapsed. It is astonishing the way they always do. As if the
entire population was in league. . . ."

"My dear fellow," the long bland pseudo-Englishman
leaned forward impressively. "You forget that the smuggler is always a popular character. Nobody loves the
gendarme. It is only human. Remember *Guignol.*"

Some one in my immediate neighborhood whistled softly.
The timid young man gave an audible sigh, flushed beet
red, and spoke with no apparent apropos:

"And his daughter seems such a nice girl!"

Following his gaze, I discovered that "the nice girl" sat
at the far end of the terrace, a fair-haired child of sixteen, perhaps, in a white organdy dress—a young girl
such as you might meet at the house of a friend in France
or England. She conversed in low tones with a black
woman in Arab costume, who leaned forward, bracelets
glinting on her bare arms, holding one of the white girl's
hands affectionately in hers.

"Nigger-crazy," a superior voice sneered.

Almost without transition, the conversation veered off
on a new topic, inexhaustible, which I had already heard
discussed from the deck chairs of the *Amboise,* the colonial
and the native. In substance and in point of view it never
varied, whether the speakers evoked Indo-China, Mada-

gascar, Algeria, or Senegal. The mysterious Abd el Hai was forgotten.

The metallic voice of the phonograph, again audible, held a hypnotized handful of listeners; but the others, singly and in groups, clapping on their helmets by force of habit, filtered away beneath the moon that hung above the square like a great arc light.

"And now, I wish you would tell me," I addressed the hotel keeper who was adding up columns of figures in a notebook, "*who* is Abd el Hai?"

He laid down his fountain pen. "You have heard what they said," he began; "some of it true, a lot just legend. The Europeans are as bad as the natives. And the Somalis, the Issas and the Danakils, all have their legends about Abd el Hai. They will tell you how, single-handed, he put to flight a whole regiment of Italian askari; how he saved a fleet of Arab boutres from the English guns. They say he can stop a bullet with a look; that even the sea creatures obey him; that once, when he ran his boat on a reef in a storm, the porpoises gathered up every plank, every rope and spar, even the anchor, and carried them all to the beach before his door!"

"Who *is* Abd el Hai?" I persisted.

"A good many people have asked that question," he remarked, stopping to light a cigarette. "You have guessed, I imagine, that Abd el Hai is not the name I knew him by first. He was Henri de Monfreid before he became a Moslem and the natives began calling him Abd el Hai. Scarcely a conversion that. More a matter of expediency. It helped him with the black men. They do despise a Christian. You have no idea. . . . Though his influence goes deeper than that. You see what the natives respect—and with the Somali or the Arab it is quite the same—is not money nor brute force. Naturally he accepts the money, and since he is no fool, he shows proper respect for men-of-war and machine guns. But in his heart he despises us just the same.

"Take the English," he went on, lowering his tone a fraction as his gaze strayed towards the solitary drinker. "They have tried to get the Arabs with gold and machine guns. There are times when they seem to have succeeded; but nothing lasts. It is all unstable. They have to keep both elements working all the time—the money and the rest. And invent all kinds of tactics. I have heard of a fellow over in Yemen who spends his time fomenting revolts, so that he can go in with airplanes and bombs and put them down.

"But that is politics. I don't think Abd el Hai has mixed greatly in politics. He is too much of an individualist; and if he has, I doubt whether he has met with much encouragement. Not from his own government, certainly. Between you and me, the French are pretty pusillanimous in this quarter of the world. They let the English keep the upper hand. . . . Though once you get away from the coast, the native does pretty much what he pleases.

"Boy! A *citron pressé* for Madame! Let me see, where was I? Oh, yes, the native. What he respects, then, is not the gun nor the money bag. His admiration goes to the man who is not afraid to stake his life on a gamble. That is the secret of Abd el Hai. . . ."

At dawn the next morning, the bi-weekly train of the Franco-Ethiopian railway carried me westward to the Abyssinian plateau. Djibouti and Abd el Hai were alike forgotten. . . . That episode was no more than a fragment—a bit of mosaic I never hoped to see completed.

Our paths crossed again by a rare coincidence. Chance brought him a year later to a laboratory on the Seine, among the fossil bones and stones of a Paris museum. One winter afternoon, I came in and, however unexpected and incredible his presence there, I recognized him at first glance. Flanked by the stocky corpulence of the Chief, and a tall scientist in ecclesiastical black, he was seated at a table—my table—on which were heaped, in neat piles, bits of limestone and flint. His brown hands moved rapidly among the stone fragments, seizing a primitive tool of rock crystal, holding an obsidian chip to the light, and talking the while—as if quite the most natural thing in the world—the technical jargon of the prehistorian and the geologist. He looked more Arab than ever in his dark suit and formal collar, which he wore with a certain stiffness, like an officer in civilian clothes.

While I still stood rooted with surprise in the doorway, the Chief beckoned me into the circle. He spoke a name—it was not Abd el Hai; in its assonance it might have been either French or English. As an afterthought he added:

"This is almost a countryman of yours, Madame." The stranger nodded.

"My father was born in Boston."

"Boston!" Back Bay and the gossip of a hotel terrace on the Somali coast. Sea-adventure and fossil bones. The pattern of the "mosaic," I began to suspect, might prove more intricate than I had first imagined.

The days that followed gave food to the hypothesis. They furnished other fragments, revealed still different aspects of the East African navigator. I was to see him seated at the piano of an Auteuil apartment, weaving together in a sort of semi-improvisation (while I remembered the story of the hypnotized British officers!) snatches of

Bach, Beethoven, and Brahms, old patois folk songs, and measures of Plain Chant.

"The sort of thing that sticks in your head when you haven't seen a sheet of music for years," he explained. "That is my quarrel with the moderns. Their things are amusing, like cross-word puzzles, but they don't stay in a layman's memory overnight."

"Music," he told me later, "is essentially an accompaniment. I cannot conceive of it as an isolated 'performance.' The Somali associates music with every emotion, with every physical effort, however humble—hauling stones, grinding durra, lifting an anchor. It furnishes a rhythm to his interminable stories. To me, music represents a background—or a stimulant—for thought. It gives the fundamental tone. You may smile, but I have worked out many a problem, come to many a decision at the piano. On land I generally manage to have a piano," he went on. "There is a German make—excellent tone and very convenient. You can take it apart and load it on a camel."

He spoke from a rug of black and white monkey skins, on which he sat cross-legged. "The most restful posture I know of, once your legs get used to it," he explained. "Though they laugh at me on trains." His features, habitually stern, relaxed in a boyish smile. Now that I think of it, I rarely heard him laugh. Even in repose his whole figure kept its tenseness. There was nothing heavy or massive about him, not an atom of superfluous flesh; as if his body, wiry and slight, had been stripped to the essential muscles. Every gesture, every movement, bore the same alert intentness. Some one commented on him later: "Abd el Hai never *walks* towards you, *il fonce!* 'He springs.'" The man himself was a steel spring, perpetually coiled and set.

Above his head, as he sat Buddha-like on the low divan, a sketch in water colors hung against the wall, a desert landscape, sun-baked and bare, a succession of horizontal planes—sea, beach, and distant table-land. About the room hung others, more desert, rock, and sea; in the foreground, an occasional dark figure or the ragged outline of a palm. All done by the same hand, a technique vigorous and simple. Abd el Hai caught my unspoken query.

"That," he indicated the sketch above the divan, "was one day in the anchorage of Ras al Ara; and that," pointing to another, "when we were held up by bad weather at Assab. The three by the window, I painted from memory during a stay—involuntary—within four walls."

"You?"

"Why not? Painting runs in the family, you know. Though I began rather late in life and could never hope to compete with my father, who was a painter by profession. Seriously, when a man spends his life in the lonely places of the globe he cannot afford to be a 'specialist' unless he expects to starve, physically and spiritually. He learns to try his hand at all kinds of jobs for which he received no training. Generally he ends by discovering possibilities within himself he never dreamed of—if nothing more than finding how to be his own mechanic, or doctor, or cook! What drove me to paint was no particular concern with art, but more nearly an attempt to give an illusion of permanence to my own relationship with landscapes and regions that had meant much to me in the past. A relationship which, as I grew older," his face darkened, "I realized could not be prolonged indefinitely. . . . Much the same motive, I imagine, that pushes the traveler to collect photographs or souvenirs. That low rocky island, there by the door, was where I fancied I

saw the funnel of the fugitive *Caiman* and made ready for
the attack; that inlet between two cliffs was my first
anchorage when I started to try out my luck in the arms
trade; that bare strip of beach is where we landed after
the shipwreck of the *Ibn el Bahar;* and that gorge with the
incense trees is where Sheik Mâki, the slaver, made camp
with me."

Out of that row of water color sketches grew this book,
pieced together fragment by fragment, arabesque by
arabesque, until the mosaic pattern was complete. As my
host talked on, the walls of the Paris apartment receded.
I felt the hot breath of the *Kamsin* sweeping south over
the Dankali desert, saw the Gulf of Tajura glitter in the
sun, volcanic peaks and black beaches, the purple wall of
Yemen, green water breaking on hidden reefs, the flare of
midnight signals; and heard the thud of heavy cases landed
on the sand and the rubbery tread of Bedouin camels.

"You must write," I said.

"No, no. I have not yet reached the age to find consolation in memoirs. I am interested in the present . . . and
the future as well!" He drew my attention to a table littered with catalogues, blue prints of motors, and estimates.

"And if some one else held the pen?" I suggested. "If
I . . ."

"But would I not offer difficulties to a biographer since
I am not yet dead!" He looked very much alive as he sat
there, crouched on the black-and-white fur, for all his
fifty years as alert as a man in his twenties. "You would
have to be polite." His eyes twinkled. "And in a certain
measure, discreet. Not on my account; but there are other
people to consider. In short, you could tell only part of
the story—the first half."

That is how the story came to be set down. It is the narration of the "first half" of Abd el Hai's life in the East.

There was no lack of tangible documents to consult: hundreds of letters; the log-books of dozens of cruises in the Red Sea and the Indian Ocean, detailed as a traveler's notebook; sketches and photographs. But most of this story of his is just as Abd el Hai told it himself the following summer in an Abyssinian garden high-perched above the blue plain of Erer, and continued in the shade of the taut canvas as the sailboat—the same one I had first seen in the harbor of Djibouti—plunged through the long swell towards Arabia.

I have tried to write it down as he told it, changing here and there the name of a person or a locality: minor modifications, made out of consideration for others. . . . Aside from that, nothing has been changed, nothing altered. The story stands as I noted it down from the lips of this blue-eyed dark-skinned man of my own race who years ago set himself voluntarily outside frontiers, outside the law, through love of solitude and the sea, and risk—irrespective of failure or success—itself its own recompense.

PEARLS, ARMS AND
HASHISH

1

Boyhood on the Cape

The first thing I remember as a tow-headed little boy, is a window looking out on the Mediterranean and the bare flank of Cape Leucate, named by the Ionian colonists who settled centuries ago on the edge of the lagoon.

My grandfather's house turned its back on the salt marshes, the sandy vineyards, and the clustered cabins of the fishing village nestled in the shelter of the cape. It looked towards the open sea in a line of windows, one of which was mine. Of the room that lay behind the window, I have no recollection. It was as if I, too, like the old house, turned my back on the land.

I had no playmates or I have forgotten them. Even the familiar figures of the household in which I spent my first eight years have grown indistinct with time. But I recall to-day with startling precision the sound of the sea wind in the pines, the smell of the cape—its silvery tufts of thyme and lavender crushed underfoot or fragrant in the sun—and more vivid still the beach, and the excitement of each new morning when I hurried across the sand to discover what the sea had brought during the night: a wealth of shells and seaweed, bright-colored fish, and strange nameless creatures, thorny and tentacled, or boneless and opaque like mysterious sea flowers.

Like all children living by the sea, I heard tales of its malice: storm, torn nets, lost boats and men—things I failed to understand and in my secret heart refused to

3

credit. True, I remember one winter nightmare of shrieking mistral, rockets and gunshots, hurrying shapes with lanterns, and dripping strangers in the family kitchen. But in the morning—lavish compensation—the Mediterranean lay still and blue, and the beach for hundreds of yards was strewn with oranges!

To me, the friendly sea seemed far less destructive than man himself. Our neighbors with their boat-loads of gasping fish, stretching snares for the migrating birds, massacring the ducks that dotted the lagoon in November, trampling the ripe grapes with red-stained feet in the big wooden wine vats; and my own family who stood constantly in the way, uncomprehending, interfering in what concerned me intimately—my relationship to the sea. . . .

Like the Ionian rock which had given it its name, and from which—I learned as a schoolboy—criminals and political offenders had been cast into the sea, the cape of Leucate owned a legend. In the days of the Moors, three sons of the Seigneur of Leucate had leaped off the point of rock to escape death at the hands of the invaders. Fishermen still point to three boulders at the foot of the cliff to prove the story. It was difficult for me to believe that the three lads had sprung to their death in the blue water, and I preferred to imagine that the sea had borne them away to a rich and foreign destiny; that their leap had meant not suicide but an escape. I often wondered, as I lay on my face in the fragrant herbs of the cape, whether if I too leaped, strange fortune would not be mine.

My mother's family, with whom I spent the greater part of my childhood, came of peasant stock. Serious, hardworking land-folk, advocates of constant patient toil for hard-won, often insignificant rewards. Though their vineyards lay along the Mediterranean, there had never been a single seaman among them. But I have heard my mother tell how my grandfather, in Paris for his daughter's wedding, astonished the barber who shaved him, by a lurid narration of imaginary adventures as a sea-captain in distant lands. But that may have been nothing more than meridional exuberance, not the smoldering passion for the sea which I was to inherit.

My father was an aristocrat and a painter. An American by birth, but of French Protestant stock exiled three centuries before. He had lived in France since a young man, one of the little group of painters, of which Gauguin and Van Gogh formed the luminous center. A jovial, easygoing individualist, my father, with Bohemian tastes acquired when to be "Bohemian" represented not so much a pose as a profession of faith. As foreign to the practical-minded folk of my mother's family (he had fallen in love with my mother for her beauty) as a cricket among ants. For all their mutual affection, radical differences in character and outlook created grave misunderstandings between my parents, struggles that marked my boyhood with their imprint, and harassed and pursued me for years to come. Outwardly, from affection, I stood with my mother during her brief lifetime; but secretly all my instincts and preferences inclined me to take my father's part.

My father loved the sea, but as amateur, not as a navigator. He owned a white-winged yacht, a two-masted schooner which from time to time dropped anchor in the lee of the Cape. It supplied the few outstanding events of my childhood: cruises in the Mediterranean, and to North Africa and Spain. I too resolved to have one day a boat of my own and cruise in distant seas, not as passenger but captain. At fifteen, I owned my first boat, an old fishing bark abandoned on the beach for years, after the death of its proprietor. I appropriated the derelict, calked and tarred it, and fitted it with a sail. First, I tried out my prize on the lagoon. Later, I ventured into the open sea, choosing rough weather by preference to test my own skill. I sailed summers with the fishers of the Cape, proud to be treated as a member of the crew and receive my share of the catch. Glorious vacations of sun, and water, and flapping sails those were, with only one cloud in the August sky—the return to the city and to school.

At eight, I had been taken to Paris, to civilize me, as my mother said, Paris—gray, maladorous, and airless— my first great disappointment. We arrived at the capital, with me dressed in an ornate sailor suit I detested. (No seaman I had ever met wore anything that remotely resembled it!) And we came out of the station into a gloomy morning, dripping and raw. Processions of umbrellas lined the boulevard, its asphalt glistening with rain. A few street lamps still glowed yellow, though I knew that the sun must have risen hours before. Then the apartment, another disappointment, with closed windows overlooking a deary landscape of roofs and chimney-pots. I decided straightway that I loathed all cities.

At school, the young Parisians made fun of my southern accent; and because I was timid nicknamed me straightway the "Savage." To avoid becoming a victim and a martyr, I had to adopt the pattern of my fellows, appear to like what they liked and hide my own preferences. I succeeded in maintaining a façade. But as I grew older I learned to distinguish two separate and distinct worlds: school and the city, the drab promiscuity of bodies and ideas made up the one—a world esteemed by my mother, my uncles, and my grandfather. The other, a free, lonely existence of sun and sea, belonged to my father and to me.

Of the two, the former only had intrinsic value in the eyes
of most people. "Art," sneered the uncles. "Egotism,"
Grandfather supplemented; his tone implying that the two
were synonymous. My mother shook her head sadly and
remained silent.

Notwithstanding my mother's admiration for her brilliant, irresponsible mate (I am sure she admired him up
to the very end), it was not he whom she held up to me as
model, but Uncle Emile—Uncle Emile, the notary from
Toulouse, always dressed in black, and carrying with him
an oppressive atmosphere of sepulchral elegance. I had
no love for Uncle Emile though I too was impressed by the
weight of his watch-chain and the amount of consideration
he aroused in others.

Aside from my father, the one man who stirred my admiration was a vagabond who came to my grandfather's
door one July night to ask for food and shelter in exchange for work. As the man of the house was absent, my
mother and grandmother admitted the stranger grudg-
ingly, trembling for the family silver, but fearful to refuse
lest he set fire to the straw-stacks and outbuildings. Such
things had been known. . . . That night, while the two
women barricaded themselves in their rooms behind barred
shutters, I slipped out through the window, to keep the
intruder company in the tool-shed.

He told me little of himself beyond the fact that he was
a florist by trade. A florist! The word alone aroused pic-
tures of exotic luxury in a district where no one thought
of cultivating flowers, since they had no market value. . . .
Something the matter with his lungs had brought him
south, covering the distance from Paris on foot. He remained with us only a day, for he decided, incontinently,
to settle on the Cape. He asked help of no one, and built

himself a cabin of stones and driftwood on the edge of the beach, where he lived alone, fishing in the lagoon and selling his catch for bread. And—amazing thing—he created a garden: roses, chrysanthemums, and carnations. In time, jasmine and *vigne vierge* covered the cabin.

My grandfather and several of the wealthier neighbors, inspired by his example, tried to get the man to plant gardens for them in the sandy soil among the pines. Stubbornly he refused. He told them he earned enough for his own needs by selling fish and he preferred to work for no one. He did not even sell his flowers, though he gave them away generously to the housewives of the village. The Cape grew to accept the newcomer with good-humored tolerance, while deploring his "lack of ambition." "Once a tramp, always a tramp," my grandmother liked to remark with acid emphasis when any one spoke of the stranger. What she and the other thrifty folk failed to grasp, I comprehended perfectly: the man was happy; living life as he understood it, asking no more than to be left in peace between his flowers and the sea. Secretly I promised myself some day I would follow his example. But not on land. . . .

Meanwhile the family began laying plans for my future. To those relatives of mine, my passion for salt water was identified with the "egotism" that had made my father a painter. As I neared the age of military service, I ventured to state my solemn intention of following the sea as a career. The statement produced an explosion. Pent-up resentment, unknown to me, had been accumulating for years. I was no match for such combined opposition, and my mother's tears carried the day. I promised to remain on land.

I set my teeth doggedly, determined to show the world —their world—that the "artist's son" as Uncle Emile scornfully termed me, could be as solid a bourgeois as the rest of them. I threw myself into my studies, docile enough in appearance, but resolved that once I had demonstrated my capacity, and was as rich and respectable as Uncle Emile, I would do as I pleased.

When I had finished with the middle-class education which fitted me for nothing, I started out to earn my living. To my mother's disappointment, I resolutely refused to become a lawyer or a notary. An office-prison was unendurable. I announced that I was going to take up business.

"Business." I smile now. I became a coffee salesman for a firm that to-day still owns a network of branches covering the whole French countryside. Not a village but receives the visit several times a month of a man with a pushcart, or walking beside a dog or a donkey that draws a box on wheels. His coming is heralded afar by the sharp toot of a horn.

"Coffee, Madam, sugar, or spices? Or a box of *petits fours?*"

I had neither donkey nor cart, for my "district" was limited to several wards in the north of Paris. I merely collected orders. Daily I climbed hundreds of back stairs, rang hundreds of bells. I learned to overcome my panic of timidity before closed doors, and to assume the "salesman's face"—beaming and affable, whatever the reception. I stuck grimly to the task. It took three years to convince me that fortune, immediate or eventual, did not lie in that direction. In fact, all my earnings barely sufficed to provide food and shelter, and to keep me in shoe leather.

My next business venture carried me a step higher on the ladder. The milk trust engaged my services as "laboratory expert." My task consisted of buying up dairies and opening new milk stations. That experience furnished me with a modest bank account, the conviction that there was money in the milk business, and a deep-seated dislike of working for a salary while the profits went to others.

After five years of the milk trust, I decided to go into dairying on my own. Cows . . . can any type of slavery be worse than that exacted by the milk-giving bovine? Even now, the mere sight of a cow gives me a shiver. I was the complete dairyman—stable boy, milker, bottler, and deliveryman; for I could ill afford to hire many helpers, given the loans and mortgages that had made the *"Vert Clos"* dairy possible. Stalls to clean, bottles to wash; milk, strain, skim, fill . . . harness the horses and start out at four in the morning on a route that kept me going until long past noon. And at three in the afternoon, begin all over again! I finished by detesting the placid beasts, but the tyrannic udders furnished me little leisure even for lamenting. I trudged through the daily round like a slave in the treadmill.

Then Fate took a hand. The blessed cows, or the goats (for I had imported a herd from the Pyrenees) gave me the Maltese fever. Eight months of semioblivion—delirium, recovery, and relapse. When I began to totter about again, debts and interest had eaten up cows and dairy. Nothing remained. I was ruined financially, but the fever had set me free.

The fever did me another good turn. During convalescence, I rediscovered my father. For years we had lived, not estranged precisely, but separated by barriers that no longer had any reason for existing. . . . Now we spent weeks together; a lazy, happy time among the red rocks and cork forests of the Eastern Pyrenees where the cone of the Canigou looks down on the distant Mediterranean. It was good to be irresponsible again, to think momentarily of other things than cows and coffee, to wander purposeless as a boy through the rich vineyards and olive groves; to spend hours at the piano and fill notebooks with timid sketches.

There was even time for an idyll. In the village five miles down the slope, I made the acquaintance of a farmer's daughter, a black-eyed, black-haired witch of a girl whose Spanish blood gave her uncommon spice and color even in a region where handsome women are the rule. My daily walks became less purposeless. My attentions were gracefully accepted; indeed, the entire family adopted me with alacrity. Evenings I had my chair in the circle round the fire, while the old grandmother told hair-raising tales of witchcraft, and the whole circle sang songs of the countryside: the "*Pardal*" that dates from the Crusades, or the "*Dama de Paris*" whose blond tresses were tied with ribbons of nine different colors. . . . Sundays, with the young folk of the village, we danced the *Cerdane* beneath the plane trees of the square to the music of a "*cobla*."

My father puckered his fine brows and sounded a friendly note of warning on the subject of mismatches. But I shook off his advice. I had done with considerations of that order which recalled all too unpleasantly the counsels of Uncle Emile! Then, suddenly without warning, I found myself the center of a typical peasant drama. I discovered that my black-eyed sweetheart already had a lover, an accredited fiancé; and that together they had counted on my credulity to supply a comfortable *dot* to the prospective bride.

Sorry ending to a country idyll! In the humiliation of that discovery, the last shreds of my tardy adolescence fell from me. I realized that I was nearing my thirties and that the period of convalescence was over. Materially speaking, I had little to show for the eight years' effort in the world in which I had promised myself to succeed so brilliantly. Failure everywhere. Not even a sentimental success to my credit. I would have to begin all over again.

But not in France. That I decided, filling my lungs with the fresh mountain air as I looked down the long slope of vineyards to the distant blue line of the Mediterranean. The drab city would see no more of me; the time had come for the leap towards the unknown. "Not a suicide but an escape. . . ."

Through a friend I got promise of employment in a French trading firm established for many years in Abyssinia. In July, 1910, I engaged passage on a liner leaving Marseilles for Djibouti.

A deck passage . . . East.

II

Rain

When it rains in the tropics, there is nothing much you can do except sit down and accept it. That is if you are lucky enough to find any shelter. There is precious little chance for philosophizing if you are caught between the walls of a cañon, following the bed of one of the dried-up streams that wriggle down from the Tcher Tcher mountains to the Abyssinian plateau and the desert. In dry weather, travel is bad over one of these primitive trails among the heaped boulders and water-worn stones. But when it rains—for all the world as if the bottom had fallen out of a lake suspended somewhere overhead—you know you are caught without any providential ark.

Gasping, pelted, half-drowned in the black downpour, you splash down a stream that in fifteen minutes has swollen to a torrent. By the half hour it will swirl nine feet deep between the rock walls, sweeping all before it: you and your caravan along with tree-trunks and stones, unless wit or luck show you a way out of the watery trap. The pack animals know the danger. Mules buck and scramble. Camels snort and groan, swaying and stumbling beneath their loads. In the blackness of the cañon bottom, the train stampedes—a panic of frantic beasts and shouting men. A mule slips; is borne away struggling in the current. To-morrow you may find it far below; though of his pack no trace. Lost or looted. Given a storm, and all that the storm can cover, chances are that few of the bales

13

of hides and coffee will ever reach the coast. And what
finally gets there will be practically worthless from the
soaking.

That, I reflected, was what was happening to my pack
train, as I sat in the doorway of a hut on the Tcher Tcher
mountainside one October afternoon watching the blue-
black sheet of rain that darkened and shut off the world
outside. Flashes and zigzags of lightning gave it brief
instants of transparency, revealing pale green patches of
coffee and *kat* and a tossing confusion of banana leaves,
far below on the valley floor. A thick smell of soaked earth
and sodden green things crept fog-like up the slope, min-
gling with the smells of the hut, magnified in the dampness:
the tang of burning cow dung, of rancid butter, and sour
milk; the stale odor of hides on the earthen floor. Behind
me in the darkness of the hut came the faint flat tinkle of
anklets, barely audible in the hiss of the downpour: the
Somali girl, moving about the fire.

If I had gone with the pack train. . . . The thought tormented me. Something, perhaps all, might have been saved.
A desperate struggle in water and darkness—with nine
chances to lose out, but always one to win. Those Somali
boys! What were my precious bales to them? Not values
to risk a life for, though their capacity for faithfulness
and devotion—profound primitive virtues—is always far
above that of the white. Ask a white man to carry a letter
to its destination, even to the nearest letter box. He will
lose or forget it, and justify the oversight with the reflec-
tion that after all this was not his business; if important,
you should have attended to it yourself. But the black man
you meet in the desert—"Will you carry a message to
X?" (It may be distant a day's journey, or two, or a
dozen.) If he accepts the errand, he will go through fire

and thirst, rain and darkness, and deliver the massage.
That you can count on. Property is another matter. It is
less sacred than the word, spoken or written; infinitely
less important. To-morrow, if the slippery ledge where
you cling shivering through the night has not let you drop
spinning into the torrent, you will still be yourself, richer
or poorer. *Inchallah.* . . .

In the shadow of the hut, the Somali girl, oblivious of
the lashing fury of the storm, was preparing our evening
meal. One must eat . . . though a thousand plans had gone
crashing to destruction and all my Maria Theresa dollars
—two years' patient combing of the Ethiopian brush—
swept jingling down to the sea. The black girl crouched
by the fire, the curved *gembia* with its razor blade up-
wards, gripped firmly between her two feet. Holding the
strips of raw mutton stretched taut between both fists,
she severed them on the blade, tossing the meat into the
boiling kettle. The firelight glinted on her arms and breast
that had the patina of old bronze. Her only garment, a
few yards of striped cotton, strained tight about her hips.
Through the cool mountain night it served her as a cover-
let, while I shivered beneath two blankets.

Out of doors the rain stopped—suddenly, as if the
celestial lake had emptied to the last drop. And as suddenly, all the familiar sounds that the rain had muted
burst forth again, explosive in their abrupt release: green
things stirring; insects; bird calls; cedars rustling, shak-
ing off raindrops, and blurred far-away voices. I had seen
other storms on the mountains; in the years to come I was
to live through many another, sheltered and in the open,
but none has stayed in my memory as vividly as that
October rain on the Tcher Tcher. Even to-day I have
only to close my eyes to see again the valley with its green

plantations, the peaked thatch of the clustered huts on the hillside, the swaying cedars overhead, and smell the damp fragrance of rain-beaten plants and the acrid odor of burning dung. Not that the fact of material disaster marked that far-away evening with particular stamp; I have known other defeats beside which the loss of that one caravan is as nothing. But, though I was far from realizing it at the time, the October downpour swept away far more than a few pack animals and the bales that represented my entire fortune—a few thousand Maria Theresa dollars. As I look back on it now, that blue sheet of tropical rain dropped an opaque curtain on the first act of a not very eventual nor successful life. It represented a break far more complete than the one I had imagined two years earlier when I watched the silhouette of Notre Dame de la Garde and the lights of the Joliette drop into the horizon from the deck of an eastern-bound liner.

As I said, I was unconscious of any portentous cleavage of my destiny as I sat in the doorway of the mountain hut and watched the tropical dusk tumble into the valley. To be sure I meditated gloomily, adding up my losses and reflecting with considerable weariness that now I would have to begin all over again. It may have been legitimate discouragement, or perhaps merely a touch of tropical spleen—that nagging depression of hot lands that suddenly, for no appreciable reason, envelops you like a cloud, distorts and discolors everything in your range of vision, gives gigantic proportions to details, and halts you on the threshold of every task with the disheartening objection: What's the use anyhow? I found myself asking with considerable dejection: why make a new effort? Strain and plan and combine, to what end? To form other pack trains? I had already lost two that season. What guarantee did I have that a third or a fourth might not meet the same fate? And if I succeeded—made tons of money like Grandjean of Djibouti, or the Mercati brothers at Massawa? What was a successful trader—a petty storekeeper, no better. I might as well have still been selling coffee for the Planteur de Caïffa, or peddling milk up a hundred Paris back stairs!

Was it for that I had come to Africa? Here I was after two years in the desert and the bush, tied to my account books and inventories, fretting with debits and credits, losses and gains, like any grocer or dry goods' merchant on the public square. Adventure? Precious little of it. Thirst in the desert; a touch of fever during the season of rains; mild skirmishes with pilfering black men. But most of the time, in a sweltering *comptoir* at Djibouti, a baked mud house in Harrar; a hut on the mountainside, juggling with columns of figures, selling, buying, exchanging, loading pack mules for Diré Daoua and the coast for the problematic profit of some one—rarely for my own. The whole race of traders, we were like some noxious breed of insects burrowing in the rich African soil. Like beetles on a dungheap. That was what Africa meant to us—desert and plateau and mountain—a marvelous dungheap to plunder and abandon. . . .

I, like the rest, had thought that some day, inevitably, I would return to Europe. All this burrowing and gorging was a means to that end: to finish my days in a white villa among dusty vineyards where the Pyrenees dip—a jagged wall of granite—into the Mediterranean. Now I found myself putting the question for the first time: was that, only that, all I wanted? Years of patient ant-like labor, bloating myself with plunder to insure a future of comfortable mediocrity . . . like Uncle Emile or any small town *rentier*.

Ever since my arrival in Africa I had viewed with derision the pitiful attempts of my countrymen, of all Europeans, to transport Europe, even fragments of it, into the African bush. Teas and *apéritifs*, stifling salons and stuffy intrigues; sweltering "correctness" of dress in a land of loin cloths; and that super-abomination, the sun helmet. . . . The vanity of applying a millimeter rule when the scale is reckoned in miles. . . . In the eyes of my helmeted, white-clad compatriots and their bloodless, heat-worn wives, I had "gone native"—unspeakable degradation. That is to say, I had substituted the loose and convenient Arab dress (and occasionally the lack of it!)—for the "superior" trouser and coat; the turban for the helmet. I slept on native mats instead of a camp bed; and when I started on an expedition, I took care not to encumber myself with tents, kitchen utensils, canned goods, and filters. And—unpardonable offense—I had limited my social contacts to Somalis and Gallas, and the taciturn affection of a black woman who took charge of my primitive household and nursed me devotedly through attacks of fever. There had been no conscious effort on my part to penetrate or assimilate the customs of a land so foreign to my own; but instinctively I found myself drawn by the life of my native companions—its reality and sincerity— far more than the transplanted sophistication of the little circle of Europeans. But at heart, our aims were identical. . . .

So I mused pessimistically from the doorway of the mountain hut that distant October evening. We had eaten our evening meal of boiled mutton and *durra*. Fatouma, the Somali girl, left her vigil by the hearthstone, and came

Gallas and Issas and Somali on the Franco-Ethiopian Railway

to squat beside me on the threshold—a silent figure of bronze.

We sat there a long time without speaking. Blue night settled down on the mountainside. Across the valley the row of peaks showed a silver outline. The moon was rising. My companion touched my arm.

"*Ammi*—(my master)" she said softly with a faint note of reproach. "*Urma abiad* . . . You have forgotten . . . *Urma abiad* . . . the white woman." That in part was a legend of Fatouma's creation. The hour before sunset I devoted daily to the clerking end of my "storekeeping," balance sheets and accounts, reports to middlemen and buyers, and the occasional letter to Europe. Once she found me poring over a sheet of paper, reading and re-reading. It was a letter—the sort of letter men take with them into the wilderness. I had carried it about with me until the folds had grown tattered—as one does with certain letters. That strange instinct of women that scents the presence of a rival must have warned her, for she hovered about me, like a lark above the whirling mirror, fascinated by that bit of yellow paper, the written words so pale that even I, who knew them by heart, could scarcely read. At last she inquired timidly—that mysterious sheet, what was it? The first time she had put such a question, pointing to the faded handwriting, I answered with cruel abruptness that the words had been written by a woman— a white woman, whom I had left in Europe. I wanted to see what she would say. To my surprise, the words gave no apparent pain, aroused no perceptible jealousy. Only an eager almost tender interest. And my cruelty received its counterthrust, involuntary on her part.

"Why does the white woman not come?

"When she comes," she added, "she will be afraid of me

because I am black. Perhaps she will kill me like a jackal. . . . But tell her, if I am black, my heart is good. You are my master, I love all whom you love. I will sleep there on the ground and when you are away I will guard your white woman so that no one may cast her an evil look."

So for Fatouma all my papers, the bills and accounts like the rest, from that one incident acquired special meaning. They were links that joined me immutably to a fixed though distant superior essence. The White Woman . . . Europe. That October night (though at the time I was as far from realizing it as the Somali girl crouching in the darkness beside me) the bond had grown so loose, it needed a single gesture to set me free. Left to myself, the liberating gesture might never have been made. The clutch of a past, however oscillating and insecure, becomes a tyrannic thing to men scattered like atoms on an immense dark continent. . . . Material failure alone rarely suffices; the carapace may crack, but it takes a broader phenomenon, a more complete disaster, to wrench off the protecting shell, releasing a creature soft-bodied and unresisting to be whirled towards a new destiny, as down a tropical torrent born of an autumn rain.

For all my dejection, that October evening in my hut on the Tcher Tcher mountainside, I felt no distinct intimation of an approaching crisis. Certainly I had no inkling that it was already installed at my hearth. Fate in the person of that silent figure at my side whose dog-like affection I had purchased and accepted, without question, almost without return, for months on end? I would have smiled to myself in the darkness, with a white man's irony at the thought. And yet that casual relationship was to become momentarily an element of tragic potency. Disaster—material and sentimental; how many men have resisted, unshaken, the double onslaught?

That night I recall even now with the distinctness of a dream from which one has just awakened. We sat for a long time on the threshold of the hut looking down on a landscape fixed in an icy rigidity of moonlight. Across the valley the peaks lifted vast silver shadows curiously transparent. From the scattered villages, unseen, drowned in the blue, drifted up the sounds of voices: children singing —melancholy cadences repeated in beating, endless rhythm. I ceased to think of the storm, the lost caravan, the Maria Theresa dollars . . . or of Europe, the White Woman, tyrannic and tender. I sat wrapped in the enchantment of the African night—numbed with ineffable weariness; a torpor that perhaps was peace.

III

Mektoub

By instinct I am no hunter. As a boy when I followed my father's pointers over the August stubble, I used to justify it with an illusion of necessity, taking delight in the fiction that the occasional partridge was to save us from famine. The thought of the plucked bird twirling on twisted strings before the campfire gave me an inner satisfaction far superior to the temporary thrill of bringing it down by a skillful shot.

In Africa my reaction was the same. In a reputed hunter's paradise I had done little shooting beyond what was required by the needs of my table. I conceived little joy in going out even for big game with a high-powered rifle. I would have preferred more primitive methods. The old native fashion of elephant killing, for instance. A solitary hunter, naked, his body greased with butter, his only arm the same blade that served Fatouma by the hearthstone. He stationed himself in the path of the great beast, wary and alert lest he be trampled underfoot. If the elephant's trunk seized him, he trusted to the oiled surface of his skin to wriggle free again. His play was to attack by surprise, swing the heavy knife with such force that it severed the trunk. His own life, he realized, was the price of that first stroke. If he succeeded, the elephant insane with pain, reared on its hind legs, its body flung backwards as if recoiling from a blow. With lightning swiftness the terrible blade struck again, slashing through the tendons of the knee, bringing the animal crashing to the earth, helpless, to be dispatched by a spear-thrust.

It stretched the imagination to picture myself succeeding at that precarious sport, but the Somali and his knife came much closer to my idea of a hunt than the sun-helmeted European, high-perched on his *mirador*, with an escort of beaters, boys and guns, and his explosive bullets,

What took me hunting that October morning following the storm on the Tcher Tcher, I can scarcely explain. A touch of nervousness, a characteristic dislike of awaiting inactive the arrival of news good or bad—though perhaps it was only a consciously futile hope of dodging an unpleasant reality through temporary flight.

At any rate the pretext that sent me out at the hunter's hour before daybreak with my two Somali boys, was a half-forgotten promise to gather a few monkey pelts as a present for the Somali girl. Our path zigzagged up the mountainside, crossing the chain a couple of miles above the cabin. From there it plunged down abruptly among the cedars through a series of deep gorges so steep among the crowded trunks, that one had the sensation of plunging down vertically, parallel to the tall black shafts. I was reminded incongruously of the elevator in my father's Paris apartment, that so terrified my childhood, dropping silently between the columns of glistening steel.

The storm of the day had not passed beyond the summit. Below us the sandy bed of the torrent twisted on the valley bottom, sun-baked and dry among the rocks, littered with bones that mark the pack trail. The Galla never kills the worn-out ass or camel; abandoned in a waterless land, they wander back over the familiar route, falling an easy prey to panther, hyena, and jackal. Their whitened bones blaze the trail through the brush along the bed of the torrent until the rains, sweeping down the gorge, **carry** away all trace.

As we climbed the opposite slope, a black-and-white animal bounded across the path a few yards ahead. "*Agoza!*" (Monkeys!) one of my Somalis shouted, passing me a gun. Overhead two flying shapes flashed through the tree-trunks. Then a whole band of rapid shadows rushing up, up towards the top foliage. We had a vision of leaping silhouettes, high among the branches. Then . . . nothing. Or was that a single shape against the sky? I lifted my Mauser, fired. Fifty or more monkeys bounded through the air in all directions. A single dark mass fell, heavily clutched at a branch and hung there suspended. I fired again. Again the panic of leaping shapes. But I had loosed the target from its branch; it dropped. Ali, one of the Somalis, rushed forward; the wounded monkey met his onslaught halfway. There was a hasty struggle; a cry of pain from Ali. The monkey appeared getting the best of it, until I put an end to the fray by seizing the animal by the tail and smashing its head against a rock.

We had little luck following the band through the cedars beneath a tangle of hanging vines. The animals carried off their wounded, or when hit clung so desperately to a forked branch that a shot failed to dislodge them. To reach them would have meant scaling a vertical trunk and fighting hand to hand a hundred feet from the ground. After three hours and thirty-four cartridges we had only six animals to our credit. Several had received as many as four shots, any one of which might ordinarily be considered mortal, but I had been forced to dispatch all of them with my revolver. The hunters themselves were in a sorry state. My left hand had been bitten through the palm. Ali's face and arms were lacerated and bloody—to the horror of my two Moslems who hated blood and for whom all monkeys were *Chaëtans* (devils).

Skinning monkeys is always an unpleasant process. Stripped of the long black and white fur, their bodies are horribly like those of young children. We loaded the skins on one of the mules—a proceeding not at all to its liking— and handing over the guns to Ali's keeping, set out for home. To avoid the interminable zigzags of the trail I selected a supposed short-cut across the chain.

Then occurred one of the ludicrous incidents that furnished the necessary touch of grotesque to the day which was to end in tragedy.

At the bottom of the gorge, as we halted by a slimy puddle among the rocks to water the animals, the pack mule that carried the monkey pelts wrested the halter from Ali's grasp and set off at a light trot up the opposite slope. Ali dashed after it, but the wily mule kept in the lead. The chase continued all the way up the slope. At the summit, I mounted the second mule, and ordering the boys to return home directly with the guns, I started in pursuit of the fugitive. There followed a sliding, scattering chase through brush and rock. Ahead I saw the clustered roofs of a village. The mule made for the first hut, dashing straight through the doorway. I heard muffled cries from within as the animal burst through the opposite wall of palm mats, upsetting a jar of durra, smashing a dozen cooking pots, and sowing panic in his wake. The chase continued down the mountainside across fields of durra, coffee and *kat*—until at last in a hollow among the rocks I succeeded in cornering the fugitive. Leaving my own mount, I leaped to the back of the runaway and set out on another mad steeplechase down the slope. I let him go full gallop

while stones clattered, bushes and boulders rocked past
and the whole landscape reeled and heaved.

Abyssinian mules are a wiry, sure-footed lot. Our headlong course ended without accident. By the time we
reached the valley floor, the temper of the animal had
worn itself out, and it turned docilely into the trail leading
up the mountainside. That little diversion had consumed
three hours. As I came in sight of the hut, I dismounted,
removed the monkey pelts from the mule, and leading the
panting animal by the bridle, climbed the rocky path.

A group stood about the doorway of the hut; white-
clothed Abyssinians and half-naked Gallas. Among them
I made out the tall figure of Abdi, the Somali muleteer,
who two days earlier had left with the pack train for
Diré Daoua. His presence could only mean bad news. This
time there was no dodging disaster; I went forward to
meet it, stumping up the steep trail, dragging the bundle
of pelts.

My approach produced a curious effect on the group
about the doorway. They stood staring down at me as if
hypnotized. Complete silence; not a cry nor a gesture.
As I drew nearer I distinguished a curious throbbing
sound; some one sobbing, the muffled cries and hiccoughs
of frantic grief. A few yards from the hut, a dark form
lay in the grass writhing as if in the agony of a wound.
As I approached, it lifted a face distorted with misery
and fear and I recognized the boy Ali, his cheeks streaked
horribly with tears and blood. My first thought—that he
was injured, shot perhaps—vanished in sick presentiment
as he flung himself towards me on all fours, clutching at
my ankles.

"Kill me, Master, for I have killed. . . ."

I kicked him off savagely and strode to the doorway.

As if his words had loosed a spell, there welled around me an instantaneous hubbub of sound. An infernal chatter in Arab and Somali and Galla. Confused gesticulating shapes blocked my way. I knocked them aside. Within the hut, black after the blinding light without, I made out a shadowy knot of crouched and stooping figures, and one lying prone. Kneeling beside it, I put out a hand in the darkness. My groping fingers touched an arm, warm but lifeless.

"Fatouma. . . ."

A woman's voice spoke at my shoulder. "She will not answer, *Gaeta* (Master; the Abyssinian title), she is dead." Cursing the darkness, I ran my hands over the body: under the left breast the flesh was broken and wet. I knelt in a pool. . . . There was nothing to be done there. I got to my feet again and stumbled out through the door. I felt heavy and sick. It was hot in the sun but I was glad to sit in the grass by the door of the hut. The boy Ali still lay sobbing quietly. He rolled an eye towards me apprehensively from under his elbow. But I felt no desire to beat him, though his silly antics with the gun had been responsible. . . . He had wanted to show the Somali girl how I shot monkeys! There was something touching in the childlike abandon of his grief.

As for myself I cannot remember feeling any distinct pang at the tragic end of poor Fatouma. I sat staring at the dark splotch on my knee, conscious only of great weariness and a curious sort of apathy. Yet her death carried with it an element of finality. While in itself, it represented no deciding factor in my life—a painful incident, no more, and soon forgotten—yet it stands as I look back on it to-day like a milestone, a terminal post marking a closed frontier.

I beckoned the muleteer who throughout the scene had hung silent on the outskirts of the group.

"And you, Abdi, are you all that is left?" I asked him. Though I knew in advance the answer. The man pushed towards me through the crowding figures.

"Three escaped: I and two others," he replied in a low voice.

"And the mules, the caravan?" His hands dropped to his side in a gesture of despair.

"All swept away in the great water." Then fixing me with dark eyes, "Be comforted, Master. *Mektoub.* It was ordained."

The words dropped like a stone in the silence. Then a murmur, a rippling eddy of sound welled from the circle of black men, an echo so soft it seemed to rise from the earth on which I sat, bereft as Job.

"It was ordained. *Mektoub.*"

IV

Return to the Sea

Among seafaring men, you find in general, two types. There are those—the majority of steam navigators, I have observed—to whom the sea is merely a highway between continents; as banal as a railroad. Hard-bitten old sea dogs they may be, yet they carry with them eternally the mirage of the port. The reality may be only the bars of the Joliette, the jostling bawdyhouses of the *Vieux Port,* the sordid water front of Shanghai, Rio or Liverpool; but it has all the glamour of the journey's end—a goal to long for and dream of, dearly bought at the price of months of tossing on hostile, watery ways. To such men the sea is an enemy, double-faced and insidious, to be fought with, mastered, never loved. While to others, the sea is a world, the inseparable companion of their existence. All the continents of the earth are but frontiers, lonely islands of exile—lifeless as the cinders of the moon. To those others, the sea alone, represents life, rich and manifold. It is an adversary one loves and battles with in a complete passion that finds its consummation in defeat as much as victory.

In all the dark hours of my life, I have turned to the sea; not for consolation, but as one turns to the rich wilderness after the parsimony of cities. It has never failed me. All that the land denied—treasure, high adventure, hope; crises that enrich the soul—it has given me, prodigal as nature itself.

When I came down from the Abyssinian plateau that

29

autumn after the wreck of my two years' experiment as a
trader, my situation from a material point of view was
no more brilliant than when I landed in Djibouti two
years earlier. Morally I was even poorer. To the crushing
sense of defeat, the death of the Somali girl had given
tragic precision and color.

When on the afternoon of the accident, the tribesmen
of poor Fatouma bore away the dead wrapped in a burial
sheet, I watched the little procession wind down the slope
until the dark forms of the bearers disappeared against
the green, and only the white stain of the shroud remained
dancing in the heat waves like a persistent gesture of farewell. I strained my eyes until the palpitating dot had
vanished, and it was as if something essential, the last
confident omen of my youth, flickered out like a match
struck in the wind. But despair is an emotion for adoles-
cents. I was a man of thirty, and I had already known
defeat.

The sense of crushing heaviness persisted during the
journey down the mountain. But when we approached the
desert I breathed again. If one must live in exile on the
land, I would always choose the desert. Impersonal as the
ocean, it is untouched in its naked immenseness, by man's
petty handiwork. As we came down to Djibouti, the gulf
stretched intensely blue under a sunlike lead. Not a ripple
of air stirred the glittering water that lay within an immense crescent of black and gold bordered on the west by
the Abyssinian highlands. Above the plain, strewn with
black stones like the slabs of a hearth, the heat waves
quivered and danced. Ten minutes would have sufficed to
burn through the soles of any European who ventured to
walk there at that hour.

Few would have recognized me, had they seen me one

morning shortly after my return to Djibouti, at work
down by the water front in the company of Abdi, my
former muleteer, who had definitely chosen to cast his lot
with mine. Abdi was a Warsangali from Cape Gardafui, a
man in his early twenties, broad shouldered and bronzed
of skin, his long hair bleached yellow with lime. A true
amphibian, he was equally at home on land, in a boat and
in or under water. As a lad, he had been a pearl diver in
the Dahalak Islands. A precious collaborator, a friend of
whom any man might be proud, during the years that followed he proved equal to every circumstance, brave, tactful, and good humored.

My costume that morning differed little from Abdi's
own. It was limited in both cases to a hip cloth. My body,
burnt almost as dark as my companion's, had been rubbed
with butter—an indispensable precaution as protection
against the sun. At that period I still wore the turban,
which I later discarded except for occasions of ceremony
—going bareheaded in the sun which I learned to support
with the indifference of a Somali.

We were busy testing the results of my first attempts at
pearl cultivating, for I had decided to turn my attention
to pearls. That meant a return to the sea and at the same
time the possibility—if luck came my way or if Allah
willed (according to Abdi's phraseology)—of building up
my fortunes with relative speed. However, to make pearl
fishing a paying game, would have meant acquiring boats
and diving crews—the expenditure of capital which I did
not possess. It occurred to me that I might try my hand
at cultivating pearls, an industry of which I had heard
and read considerably in the past. It had succeeded in
Japan; why not in the Red Sea? At any rate, to put the
idea into practice required little outlay of money.

A word about pearls.

Even the layman knows, I imagine, that the pearl is a foreign body that has penetrated within the flesh of the oyster and which the bivalve encloses, as time goes on, in a prison of mother-of-pearl. It lies enveloped in a little pocket in that part of the oyster, which secretes mother-of-pearl. An Indian legend, believed by the Soudanese fishers, relates that the pearl is a dewdrop fallen into the sea during the full moon; that moonlight gives the gem its luster or "orient." That is why, they maintain, rainy years are always good pearl years—a fact, surprisingly enough, which seems to be true.[1]

What the layman does not realize is that the formation of pearls is not a rare phenomenon. Nearly every oyster contains a pearl at one time or another; but ordinarily the pearl is expelled before it has attained the size of a grain of sand. Only under very special circumstances does a pearl remain within the oyster until it reaches a considerable size.

Such "special circumstances" the pearl cultivator attempts to create. As for myself, after experimenting with various substances, I adopted as nucleus for the future pearl, a little ball of mother-of-pearl pierced with two tiny holes to admit a fine strand of catgut. I made the oyster "yawn" by exposing it to the air, and inserting a bit of wood to hold the shells apart while I proceeded with the "operation." With a fine drill, I bored a hole through one of the valves. Through the hole, starting from within the

---

[1] If it is a fact, as certain scientists maintain, that a minute parasite eliminated from the intestines of the stingray, is the origin of the pearl, it seems very possible that the surface currents of fresh water (which I have noticed ten miles from the coast during the rainy season in calm weather) attract the ray in large numbers, so that the intestinal parasite penetrates a greater number of oysters than is customary in the dry season,

shell, I passed the fragment of catgut; pulled it taut from
the outside so that the little ball of mother-of-pearl lay
in tight contact with the inner surface of the shell, and
cemented the strand fast on the outside by filling up the
hole I had drilled. A nucleus thus planted should in four
or five months produce, on the inner surface of the shell,
a protuberance covered with an iridescent layer of mother-
of-pearl. This, when sawed through with great care, produces a half-pearl. To produce an entire pearl requires a
more complete operation. The nucleus must be inserted
within the body of the oyster. If inserted directly, the
oyster dies. The "operator" sacrifices an oyster, cuts a
piece of its flesh in which he envelops the nucleus as in a
little sack. He then makes an incision in the living oyster,
taking care not to use steel instruments, for their contact
kills the oyster instantly, inserts sack and nucleus in the
wound, assuring a contact between the "mouth" of the
sack and the living muscle. If all goes well, the two muscles
grow together and the nucleus, now in the normal position
of a pearl, receives its iridescent layers and in time becomes a "pearl." As I considered myself too much of a
novice to attempt anything so complicated, I contented
myself for the time being with the simpler operation.

With Abdi's assistance, I prepared a modest "nursery":
a packing case coated with cement. From diver friends of
his, Abdi procured a dozen live oysters of different species
and sizes, and into the shells of these I carefully introduced my little spheres of mother-of-pearl. Afterwards we
carried the box half a mile from shore and sank it on a
shoal. Ten days later we brought it to the surface again,
for I was eager to learn whether my patients had survived
the treatment.

On the morning of which I write we were busily exam-

ining the oysters, nearly all of which, I was delighted to
discover, seemed none the worse for the treatment. I resolved to repeat the experiment on a great number of bi-
valves, confining my efforts to a type that had shown the
lowest rate of mortality.

Two principal species of pearl oyster are found in the
Red Sea—the *sadaf* and the *bil-bil.* The *sadaf,* the big
pearl oyster (adult, it is large as a plate, and the two
valves weight two pounds or more), contains rare pearls
(one in 10,000 shells). These are generally the "solitaires"
remarkable both for size and quality. The shell of the
sadaf has a market value as mother-of-pearl. Often the
pearly layer is fully half an inch thick. In the *bil-bil,* the
smaller species, pearls are far more common, but these are
generally insignificant, both in quality and size. The shell
of the *bil-bil,* of paper-like thinness, has no value as
mother-of-pearl.

After my initial experiment, I gave my attention entirely to the *sadaf* which, from every point of view, offered
better chances of success. That meant I had to carry my
research farther afield. There were no pearl-bearing
oysters in the neighborhood of Djibouti, and I found it
almost impossible to procure live oysters from the few
natives of the region who fished them, as they invariably
opened all they found, hoping to discover pearls. I had to
go oyster fishing on my own account. That meant renting
a boutre—a native boat with a lateen sail. Abdi found me
one that seemed suitable, and two Soudanese divers to
whom I promised a rupee an oyster. For provisions I
bought a sack of dates, one of rice and a third of durra
and several quarts of butter. (In these regions butter
takes the form of oil.)

In order to clear the port, I had to show papers of some

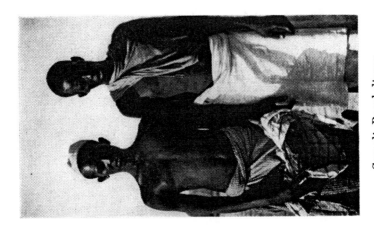

Somali Pearl-divers

Opening Pearl-oysters (*sadafs*)

sort. I obtained a fishing permit, being careful not to
specify what type of "fishing" I expected to engage in.
(If my experiment failed, I could see no need for adver-
tising the fact. If I succeeded, I had still greater reasons
for discretion.) The employee who handed me the papers
specified that the permission to fish in the waters of the
gulf in no way implied the right to touch anywhere on the
Dankali coast, reputed to be unsafe for Europeans. That
restriction did not disturb me particularly. The papers
would be useful merely to clear Djibouti; beyond that
point, I was indifferent alike to permissions or proscrip-
tions.

We got under weigh one moonlight night about ten
o'clock. A steady breeze carried us due east, all sails set.
The dead calm that in these waters comes at daybreak
found us well out of sight of land. When the morning wind
reached us, it brought a heavy swell from the Indian
Ocean and by noon the sea was rolling heavily. Twice we
shipped a ton of water that washed knee-deep from bow
to stern, our boat—like all the boutres of the coast—
having no deck. I changed our course to the west, running
with the wind to avoid capsizing. By sunrise we lay off the
Dankali coast—ragged black cliffs rising sheer six hundred feet above the sea. We put out the houri (a native
dugout) and I landed on the sand of a little cove that cut
into the rock for a hundred yards or so.

My two Soudanese made ready for their morning's
work, launching a second dugout manned by two *ghaouas-
sins* (divers). As is customary, they prepared to work in
shifts, one man scanning the sea floor through the
mourailla—a glass-bottomed box, generally the inevitable
tanika or four-gallon oil tin of the Shell or Standard Oil,
which in the Near East serves every imaginable purpose,

from water can and soup kettle to slop jar, and is hammered out for walls and roofing! The Soudanese companion did the diving. In a calm sea it is possible to make out the bottom beneath sixty feet of water. When the man with the *mourailla* catches sight of a pearl-bearing *sadaf* or *bil-bil,* he gives the signal and the second *ghaouassin* dives overboard. His eyes glued to the *mourailla* the man in the dugout keeps watch of what goes on below. He is armed with a long pole sharpened at the end—a weapon that served to ward off inquisitive sharks, for the diver under water is blind to what goes on about him beyond the radius of a yard or so.

With one Soudanese scanning the sea bottom while his companion paddled, the dugout slipped quietly over the surface, glassy-still in the morning calm. The couple would not return to the boutre until evening. After a brief examination of the little cove in which I discovered a spring of brackish yellow water, I went on board again; for as the sun rose the heat grew intolerable at the foot of the black wall. I had stretched myself down to nap in the shadow of the sail when Abdi, my Somali boy, roused me with the news that four Danakils had come into sight following a ribbon of sand at the base of the cliff. With the glasses I made out that one of them carried a gun half-concealed in the folds of his *chamma.*

When they had come within hailing distance they called to me in Arab asking me what I was doing there, where we were going, and offering to sell us milk if we would come on land. During the dialogue I did not take my eyes off the man with the gun—a Gras rifle. I could make out the glitter of its brass fittings though he continued to keep it discreetly out of sight. My revolver, our only arm, lay conveniently at hand. Ordering my men to attach the furled sail to the yard with cords of palm fiber, so that a single tug at the sheet would release it, I informed our visitors that for the time being we had no intention of landing. At my words, the four plunged into the water. It was low tide; they could have come within thirty feet of the boutre without swimming. Whatever their intentions may have been—whether to loot us in the classic fashion of the coast, or simply to extort a baksheesh—I saw no need of courting the risk. Without losing a gesture of the Dankali with the rifle, I bade my men lift the anchor and we took the wind, while a chorus of noisy invective followed us from shore.

I smile now when I think of my first uneasiness with regard to the Dankakils. But remember, my head still rang with terrifying tales current at Djibouti. It is true when the Dankali warns you to keep away from his country, you might better pay attention to the warning. Journeying across the mountains, I have often seen immense piles of stones heaped on the edge of narrow cañons at the bottom of which passes the only practicable trail; so that one man with a billet of wood as lever can set loose a veritable avalanche. . . .

Of the three great groups, closely related ethnically—the Somalis, Gallas, and Danakils—the latter have remained by far the most independent and primitive. "Savage," I suppose most Europeans would say. Their taste for freedom has made them difficult to "colonize"; hence their bad reputation. Personally I consider the Danakils a noble race—they have great physical beauty possibly because of Egyptian origin—proud and self-respecting, and as individuals absolutely trustworthy once they have given you their word. If they have accepted me, it is, I fancy, because I never interfered with

their customs, always took care to be as scrupulous in
my dealings with them, as they with me, and perhaps most
of all, because I had no official governmental connections.
On the contrary.

After our ridiculous flight before the curiosity of the
four natives, skirting the coast, we took the houri with
the divers in tow. Their catch that morning had not been
brilliantly successful—only three *sadafs*, owing to cloudy
water after the night's storm. The morning wind had
risen, carrying us along at a spanking pace—too rapid
for the dugout which shipped a wave and capsized. I cut
the tow line and brought the boutre about. By that time
the two divers had righted the houri and gathered up
oysters and scattered equipment. But the glass of the
mouraille was broken—a real disaster, for without that
submarine eye the divers were useless.

Notwithstanding our loss, irreparable on that uninhabited coast, I kept to a northwesterly course. By nightfall we gained the inlet of Ras Ali, a fiord-like arm of the
sea that cuts into the rock wall for a half mile or so,
forming a narrow lake, Khor Ali, that communicates with
the sea only at high tide. Its bottom, I discovered the
following morning, was carpeted with a marvelous vegetation of rainbow-colored coral, a garden of feathery
branches, rose and blue, and a hostile population of long-
spined poisonous sea urchins. Along the beach lay beds of
edible oysters, that furnished us with an abundant breakfast. We had just returned to the boutre after our meal
when we were hailed from the shore by a Dankali carrying
a jar of goat's milk. As he carried no arms, we let him
come on board and offered him dates and tea—an attention which made him volunteer to show my divers places
along the coast where they would be likely to find *sadafs*.

That afternoon, I accompanied the Dankali on shore to visit a grove of incense trees. By a goat path that zigzagged among the rocks, we climbed the steep wall of the fiord to a plateau several hundred feet above the sea. The hot stones burned my feet cruelly; I had left shoes along with my "civilized" clothes in Djibouti.

· Two miles inland a second wall of volcanic rock rose above the plateau, cut in two by a deep gorge, its bottom strewn with a confusion of immense blocks. On the steep walls of the ravine grew the incense trees, in shape not unlike fig trees. When the bark is cut, a milky sap oozes through the slit. It solidifies rapidly, forming a sort of whitish rosin that hardens into transparent crystals—the incense as we know it—after a few months' exposure to the air.

We clambered several hours among the blistering rocks. Night had come before I returned to the boutre, footsore and exhausted, my throat and tongue literally raw with thirst; for I was learning to adopt the native habit of not drinking when on the march. . . .

The next morning, our Dankali was on hand early. The tide had dropped, and the entire crew including myself set out to hunt for *sadafs* in shallow pools among the rocks. All day long we splashed about the warm water, collecting in all twenty-five oysters. I judged that the number would suffice for my experiment, and at sunset we hoisted sail for Djibouti.

That mysterious trip of mine set my countrymen at Djibouti to conjecturing. They besieged my men with questions, learning little; for a Soudanese can be taciturn when it is to his interest . . . and Abdi had seen to that. As for myself I let them gossip and surmise at will. I was busy operating on my oysters.

I installed them in a temporary nursery while I prepared the future pearls—each tiny ball of mother-of-pearl
cemented to a fine silver wire. (I had not yet learned the
utility of catgut.) It took me a couple of days to pierce
the shells and insert the nuclei. When all was ready, Abdi
and I loaded the cement box with the *sadafs* on the dugout—a perilous proceeding, for the case was heavy and
the dugout characteristically unstable. While I paddled,
Abdi swam alongside supporting the case with one arm
and maintaining the houri on an even keel. We deposited
the box on a shoal about four miles from the coast. While
Abdi paddled me back to land, I lay in the bottom of the
houri well pleased at having carried out the first step of
my plan and making enthusiastic schemes for future pearl
plantations on a large scale, with acres of oyster parks
and a fleet of boats and divers. Within a few years, pearl
cultivating was sure to become one of the leading industries of the coast. . . .

My enthusiasm proved unfortunately premature. On the
following day, when I paddled out to the shoal to take
a look at the submerged nursery, I discovered to my discomfiture that all the *sadafs* were dead. Either my methods
had been too brutal, or the cement had contained too much
lime. In any event, my brilliant future as a cultivator of
pearls seemed gravely compromised.

"Nothing to do about it, but begin over again," I remarked ruefully to Abdi as we surveyed the litter of
gaping shells.

The Warsangali gave a dubious shrug. "*Al'allah*—as
Allah wills," he muttered; his tone conveying that Allah
undoubtedly disapproved of my tampering with the proc-
esses of nature.

Nevertheless, the following evening we set out again in

the rented boutre to gather a new supply of *sadafs* along the Dankali coast. That time we were held up nearly a week by bad weather in the inlet of Khor Ali. I began to suspect that my luck on the sea might not prove superior to my luck on land—when one night I received a singular visit.

It was about ten o'clock. The men were asleep forward, tumbled heaps among the ropes and sails. I lay on my back along the steering-bench, wide awake, watching the stars and listening to the silence. There was not a breath of wind; we lay as if fixed to the coral bottom of the inlet. All at once I was conscious of a soft splash, splash, along the side of the boutre. At first I took it for a fish, but as I leaned over the stern, I made out the silhouette of a swimmer, moving in a fiery star of phosphorescence. As my face showed above the rail, the man spoke a low "*Salaam*," and seizing the rudder, swung himself aboard.

On deck, the stranger—a Soudanese—squatted on his heels uttering the polite phrases of the casual visitor, as if it were the most natural thing in the world to swim out to a boutre at that hour for a bit of conversation. Propped on my elbow, I replied to his questions with equal ceremony, wondering meanwhile what had brought him.

Finally came the revealing question. "Do you buy pearls?" At that, I understood. . . .

Pearl fishers work in groups. Several couples working together make up the crew of a fishing boutre whose *nakhoda* directs their operations. Every morning they go out, two by two, in the dugouts to fish. At night they return with their oysters intact. These are opened on board the boutre in the presence of the entire crew, all of whom share in the eventual sale. To avoid temptation, no diver is allowed to take a knife with him in the dugout.

Occasionally it happens that a diver does open an oyster and that he finds a pearl which he subsequently tries to dispose of in secret. You may wonder why this does not happen oftener; but the pearl market is a tight little circle. When a valuable pearl is bought, every one knows who the buyer is, and who the seller. It is difficult for a diver to sell a pearl secretly through the regular channels. Sometimes, however, he is fortunate enough to meet a stranger who has no connection with the pearl market, but who may be interested in acquiring a fine pearl. . . .

So when the nocturnal caller asked me: "Do you buy pearls?" I understood and nodded. The diver untied a knot in his dripping *fohta* and taking something from the fold of cloth, stretched a hand towards me. Something lay in the hollow of his palm. At the time I knew practically nothing about pearls, but to my layman's eye, the specimen looked worthy of interest. It was smooth and round, about the size of a small pea, and glistened frostily in the light of the match I struck to examine it. I should have liked Abdi's advice; an experienced diver, he undoubtedly knew how to recognize a good pearl when he saw it. But I feared arousing my visitor's apprehension if I waked my men.

I decided to risk the purchase, and offered the Soudanese four English pounds for his find, which at the time represented just one half of my entire fortune. I suspected and hoped that the market value of the pearl would prove tenfold that figure. I knew also that the diver under the circumstances could not afford to be particular about his price. He seemed satisfied with my offer, accepted with alacrity, and swam off into the night, my four pounds tucked away safely in his cheek.

As it happened, that little transaction turned out a better gamble than my hope. Less than a week later I sold the pearl in Massawa for 400 pounds!

So it was that my first stroke of luck came to me directly . . . out of the sea.

V

Diplomacy and Pearls

Thanks to the pearl—which Abdi persisted in viewing as evidence of divine favor—I now had a boat of my own. Nothing more pretentious than a five-ton native boutre, with a triangular lateen sail, manned by a crew of four Somalis; but it meant that I was no longer a prisoner of the land. What use I was to make of my new liberty, I had as yet no notion. First I had to learn a type of navigation, compared with which my boyhood cruising along the *Côte Vermeille* appeared as hazardous as a small boy's sailing of a toy boat in the fountain of the Luxembourg gardens!

As I said, I had no definite plans when I bought the *Sahala*. . . . I had a vague project of going in for pearl fishing on my own, with crews of Soudanese divers, north of the Straits of Bab el Mandeb. The richest pearl fields lie in the Red Sea, a perilous region, as I well knew, for the amateur navigator. I contented myself at first with getting the hang of my newly acquired craft, cruising along the Dankali coast, and making brief excursions into the Gulf of Aden. In the meantime, with Abdi's help, I continued my experiments at pearl cultivating. We fished for more *sadafs*, and I succeeded in operating a fair number of oysters. I had shifted my nursery to Mascali Island, five miles north of Djibouti, for three times the cases of oysters we deposited on the shoal off Djibouti disappeared mysteriously. Out of half a dozen cases sunk with infinite pains, I recovered only one that had slid off the shoal into deep water—a delicate task, in the course of which I came near losing one of my best divers. My nursery on the island I placed in care of the lighthouse keeper, a Dankali named Bourha who with his family constituted the sole population of Mascali. He had lived there for eighteen years on a princely income of twelve francs a month, raising goats and sheep and a family of several dozen children, for as a prosperous citizen he possessed four legitimate wives.

He had proved only too willing, for a modest increase in his monthly income, to keep a paternal eye on my pearl plantations. But as Abdi remarked: "Pearls grow with time," and I had no prospects of even a modest crop of half-pearls under several months. I resolved to track my still elusive fortune farther afield. . . .

One evening I dined at the Residence with the Governor of Djibouti. While a deep-seated dislike for the usual state "functionary" led me to avoid the majority of my countrymen in the colony, I had maintained friendly relations with that particular official, a thickset Gascon to whom neither alcohol nor over-feeding had given the liver-pale complexion of the average colonial. As we sat smoking on the terrace after dinner, he led the conversation adroitly from a general discussion of Abyssinian affairs, to my return to the Somali coast and concluded with a pertinent question.

"So you have made up your mind to try a hand at pearl fishing?"

The remark did not surprise me. The goings and comings of the *Sahala* were known to every one, and I had made no secret of that part of my project. I replied with a laugh that Red Sea pearls, I hoped confidently, might prove more profitable than Ethiopian hides and coffee. The governor rolled the end of his cigar meditatively in his thick fingers. Then he spoke casually out of the dusk.

"Had you thought of making a trip to the Arab coast . . . perhaps to Yemen?"

It was my turn to puff silently at my cigar before I replied in a tone as careless as his own, that I might easily take a tack in that direction on my way north to the pearl market of Massawa. As His Excellency was aware, no doubt, I had already fitted out my boutre for an initial trip into the Red Sea, to look over the ground before beginning operations.

"There is a little matter I would like to talk over with you." The governor tossed his cigar into the gravel and drew his chair closer to mine. "A slight service, a little mission of no great importance. . . . But I think you are the man to undertake it. You have heard of Sheik Said?"

I nodded. What man in the colony did not know Sheik Said? Sheik Said, like another Cherbourg "aimed at the heart of England"; in this case, a Turkish citadel that dominated the British coaling station of Perim, that key to the Straits of Bab el Mandeb—a Cerberus keeping watch over the southern end of the Suez route to India.

"You are perhaps aware that Sheik Said was formerly French property?" the governor went on. "In 1860 the commercial house of Ronbaud in Marseilles purchased the port from the Arabs and established a trading station there. It was abandoned during the war of 1870. To-day there is a small Turkish fort and a telegraph line from the fort to Moka—which may or may not still be in use. In fact, the whole question of Sheik Said has little direct concern for us. However, it might be . . . interesting, in a general way you understand"—the governor weighed his words carefully, "to have some one take a look about over there, see briefly what the Turks are doing and incidentally . . . bring back a few photographs. The annoying thing about it is that it will have to be done on the quiet. Which always gives exaggerated importance. . . . The Turks don't welcome European visitors at Sheik Said. A European might have an unpleasant time of it, if they discovered him there. But you—you can easily pass for an Arab." He paused suggestively.

At the time I was still unfamiliar with the crossed and tangled meshes of European policy in that part of the world. I knew in a vague way that four jealous powers, like four hungry terriers, kept an alert and watchful eye on the southern issue of the Red Sea. And that three of them looked on with growing envy—however diplomatically dissimulated—at the British bulldog who had locked his jaws on the coveted morsel. While the words of the governor aroused my curiosity, what appealed to me most was the nature of the mission to which he attributed— officially—so slight importance. The element of actual risk, whether at the hands of Turk or pirate, gave an additional zest to the anticipatory thrill of piloting the *Sahala* into unknown waters north of the strait. The ultimate value, diplomatic or political, of whatever information I might obtain, interested me little; but the getting of it offered possibilities.

"You understand of course . . . I count on your discretion . . . to avoid misinterpretations and misunderstandings. . . . And if you should happen to meet any of our friends from the Rock," he gestured in the direction of Perim, "it might be well to remember that your only interest . . . is pearls."

True enough. Although the morning when I swung the

Sahala under full sail out into the Gulf of Aden, I felt all the emotions of a small boy on his first ocean voyage. A temporary oblivion buried pearls and delicate missions alike. . . . I was conscious only of the keen joy of departure; and the *Sahala* slid swiftly on an even keel through the dawn wind as if she too shared my eagerness to tempt unknown horizons. A single unlucky incident marred the morning. Off Mascali Island, we scraped a reef. The wind had dropped, and thanks to our feeble headway the shock did little damage, though the hollow sound of the blow brought concretely to mind all that I had heard of the dangers of coast navigation in those waters.

Eight hours later we were in sight of Perim, a horse-shoe-shaped island of black basalt and lava-rock that rises at its eastern end two hundred feet above the sea. A channel two miles wide separates Perim from Sheik Said and the Arab coast. As I pointed the *Sahala* into the channel, I noticed against the black wall of the island at my left, the hull of a steamer gone aground among the rocks. Only the bow emerged. It must have been a recent disaster; through the glasses I could see the pumps were still at work. The sight of that victim of wind and current made me remember with particular vividness that Bab el Mandeb means Gate of Tears. A few minutes later I came near discovering the fact on my own account. Suddenly, with no warning, we were caught by the wind that ripped through the channel with the speed of a hurricane. Waves thirty feet high towered and crashed about us. At every plunge we shipped a sea; the crew bailed away frantically, in water to their waists. All happened so suddenly there had been no time to take in the sail—no easy task in that type of craft, with the wind astern. Abdi made a mad attempt to haul down the yard and was swept overboard. I caught a flashing glimpse of his dark body in the foam alongside. Flinging him a coil of rope, I abandoned the helm long enough to slash a knife through the sail just above the bolt rope. With a report like a gunshot, the sail ripped to the mast and hung flapping like an immense flag. To replace it, we succeeded in hoisting a jib. As we rolled helpless, Abdi captured the end of the rope and climbed aboard. Without taking time to sneeze, he joined the bucket gang in the hold while I braced myself against the bar and let the boutre drive ahead, quivering in the impact of the seas and shipping water at every wave.

Nothing but luck could save us, I knew. My Somalis, experienced sailors all of them, and equally aware of the danger, bailed stoically. It was useless to annoy Allah with prayers and promises. Allah himself cannot change what is written; though I noticed that Abdi from time to time threw a glance over his shoulder towards Sheik Said, while his lips moved. What one may not ask Allah may be sometimes obtained from his "Saints." He was begging the deceased holy man to give aid.

Half in bravado, half in earnest I shouted through the howling wind (Abdi stood almost at my elbow) "If Sheik Said brings us through, I become a Moslem."

The words came without conscious premeditation; though it was true that for some time, ever since my return to the coast, I had contemplated taking the step. It represented the one way to approach my black companion as an equal. None knew better than I their contempt for the white eaters of pork, blood, and carrion. Also, I knew with what ease they penetrated the cunning European who thinks with a turban, a *chamma*, and a few prayers learned by heart, to pass as a follower of the Prophet. A simple

statement of my "change of heart," would never have
sufficed. For my conversion, I needed a pretext. Our predicament that afternoon in the Strait of Bab el Mandeb
offered itself.

From the Moslem's point of view, the situation was
clear. In deadly peril on the sea, I made a vow. Had I
been insincere, the Sheik invoked would have punished me
with death. A miraculous rescue, on the other hand, proved
my sincerity and showed plainly that my change of religion was acceptable in the eye of Allah. As it was,
whether luck, fate, or Sheik Said kept us afloat, we came
through unscathed. After three hours' desperate tossing,
we made calm water in the lee of the cape.

In my relief I felt an instinctive longing to thank whatever power had pulled us through. But my Moslems, I
noticed, were unmoved. If Allah had saved us, it was because it pleased him to do so, hence there was no need of
thanking him. . . . Secretly, I suspect we owed our safety
to the *Sahala's* leaden keel. Had we carried the customary
stone ballast, I believe my career as a navigator would
have been cut short that day. Actually, none of our losses
were irreparable—aside from the damaged mainsail, and
a sack of sugar that had gone in the form of syrup to
sweeten the tears of Bab el Mandeb.

We spent the night at anchor in the shelter of the coast.
When the sun rose on a wild, windy morning, I made out
a cluster of native huts on the ridge of sand that hid the
inner bay. Placing a couple of revolvers and my camera
in a tin *tanika*, I had the houri lowered and ordered one
of my Somalis to carry the *tanika* to the beach. When he
returned, Abdi and I embarked in the dugout, carrying
with us two Gras rifles. I left three others on board with
the crew, telling them to keep an eye on the dugout, and

Abd el Hai goes Ashore (Arab Coast)

in case any one should approach it in our absence, not to
hesitate to fire. The crew preferred to remain on board,
for all knew the reputation of that part of the Arab coast,
where the stranger, if he escaped being shot by the Turks,
ran the risk of being plundered by the Arabs.

Our landing seemed to pass unperceived. A few rods
from the beach Abdi prostrated himself before a straw-
thatched hut bearing the red pennant of the Prophet, so
marking the tomb of a holy man or Sheik. The time had
come for me to execute my vow. Throwing myself on the
ground beside the Somali sailor, I spoke the profession
of faith:

"*La iloha illa Allah; Muhammid rasul Allah* (there is
no God but God; and Mohammed is his prophet)."

Then while the wind whipped the sand about us in
whirling eddies that stung and blinded, I repeated after
Abdi the words of the *Fata* (the most important of Moslem prayers).

So was my change of religion consummated. From that
moment, I ranked among the followers of the Prophet. At
my leisure, I learned the rite of the five prayers; and
several months later I took time off in Djibouti to have
performed by a European surgeon the little operation essential to every True Believer. But from that morning at
Sheik Said, my position was assured. The story of my
"miraculous" conversion was told on both shores of the
Red Sea, and from that day I was known to Arab, Somali
and Dankali, as Abd el Hai, the "slave of the Life-Giving."
To-day, I am not what one would call a practicing believer. That is to say, like the average Turk, I never go
inside a mosque: I have not recited a prayer for years.
But when in the Near East, I never eat pork, nor meat

that has not been bled. It has become a matter of habit;
and besides, that remains the one unpardonable offense.

To return to Sheik Said: leaving the tomb of the holy
man, Abdi and I climbed to the top of the sandy ridge
dominating the inner bay—a shallow lake of greenish
water opening to the sea by a channel crossable on foot
at low tide. All about the bay rose jagged volcanic hills,
curiously splotched with red and apple green, like immense
heaps of waste from a chemical works. Not a grass-blade
nor a shrub anywhere.

Two fishers, busy with casting nets at the water's edge,
were splendid fellows, with copper-colored skin, and hair
that fell over their shoulders in long curling locks. Each
time one of them caught a fish, he bit it behind the head,
breaking its backbone, and strung it on a cord that
floated behind him in the water. We hailed them in Arab,
causing considerable consternation with our display of
arms. But I hastened to reassure the fishers, offering to
buy some of their catch. For ten cartridges they gave us
enough to feed my entire crew. Then the four of us
squatted down by the water's edge to talk.

The village of Sheik Said, I learned, was composed of
250 Arabs, who lived by fishing, and sold their catch dried
and salted to Arab merchants. For four months of the
year, the northwest wind kept them locked in the bay.
Their only water supply was a brackish spring four miles
inland. The proximity of Perim had ruined the slave trade
between Sheik Said and the African shore; it had moved
north, they said, to the coast beyond Moka. On the height
above us, I noticed a Turkish barracks in ruins and apparently uninhabited. Farther to the right, a Turkish fort
looked down on Perim.

"There are a hundred soldiers up there," one of the

fishers told us, "but they never come down to the coast. They will not disturb you—neither you nor the others . . . *who bring arms from Djibouti.*"

This was not the first time I had heard of the trade in contraband arms of which Djibouti was, at that time, the center. Later I learned still more about the arms trade . . . but that does not yet belong to the story.

Leaving Abdi with the two Arabs, I strolled along the shore of the bay, my camera concealed in the folds of my *chamma.* Avoiding the village, I reached the site of a former French telegraph station, fallen in ruins, with the wires hanging in rusty tassels from a dozen tilted poles. Neither there nor in the vicinity of the abandoned barracks did I meet a soul. The whole coast seemed deserted under the vertical sun; as empty as a landscape on the moon. At dusk we paddled back to the *Sahala.* I was pleased at the success of my first "delicate" mission, and at the same time a little disappointed at the ludicrous ease of the performance. The governor, I felt, had distinctly overstated the danger.

The one definite cause for satisfaction was that neither of the two fishers seemed to suspect my European identity; to them I was merely Abd el Hai, follower of the Prophet and fisher of pearls. I decided to waste no more time sight-seeing but to set off without delay on my own business on the opposite shore of the Red Sea. As I sat cross-legged on the deck with the map spread out before me, Abdi called my attention to a big dugout carrying a sail and manned by eight Arabs, which had put out from the coast and was bearing down on us rapidly. At the sight I ordered my men to charge their rifles and place them within reach, conspicuously on display. There could be no doubt that our visitors belonged to the population of

beach-combing pirates who had given this part of the coast
its bad reputation. It may be—and doubtless was—the
sight of our arms that changed the object of their call.
The dugout drew alongside and after the customary
salaams, the spokesman asked if we had need of water or
provisions. At our reply in the negative, our visitors tacked
about and with a chorus of *salaamaleks* returned docilely
to the shore.

All in all, the adventure of Sheik Said was scarcely
worth the telling. Except that it was to have one far-
reaching consequence of which, at the time, I had no
inkling.

In the breeze we hoisted sail for the west coast. I decided
before proceeding north to Massawa, the great pearl
market of the region, to touch first at Assab to replace
the mainsail. The strong monsoon from the south piled up
the sea in heavy rollers and drove us out of our course,
so that we had a hard time beating our way back to the
Haleb islands—a dense archipelago overgrown with mangroves, which give the shallow waters about Assab the appearance of a calm lake.

Assab has no port, beyond a stretch of white beach and
dunes overgrown with palm and mimosa. The town lay half
abandoned and in ruins: Arab houses of white stucco and
tumble-down European shacks with only the walls standing. Clustered along the shore were date palms and candelabra-like palms, whose fiber the Danakils use for weaving
mats.

We dropped anchor in a little inlet beside a big boutre
that was loading young camels. From the shore came a
hideous noise of groaning and screaming. Some Somalis
were throwing and binding the poor beasts, tying their
legs together like chickens trussed for market. Dragged

to the water's edge, the camels were towed by the neck out to the boutre, floating like unwieldy animated sacks, and hoisted aboard. The men had loaded fifteen camels on a thirty-foot boat so that it looked like some strange sea monster—a many-headed Hydra, floating in the still, dark water. The camels were to be sent to the Arab coast. Sometimes the crossing took a week, during which the animals lay bound in the bottom of the boutre, without food or water.

Taking Abdi with me, I went to pay my respects to the authorities on shore. I had much the feeling of being in Spain—everything indefinite and disordered. An Italian doctor acted as police commissary; and the postmaster was also port commissioner. Not that that implied however a simplification of the customary red tape.

"You say you have arms on board? Then you must bring them to shore at once—*prestissimo*," ordered the Postmaster-Port Commissioner, a rabbit-like little man with a mustache screwed in quivering, oily points. I protested that the rifles were merely for self-defense; that I possessed a passport from the Governor of Djibouti. Besides, I meant to remain only a few hours at Assab; I had touched there merely to buy sailcloth. The Commissioner waved aside my explanations with a tobacco stained forefinger. Would I have the kindness to deposit our arms on shore—*prestissimo?* In a tone as formally courteous as his own, I replied that I had no intention of doing so and took my leave. Sending Abdi in haste to purchase the sailcloth, I hurried back to the boutre, determined to hoist sail if any further difficulties developed.

We had anchored about four miles from the town. At ten o'clock voices hailed us from the shore. The spokesman of a squad of askari in Italian uniform ordered us peremptorily to come on land.

"Wait until day," I answered shortly. "At night I recognize no one." They continued shouting for a half hour and getting no answer, started to launch a dugout. I hailed them, bidding them stay on land or I would fire. The askari paid no heed, but tumbling in the houri began to paddle in our direction. Upon which I let off a few shots in the air; the boat turned about and made for the land.

At dawn, we hoisted sail. I had the idea at first of striking north at once for Massawa, but thought better of it, and we dropped anchor off the town of Assab. Hailing a young Dankali who swam out to us from the beach, I gave him an indignant letter for the doctor-police officer, asking whether it was by his orders that a band of natives had tried to board my boutre in the middle of the night. An hour later I received a letter of excuses from the official: his men had "misinterpreted" his orders and I was free to come on land without further formality.

But I had no wish to linger in Assab. I had hoped to pick up a Dankali familiar with the coast, but failing in that, I decided to worry my way north with the marine charts. As soon as the sail was finished we made for the open sea. With the wind still astern, we passed to the lee of the bare islands of Ras Beilul covered with a thick layer of bird droppings, splotched greenish-black and white like blocks of ripe Roquefort cheese. Then came Cape Rakhmat with its rusty hills rising abrupt from the water; a burnt-out landscape like that of another planet, or belonging to a geological age other than that of the earth to-day. In the distance, a peak higher than the others gave off a steady jet of sulphur-colored smoke. A volcano. Then more is-

lands, Mait, Abayil, and a garland of reefs on which the
swell broke in white circles of foam. My men had never
seen any one navigate by chart before. It amused me to
tell them in advance what we would sight along the coast.
They received my predictions with a sort of superstitious
awe, eyeing with timid respect the marvelous paper that
spoke to me of so many things.

We passed the rust-colored rock of Kad-Ali, its flanks
spattered with an untidy clutter of mining shacks. Two
years before a couple of Danakils had found a handful of
shiny crystals on the island. They shared their find between them and one left for Aden and the other for Assab
to find out whether the stones were salable. At Assab, the
Dankali carried his find to the market. The Italian Governor got wind of the matter, had the man brought to him,
and when he found out that the stones were diamonds, he
ordered the Dankali chained and put in prison, on the pretext that he had no right to steal so considerable a treasure. At the same time, he sent soldiers to take possession
of the rock of Kad-Ali which no one had bothered about
until then, and which in reality belonged to no one.

In Aden, the second Dankali met with better treatment.
That is to say—less brutal. He was given a rifle in exchange for the handful of crystals and went away content.
The English authorities hastened to send a boatload of
askari to occupy the island; but when they arrived there
the found the Italian flag already flying over Kad-Ali.
And the moral to the tale, according to the Danakils, is
this: "When you find anything you don't understand, take
care not to show it to Italians!"

We put in at Eid—two mosques and a hundred native
huts on an inlet among the dunes. One of my men told me
the story of the origin of the Somali colony as we lay at

anchor close by a little fleet of Arab boutres that had put
in there to wait for calmer weather. Years before, two
Somalis belonging to the Warsangali tribe of Cape Gardafui took refuge in a storm at Eid with their bark. They
found the town to their liking, settled there and married.
For a time all went well. But eventually the jealousy of
the Danakils provoked a tragedy. The wives of the
"strangers" attempted to poison the two Somalis. One
succeeded. The other Somali escaped to carry the news to
Cape Gardafui, and prepare plans of vengeance. One
night he returned to Eid, accompanied by ten boatloads
of his countrymen. Two by two they stationed themselves
before each sleeping hut and when their leader gave the
war cry, flung themselves on the sleeping inmates. All the
male Danakils, big and little, they massacred. The women
and girls were spared; but they received the usual treatment allotted to females on such expeditions, and the day
ended with an orgy of feasting and rape. In a few days,
the Danakils rallied their forces and drove the invaders
from the coast. But the expedition had left its mark on
the town—in due time finding expression in a whole colony
of little Somalis. Not one of my men dared to set foot on
shore. The Danakils of the region killed without mercy
every Warsangali who fell into their hands.

Leaving Eid we continued along the coast. In the little
bay of Anfalay where we put in for a night, we found an
Arab boutre which Abdi assured me was carrying slaves
to the Arab coast. We anchored alongside and Abdi, who
owns a grim sense of humor, hailed the *nakhoda* whom he
knew personally, with the statement that the *Sahala* had
on board an Italian customs officer. His words produced
great consternation. Without delay, the *nakhoda* put off
in a houri to visit us, bringing gifts of fish and dates.

When night had fallen, the slave ship slid discreetly out of the bay, glad no doubt to get off so easily and obviously mystified at our lack of interest in its proceedings. I had seen no evidence of slaves on board, but Abdi assured me that they lay pell-mell in the bottom under a tarpaulin. When a slaver meets a suspicious bark, he explained, the *nakhoda* stretches a tarpaulin over his cargo and the whole crew walks unconcernedly over the recumbent forms as if under the canvas there was nothing more animate than the usual load of dates, *taffi*, or dried fish. I expressed my astonishment at the docility of the human cargo. Abdi grinned.

"Of course they don't object," he explained. "They know they will be many times better off in Arabia than here in the desert. And besides, they are only stupid Soudanese. . . ."

At daybreak, we continued our cruise northward, picking our way among coral islands like tables of flat rock, lifted eighteen or twenty feet above the sea, overgrown with thorny bushes, mimosas, and a thick-leaved green plant that supplied a scanty population of goats with food and drink. On one of the islands—*Um al Sarig*—I noticed a Dankali cemetery, each tomb marked by a heap of shells of the sea tortoise. None of my men could explain the origin of this custom, though all assured me that every time one of the relatives of a dead pearl diver or fisher captured a sea tortoise, they carried it piously to the tomb. From a distance, one would have said that bones of the defunct were heaped lugubriously on his own grave.

We gave a wide berth to the island *Um al Namis*—the "mother of mosquitoes"—rising from the sea in a bouquet of green and universally shunned because of the clouds of huge mosquitoes that have given it its name. And on the morning following we reached Massawa, a tumbled pile of Arab houses in white relief against a background of mountains. Narrow alleys twisted among tall façades, their latticed second story projecting cage-like above the street. A labyrinth of dark passages formed the quarter of the *souks*, roofed over with planks and branches, and lined with dozens of little shops with rice, and spices, and piles of dates half hidden by clouds of flies. A crowd, chiefly of Arabs, mingled with Somalis and Soudanese from the pearl boutres that put in to Massawa for provisions, pushed and jostled—naked to the waist, bareheaded or wearing the fez of braided straw about which the Arab winds his turban.

Massawa is built on an island, joined to the mainland by a dike. Its climate, fully as hot as Djibouti, is even more difficult for white men to endure. It lies in a region of perpetual calm; the Dahalak Islands shut off the breeze; and the water among the reefs often reaches a temperature of ninety-eight degrees or more. The nearness of the Dahalak Islands—the center of the pearl fishing industry in the Red Sea—has made Massawa one of the great pearl markets, visited constantly by buyers from Europe and the Orient.

On that first visit, I had the good fortune to meet a representative of one of the principal pearl merchants of Paris, a Levantine by the name of Chouchan, a "Parisian" from Cairo, elegant and perfumed, wearing a dozen heavy rings on his slim fingers. Delighted at meeting a French colleague (on the strength of my first lucky purchase I styled myself "pearl buyer") he invited me straightway to inspect his collections. At the time, in spite of my initial stroke of luck and my not very brilliant attempt at pearl cultivating, I knew little about pearls—beyond the one

fact that you found them in oysters. Of the technique of
the pearl trade my ignorance was complete. So when the
affable Monsieur Chouchan showed me his purchases, I
maintained a discreet silence.

"You find nothing here that interests you?" he inquired
at length after an hour's monologue, during which he had
shown me a dozen lots of fine pearls. I shook my head.

"Perhaps you would prefer to see a few 'solitaires'?" he
proposed, and the inspection continued.

My manner seemed to intrigue the Levantine. He grew
curious to discover my methods of operating. Would I
care to be present while he received an Arab who was
bringing several new lots? Nothing could have pleased me
more; that invitation was the very chance I had been
waiting for.

That afternoon, and for two or three days following,
I sat at the elbow of the amiable Monsieur Chouchan, to
whom I owe, though I fancy he was far from suspecting
it, my initiation into the mysteries of the pearl.

Estimating pearls is a very definite, technical process.
The owner, generally the *nakhoda* of a pearl fishing boutre,
accompanied by two witnesses, one of whom represents the
proprietor of the boutre, and one, the crew,[1] presents the
prospective buyer with a "lot" of pearls, a tiny package
about the size of a walnut, enveloped in a bit of red cloth.

The "lot" contains pearls of all sizes and shapes: from
the *douga*, or seed pearl, to those of respectable volume.
The "solitaires," those of exceptional size or beauty, are

[1] Pearl fishing in the Red Sea is organized, so far as the fishers are
concerned, on a profit-sharing basis. The owner of the boutre has a
right to a fifth of the profits, after all expenses (the *masrouf*, food,
etc.) have been deducted. The *nakhoda* takes generally a third. The
rest is divided in equal parts among sailors and divers. The *nakhoda*
is entrusted with the sale of the pearls, but his transactions take place
in the presence of the two witnesses. As Chouchan remarked: "You
have to divide your bribes in three parts! . . ."

sold individually. The first task of the expert is to sort the pearls. This he does with the aid of a series of little screens. In each group, he puts carefully aside the round pearls and the "buttons" or half pearls; all of the others are considered as "baroque." The value of a "lot" is based on the calculated value of the round pearls and the "buttons"; the "baroques" are considered as "by-product" and are lumped together and sold by weight.

To determine the value of a round pearl the expert first weighs it. He reckons the weight in grains (the weight of a grain of rice). The weight is then squared, and a theoretical value of one gold franc per grain (as the pearl market of the West is Paris, the price is reckoned in francs) is given the pearl. For instance, if a pearl weighs three grains, that weight is squared to nine, and the initial value of the pearl is stated to be nine francs. Or in the jargon of the pearl merchant, it is worth nine francs "once the weight" (*une fois le poids*).

The next thing to determine is the quality of the pearl. The expert examines its form, color and orient. According to these, he determines *how many times its weight* the pearl is worth. A professional pearl buyer will never say: "This pearl is worth X francs." Instead, he uses the classic expression: "It is worth 20, or 50, or 200 '*times*'," as the case may be; meaning 20, or 50, or 200 times the initial value based on the square of the weight.

All this I learned during the hours I sat at the elbow of my accommodating countryman, nodding an occasional affirmative, or negative, but for the most part wrapped in an indifference I was far from feeling.

After the lesson in estimating pearls, came the real business of purchase. Always a long and complicated affair. Picture the seller—the *nakhoda* and his witnesses—

the prospective buyer, and the *dallal*, or mediator, who is present at all sales of pearls. The seller states a price; far in excess of what he considers the real value of the lot. For instance—10,000 rupees. The buyer replies: 100 rupees, a figure which he is well aware represents the merest fraction of what the pearls are worth. The conversation continues with grudging concessions for hours at a time. Finally, when both parties have reached a deadlock, or when their relative demands tend to approach a common figure, the *dallal* intervenes.

Spreading out the cloth of his turban over his knees, he takes the right hand of the seller in one of his own; and that of the purchaser in the other. The hands are hidden beneath the cloth of the turban. Then alternately he suggests a price, by squeezing the fingers of the hands under the cloth. One finger means 1, 10, 100, or 1,000. Two fingers mean 2, 20, 200, or 2,000, as the case may be. The hand-holding may go on for hours; sometimes even for days. In that case, a seal is placed on the lot of pearls, and the "conversation," broken off at evening, is continued on the following morning.

But if the *dallal* esteems that his clients are ready to conclude a bargain, he places the hand of the buyer in that of the owner of the pearls.

"Say: 'I purchase' . . ." he orders the one; and "Say 'I sell'," he tells the other.

When each has repeated the phrase, he states the sum he has fixed upon as the selling price. His statement is inevitably followed by a storm of objections and protests. The owner declares he is ruined; the buyer, that he has been robbed. But the bargain is consummated; the noisy comments of the two clients represent nothing more than a matter of form. The little sack of pearls changes hands, and the *dallal* pockets his commission: one per cent of the value of a lot; or five per cent, if he has arranged the sale of a "solitaire."

Needless to say, during my stay in Massawa I bought none of the collections that passed through the hands of Monsieur Chouchan. I found none of them "interesting," chiefly, I admit, because they represented a figure considerably in excess of any sum I could lay hands on at the time. But I did make a single purchase. As I remember, it belonged to the last lot we examined. By that time, I was beginning to calculate values fairly accurately. Among the pearls of that lot was one perfect sphere weighing about twenty grains. Chouchan pushed it aside with the "baroques."

"You can count that out," he remarked to the *nakhoda*. "It is dead."

Even I knew enough to recognize a "dead" pearl—a pearl that has no orient, like a lusterless ball of white mother-of-pearl, or the boiled eye of a fish. Pearls "die" if they remain for a time in a dead oyster. That is, a prolonged soaking in salt water robs the pearl of its luster.

I picked up the pearl Chouchan had discarded. It was not completely "dead"; the faintest ghost of an orient saved it from being entirely worthless.

"If you don't want it, I will take it off your hands," I suggested, turning the smooth little ball in my fingers. Chouchan gave me a quick look of astonishment. Then he grinned.

"It will make a nice gift for some one," he insinuated. Among professionals, pearls with flaws that make them worthless for the trade are generally reserved as presents for the layman. "You can have it cheap."

As I recall, I acquired the sick pearl for "two times,"

about 800 francs (at that time $160) which under the circumstances was far from being dirt-cheap. But as the Levantine pointed out, and I as a fellow-expert was forced to agree, the luster though faint, was sufficient to give my acquisition a minimum value. For my part, I was willing to risk the amount, though not as Chouchan thought, for the sake of acquiring a reputation for generosity for the sum of $160. I had in mind an experiment.

Chouchan, of course, knew quite as well as I (I owed the information to Abdi) that a "dead" pearl may only be dead in appearance. Sometimes, within the living oyster, the pearl shifts its position to a point where the nacreous secretion is not iridescent, but dull white.[1] So that in time it acquires an outer layer, opaque as that of a dead pearl. If this outer layer is removed, one uncovers the true pearl, with all its orient. Such an operation is precarious; unless the operator proceeds with extreme care, he risks destroying the pearl. Moreover, in the case of my own purchase, the "sick" pearl, because of its feeble luster, had a market value of $160. If I removed the outer layer to see what lay underneath, there was a chance that I might discover only an opaque substance—with the result that my "pearl" would no longer be worth $160—but zero.

An expert like Chouchan, who handled yearly many thousands of pearls, had little time or taste for such experiments. But remember, I was an amateur,—like a good many beginners I had more than the usual share of superb self-confidence.

As it happened, the gamble proved worth taking. When with infinite pains and a sharp scalpel I had scraped off a thin layer of opaque deposit, I uncovered a perfect pearl

---

[1] Certain oysters like the *Portugaises*, contain pearls, but these are always "dead" as the nacreous secretion has no luster.

lustrous and glistening. A pearl that a week later Abdi sold the unsuspecting Chouchan—for "forty times." So that one little operation netted me the considerable sum of 15,200 francs—$3,040. Not a bad beginning for an amateur "expert."

So for the second time, luck pressed my hand.

VI

Pearls and "Intelligence"

With 15,000 francs buckled fast in my money belt, and Abdi by my side I picked my way through the dark streets of Massawa, towards the port. The town slept fast, though it was barely eleven. Huddled along the wharf like bands of penguins, the native boutres creaked to the slow rhythm of an invisible swell.

Anchored out from the rest, the *Sahala,* too, rocked on the black water, glassy smooth as if ironed out by the sheer weight of the heat. Our pirogue slid towards it, trailing two long ribbons of green phosphorescence.

In the east, the horizon paled. A jackal barked. Cocks crowed on the terraces of the town. A white half-moon shot over the rim of the sea. Slowly it climbed the sky. At midnight a little land breeze crept down from the mountains in timid gusts, bringing the smell of sheep-folds and dried grass—the familiar odor of the African bush.

The lateen sail spread its broad triangle, white in the moonlight. With a land breeze astern we slid out of the silent port, past the red and green light buoys tugging gently at their chains, out towards the horizon that little by little crept round us in a circle.

In those waters, dawn brings dead calm. As the sun mounts, the sea lies, a blazing mirror of yellow light, its surface ruffled here and there by passing gusts or bands of leaping fish. The sail hangs dead from the yards, its sheets sweeping the deck, and the whole crew crowds into its shadow, a welcome shield from the fiery sun rays and the reverberation of the water.

Towards ten o'clock, the horizon is barred by a dark line that widens and advances, marking the return of the east wind that blows from the open water when the sun is high.

All day long we beat our way into the wind. Night found us in the Elbis Archipelago. Impossible to anchor; the lead showed 300 feet everywhere. So, posting a lookout forward, I pushed on in the darkness. Suddenly at midnight, I made out land—a black wall that seemed to rise up suddenly a hundred yards ahead. We veered; the lead still read 300 feet; then without warning we ran afoul of a reef. We were caught in what I learned later was a network of sharp coral ridges that rose within a few feet of the surface, separated by deep "trenches" from 150 to 300 feet in depth.

At the shock of the *Sahala's* keel against the reef, my four Somalis dived overboard.

All night long we splashed among the knife-like corals, straining and tugging at the heavy hull. At daybreak we were clear. A miracle that the boutre had sprung no leak! The crew's feet were full of spines of the poisonous sea urchin, painful sores that fester for days. The Somali remedy is primitively simple. To prevent the barbed spine from penetrating deeper, they break it by biting the flesh around the wound. An application of urine—the usual treatment for all flesh wounds—serves as disinfectant. . . .

Late that morning we reached Djumelay, principal fishing port of the Dahalak Islands where thirty boutres lay at anchor in the inlet. Along the shore in a row of huts, made of branches and palm-fiber, lodged the families of the pearl fishers—Soudanese, Dankali, and Arab. The

divers were easily recognizable because of their exaggerated chest development. Invariably they were young, rarely
over twenty-five years of age. In these regions men begin
diving as mere boys and abandon the profession after a
few years, to avoid the eye and bladder troubles inevitable
if they prolong the dangerous occupation over too many
years. Every man in my crew had in his youth dived for
pearls.

If the Dahalak Islands have become one of the principal
centers for the pearl and nacre industry in the Red Sea,
it is not because pearl-oysters are more plentiful there
than elsewhere. One finds the *bil-bil* and the *sadaf* from
one end of the Red Sea to the other. But because of the
pervading calm among the reefs that lie about the archipelago, these waters are almost always clear, so that pearl
fishing is possible for longer periods than anywhere else.
In troubled water, the diver is "blind"; a spell of bad
weather may interrupt pearl fishing for weeks at a time.

For several days we lay at anchor in the little bay of
Djumelay and let the news spread through the islands that
a *Mograbi* (one who lives west of the setting sun) had
come to buy pearls. Nearly all the fishing fleet was at sea,
but I received the visit of a dozen or more *nakhodas* who
had small lots of pearls to sell. Insignificant lots for the
most part—nothing at all to compare with what I had
been shown at Massawa.

"Go to Saïd Ali," Abdi advised, when I complained that
only "seconds" were to be found at Djumelay. Saïd Ali
was a rich Arab whose collections. . . . "If you have not
seen his pearls—you have seen nothing." Such pearls,
Abdi added, with an air of mystery, were not to be found
in Massawa, nor anywhere else!

On the strength of Abdi's fine tale, early one morning

I sent a sailor to Saïd Ali to announce my visit. Two hours later he returned to the beach accompanied by a Soudanese slave, bearing an enormous curved sword, and leading a saddled ass.

With the Soudanese marching ahead, we set off under the torrid sun across the sandy island dotted with tufts of the candelabra-like palm the Arabs call *doum*. (A useful tree: its fermented sap gives the *doma* or palm-wine; from the fiber or *taffi*, the natives of the coast weave their mats; out of its hard fruit, they carve buttons.) From each little hillock we looked out on the sea that lay about the island like a ring of hot white metal.

An hour's walk brought us to an oasis of date palms, shading a dozen flat-roofed houses, built of stone and earth.

I was led across a court, white with a layer of fine shells, to a house, freshly swept and prepared to receive me. On the floor of beaten earth, a pot of coals and incense smoked fragrantly. An *engareb* covered with rugs, stood against the wall. A slave brought me the usual refreshments—cakes of *durra* fried in butter, goat milk and dates, and an earthen bottle of *keshir* (a hot drink made from the ground pod of the coffee bean, mixed with ginger, cloves and cinnamon).

An hour later, another slave came to escort me to Saïd Ali. We crossed the court to a second larger house. Some twenty persons—slaves, servants and neighbors, I gathered, squatted on their heels outside the door. Nearly all of them rose as I approached, and crowded into the room after me. Leaving the brilliant sunlight of the court, the room seemed particularly black, but I caught the glitter of the silver fittings of a water pipe and pale splotches of turban. As my eyes grew accustomed to the darkness, I made out the silhouettes of six Arabs seated cross-legged against the wall. Addressing the central figure, whom I took to be the host, I made the customary salaam—touching his hand and lifting my own to my lips; repeating the same gesture afterwards before each of the men present.

Saïd Ali, a big Arab, stout and bearded, draped in the folds of a *chamma*, motioned me to a seat on one of the *engarebs;* a slave passed the water pipe, and we began one of the conversations that precede all discussions of business of any sort in this part of the world. On the part of Saïd Ali, a long series of questions.

"You come from Massawa? From Djibouti? Have you seen Salim Mouti? Are his affairs progressing? Have the Hakmi made peace with the Turks? Are you friends with the Hakmi? Is it not dangerous for you, a stranger, to visit their country?"

"What have I to fear?" I replied to the last question, having answered as best I could all that proceeded. "If I go to the country of the Hakmi, it is on my own business. For reasons of trade. Even as I come here, Saïd Ali."

"For reasons of trade. So—," very casually, "you buy pearls?" And I, equally casual,

"Yes, but not at present. I have already completed my purchases at Massawa."

"You ought to have come to me sooner. For I too own a few."

"Should you still care to show them . . . ?" I suggested.

In answer, Saïd Ali had a low table placed before me and beckoned to a slave who brought him a small coffer, bound with copper. He tossed on the table a handful of small lots of pearls, each tied in the inevitable red rag. Even to my unpracticed eye it was evident that none of the lots were exceptional. I shook my head.

"This sort of thing does not interest me at all," I told him with a shrug. "That is why I did not come to Dahalak before. At Massawa they told me I would find here only mediocre pearls."

Saïd Ali's yellow fingers dug deeper in the coffer.

"Here are others," he observed calmly, bringing out a fresh series of red knobs. A slave unwrapped the lots and I brought out my screens and weighing-scales. These lots were infinitely finer, much finer in fact than I could hope to purchase. After a careful scrutiny, I laid aside my tools.

"No," I remarked, feigning indifference. "I find nothing here."

Saïd Ali clapped his hands. His eyes glittered under their heavy brows. "If you want to see pearls," he said quietly, "I will show you . . . pearls." A Wallamo slave stepped from the group behind me. Taking a key from his hands, Saïd Ali rose from the *engareb*, and beckoning me to follow, preceded me across the court and through a low door into a room with an iron chest built into the wall. Two slaves, each with a curved knife belted at the waist, slipped through the doorway behind us.

At a turn of the key, the lid of the chest swung out like the door of a safe. Three shelves barred the interior. On each shelf stood a row of little glass jars, filled to the brim with a transparent liquid, that covered layer upon layer of iridescent white spheres. Pearls—hundreds of them—like peas in a can, and what pearls! The Arab held out a flask for me to examine. It contained perhaps a hundred pearls of a faint rose tint, carefully matched as to size and luster. And there were dozens of such flasks in the chest.

"What is the liquid?" I inquired. Saïd Ali smiled.

"Rain water. As you know, it takes away the slightly greenish tint of the fresh pearl. You can preserve them so, for hundreds of years."

Later I was to hear of other pearl collectors, Arabs like Saïd Ali, for whom pearls are a veritable passion. If they buy and sell, it is merely to better or increase their own collections. Every time they discover a prize, they put it carefully away in a jar of rain water on one of the shelves of an iron chest. Some of these collections which are never for sale, represent tremendous fortunes,[1] guarded by a handful of slaves—and by the reefs and the desert.

After I had feasted my eyes for an hour or so on Saïd Ali's treasure (he gave me to understand that only under very special circumstances would he consider parting with any of the collection), we returned to the room where the other Arabs sat crosslegged and impassive, smoking the *medaha*, Saïd Ali paused before the table where the lots of pearls we had examined still lay exposed, each on its square of red cloth.

"These interest you not at all?" he inquired. I hesitated; I had no wish to appear discourteous. I felt that my rôle of merchant demanded at least that I make an offer. Picking out one of the lots at random (I had previously examined them all) I proposed a figure ridiculously low, according to the value I had estimated. Saïd Ali met the offer with a smiling wave of disdain and I prepared to take my leave. I was already at the door when he called me back.

"Abd el Tai," he said affably, "the price you offer is far below the value of the pearls. But as we have never yet

---

[1] At the death of Saïd Ali, a few years ago, his heirs sold the pearls I saw over fifteen years ago for $5,000,000.

had dealings together, and as I wish to preserve our contact—which I trust will be prolonged and fruitful—you may take the lot at the price you have named."

If the roof had fallen in upon me, I would have been no more surprised. Surprised and overwhelmed, for the sum I had mentioned represented twice as much money as I owned in the world. I was instantly convinced there must have been some mistake in my calculations. No Arab, I knew, would have accepted an offer with such precipitation if it had not been to his advantage. So that my offer instead of being ridiculously small, as I had thought, had probably been far in excess of the real value of the pearls! Gathering my wits together, I bade Saïd Ali seal up the lot in question, stating that I would return the following morning to conclude the deal.

After the lot had been tied and sealed in my presence, I took leave of Saïd Ali and his silent friends, and rode back through the heat to Djumelay, racking my brains to find a way out of the bargain, without jeopardizing my future in the pearl market of the region.

As I came down to the port I noticed a boutre flying the Italian flag, that had just dropped anchor a hundred yards or so from the *Sahala*. An Italian askar from the customs service at Massawa had come to relieve his colleague charged with the supervision of the port. The sight of the boutre furnished me with an idea. Not too brilliant, but it sufficed.

I forthwith bribed the askar to spread the news that he had been ordered to recall me to Massawa at once for an affair of extreme gravity. In haste I sent a messenger to Saïd Ali with the same information, my excuses for the hasty departure, and the request to postpone our affair until my next visit. At midnight, the *Sahala* hoisted sail for Djibouti.

Outside the reefs, the monsoon caught us. Three days and two nights we fought our way south, making little headway, and taking no time to eat nor sleep. After fifty-six hours at the helm, I was thankful to find an anchorage behind Ras Rakhmat, within sight of a Dankali village of the same name.

Before us stretched a black-and-white landscape—sand, lava-rock and basalt, with a background of cone-like craters, one of which smoked lazily. A shore sterilized by flame, that seemed like the slag from some enormous furnace, so desolate that one might fancy it was only yesterday the great volcanic upheavals occurred that lifted the first land out of the sea. Not a blade of grass. To feed their camels, the Danakils drove the herds several miles inland, or gathered mangrove leaves on the islands of the little archipelago. The population itself lived on camel's milk and fish and the sea as snails that the women and children gathered on the reefs at low tide.

Several houris put out from the shore, manned by mother-of-pearl fishers, their brown bodies crusted with white from the salt spray. They brought us fish, to exchange for rice, dates and *durra*.

After a night at Rakhmat we tried to put out to sea, but the monsoon drove us back. We moored in the shelter of Dakhmat island, a bare rust-colored rock uninhabited save for a species of falcon, whose nests lay everywhere among the stones. To my mystification I observed hundreds of broken *trochi* shells. As we watched the falcons we found the key to the mystery. Swooping down to a reef left bare by the receding tide, we saw one of the birds seize a snail (the snails are as big as a man's two fists) in its claws, then darting up to a great height let fall the sea snail on the rocks. In an instant the bird dropped like a stone from the sky, and picked away busily at the shattered shell. We took two young falcons from a nest. Each weighed about four pounds. Skinned and roasted, they made an excellent meal.

For two days we lay in the lee of Dakhmat while the storm howled, and the sea broke on the windward side of the islands with the noise of distant cannon.

On the second day I came near losing Abdi. At three o'clock I waked out of a long nap in the shade of the big yard and called to Abdi to make tea. But Abdi was not on board. The houri too had disappeared. I concluded that my *nakhoda* had paddled to the island, but to my surprise, I saw no trace of the houri on the beach. One of the men called my attention to something black bobbing among the waves, a mile away. With my glasses I made out the empty houri, which the wind was rapidly carrying out to sea.

Hoisting a jib, we set off in pursuit of the dugout, which we did not recover until we were in shallow water two miles from the island. Dropping anchor, we set about preparing a larger sail to beat our way back to shelter. While we rolled and pitched in the heavy sea I sighted a black speck on the beach, and with the glasses discovered it was Abdi. Then the speck disappeared; he had started to swim out to us. It was a mad thing to do, a two-mile swim against the current. I called to the crew to lower the sail; had we lifted anchor, we would have destroyed Abdi's one chance of reaching us safely. For a long time I lost sight of him; then I caught glimpses of him plunging ahead through the waves. When he was

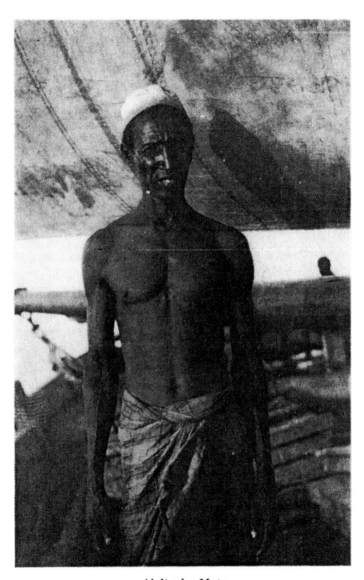

Abdi, the Mate

within a few hundred yards of the boutre, I noticed that
he kept throwing a bundle ahead of him as he swam.

As we hauled him on board, his first question was;
why had we left without him? The poor fellow had swam
to shore to fish among the rocks for our dinner, and the
precious bundle he pushed before him through the waves
contained four fine specimens wrapped in his *fohta*. The
dugout must have snapped its hawser as we lay at anchor.

The *Sahala* was not the only boutre to take shelter that
day among the islands of Rakhmat. Late that afternoon,
a *zaroug* slipped between the reefs and anchored a cable's
length from our boutre. Now the *zaroug* is the favorite
type of boat utilized by smugglers and pirates on both
sides of the Red Sea. Slender of line, light and swift, the
zaroug carries no ballast. It is manned by a crew of six
or seven men, who keep the craft from capsizing by coun-
ter-balancing the pressure of the wind by the weight of
their bodies.

Its sail furled, our neighbor settled down for the night.
The cook lighted his fire, and a tall figure in white whom
I took to be the *nakhoda* seated himself in the stern with
his water pipe. Two of my Somalis, whom I sent in the
dugout with a gift of rice and dates, returned with a
provision of salt fish and the news that Sheik Mâki was
on board.

"Sheik Mâki," said Abdi, speaking the name with great
respect, "carries arms to Arabia and slaves from behind
the mountains (he meant Abyssinia) to the land of the
Hakmi. He, himself, is a Hakmi, but he has Dankali wives
in Tajura. So he is at home here and in Yemen where he
has other wives. Sheik Mâki is a very holy man. In a night
he can ride a hundred miles on a mule. He does not fear
shipwreck, for the dolphins always save him."

Curious, I bade Abdi paddle me over to the *zaroug* with a present of tobacco. I was met by a tall Arab, clean shaven and spare, with fine regular features that in repose had an air of great severity. As he spoke, the impression vanished.

"I have heard of you, Abd el Hai," he said, cordially, after an exchange of salaams. His use of my newly acquired Arab name did not surprise me. News travels rapidly along the coast.

"They speak well of you in Tajura," he added, his dark eyes fixed on mine. "When you wish to land arms there come to me. I have friends who can be of use to you, and I too perhaps—if ever you have need of me."

Again that intriguing reference to the arms trade. After the fishers at Sheik Said, Sheik Mâki. . . . The Sheik's parting words left me with further food for thought.

"On the Arab coast, be prudent," he counseled. "They have been warned—and are on the lookout for you."

Just who "they" were—and who it was that had taken sufficient interest in my movements to advertise them in advance, I neglected to inquire. It amused me to have the great Sheik Mâki mistake me for a colleague and I made no attempt to undeceive him. I thanked him for the warning and promptly forgot it, since I had no intention, at least not during that particular cruise, of heading east for Arabia.

But I had counted without the monsoon. Next day the weather let us free from our prison at Rakhmat and we headed south along the Dankali coast, skirting barren stretches of pale sand dotted here and there with the silhouettes of camels grazing among the thorns. After a night of dead calm among the coral islands of Assab, the

Sahala sailed eastward in the morning breeze, and we planned to veer south and reach Bab el Mandeb on a second tack. Towards two o'clock the breeze freshened; by nightfall the monsoon blew steadily. With our sail reduced to a jib, I tried to hold the *Sahala* due east, but I could feel the monsoon pushing her steadily out of her course. At moonrise, its violence redoubled; there was nothing to do but run before the wind. Towards one o'clock, a liner loomed suddenly out of the night and bore down on us rapidly from the north. At that moment our one lantern, which the wind had already extinguished half a dozen times since dusk, went out completely. I tried to improvise a flare with a handful of tow, but the wind drowned it instantly. A couple of gunshots, however, had the desired effect—the steamer veered in time, passing at a cable's length. I thought with envy of the passengers snug in their cabins, while drenched and shivering, I gripped the helm of my little bark, plunging like a mad thing in the waves that piled up astern as if racing to pounce upon us.

It seemed hours later, though I imagine it must have been around three, I made out ahead the dark outline of a ridge of mountains. Lighting a match underneath a blanket, I hastily looked at the chart, and concluded that we were approaching Mount Doubaba (Fly Mountain). From that point to Moka, the coast offered no shelter. But as we neared land the sea quieted down; half a mile from shore we were able to drop anchor and wait for day.

At dawn I let the wind carry us north along a coast fringed with date palms and dotted with the white cubes of Arab houses. Towards noon we sighted Moka, a natural harbor sheltered behind a long strip of sand. Seen from

the sea, one would have said a great white city, bristling
with minarets. Closer up, it seemed to crumble before our
eyes. The fortified walls stood in ruins; in ruins, too, the
tall Arab houses that, roofless and with gaping windows,
lined the deserted beach. The *Sahala* dropped anchor before the phantom town while I wondered what sort of
fantastic creatures still crept hyena-like among the ruins.

I discovered all too soon! Scarcely had I set foot on
the beach, when an Arab, presumably a Turkish soldier,
belted with cartridges and daggers, and carrying a Remington, appeared from nowhere, and demanded my papers.
He looked them over disdainfully, incapable of reading
a line of what was written, and ordered us to follow him.

For half an hour I tramped after my guide through
what had once been the streets of Moka. At every step,
houses four stories high, carved with intricate arabesques,
testified to the splendor of the once great coffee port which
the Suez Canal had ruined. Here and there an Arab camping in the midst of the débris with his hens, goats, and
ass, gave an illusion of life to the deserted quarter. Of
some structures, only the foundations remained; and I
noticed open spaces littered with stones and wood, as if
earthquake or tornado had been the destroyer.

At last we came to a halt before a big building, tumble-
down certainly, but still relatively intact: the barracks.
We entered a room lighted only by the doorway, that
stank prodigiously of goat dung. A fat fellow in uniform,
with bulbous purple features and a vast white mustache,
sat smoking a water pipe. He continued with his put-put
and gloo-gloo-ing for quite a long time before returning
my salaam.

Then, with military abruptness, he began to question
me in Arab.

"Where do you come from?"

"What is your business?"

"Where are you going?"

At each of my replies, he exchanged glances with other uniformed and mustached individuals who squatted about him in a semicircle.

After the grilling, four brigands armed to the teeth received orders to escort me to the governor. Again we marched through a labyrinth of narrow alleys between crumbling walls to a second house. Through a succession of corridors, dark stairways, and terraces, I was led into the presence of a young Turk wearing pajamas and red leather *babouches*, who sat on a divan sipping coffee out of a tiny gold cup, flanked by two languid officers in uniform. Two red-and-blue-paned windows high up on the wall softened the hard sunlight.

"Your nationality?" I was asked in Arab.

"A citizen of France." At the words, the governor favored me with a smile, ineffably amiable. A Frenchman! How fortunate that he himself spoke the language of my country! I changed from Arab into French with small success. As I spoke, the governor opened his eyes, pursing his lips as if about to whistle. He made every effort to comprehend. But I knew that he understood not a word of what I said. This was no time for misunderstanding. . . . I switched from French back into Arab. Followed, the same sort of questioning to which I had already been subjected.

At length, apropos of nothing, the official murmured carelessly:

"Have you ever been to Sheik Said?"

So that was what! Useless to deny the fact; bad weather,

I said, had obliged me to put into port there for twenty-four hours.

The governor's smile became even more amiable.

"And—by way of distraction it occurred to you to take a few photographs?"

"Quite so, Your Excellency," I replied in as indifferent a tone as I could muster.

The Turk regarded me gravely. Then again he favored me with the elastic smile.

"I regret, infinitely, Abd el Hai" (from his lips, the name sounded incredibly strange), "but I am obliged to ask you for those photographs."

"Gladly," I acquiesced, "if you find them of interest."

"Of very *particular* interest," the governor answered, stressing the word with a quick glance towards one of the two officers. "If you will tell where you keep the negatives, I will send some one instantly—"

"I am extremely confused. . . . (It was my turn to be exquisitely polite.) I am afraid I should have to find them for you myself. Frankly I do not remember at this moment where I put them." That seemed a bit broad—considering the restricted proportions of the *Sahala*. But my interlocutor, evidently no seaman, took no exception to my statement.

"Certainly," he conceded. "I shall be glad to give you an escort to your boutre *and back again*. Here in Moka," he deplored, "the streets are not safe for strangers." An opinion my experience inclined me to share.

Leaving the governor, I set off for the port escorted by the same four soldiers bristling with guns and daggers.

On the way, I explained to my guard that I desired to buy provisions. All four offered eagerly to make the purchases for me—in the hope of scratching a *manassir* or

two from the total sum. I gave three *thalers* to two of the
men with orders to buy me a sheep. The third, I sent to
buy chickens. As for the fourth askar, I suggested slyly
that perhaps he might like a bottle of wine. (The Turks,
as I well knew, are rarely orthodox in the matter of wine.)
He accepted with alacrity, urging me to give him the
bottle before his companions returned, so that he would
not have to share it. Whereupon, we hastened our steps
towards the port. On the beach, I told the Turk to wait
while I paddled out for the bottle. Nothing loath, he
squatted contentedly on the sand, while I made off in all
haste to the *Sahala*.

The crew were all on board, considerably upset at my
absence. Hurriedly explaining the situation, I dispatched
a Somali with the promised bottle and a box of photo-
graphic plates—unexposed—to be carried at once to the
governor. From the deck of the *Sahala* I saw the soldier
set off precipitously across the beach, the flask tucked out
of sight under his vest.

To leave Moka in all speed should have been our move.
That, unfortunately, was out of the question, as the wind
still held, blowing with such violence that even in the
harbor the *Sahala* rolled heavily at her moorings. I decided to shift our anchorage to a point near the lighthouse that lifted its steel column 150 feet above the sand
bank, two miles from the town. It belonged to a French
company, the proprietor of all Turkish lights in the Red
Sea and the Bosphorus. In its neighborhood, I would feel
comparatively safe.

As an additional precaution, I thought it wise to call
on the lighthouse keeper. Barely had I grounded the
houri on the sand, when a pack of dogs rushed from behind
the fence around the lighthouse. I threw myself on all

fours—the old burglar trick which had already saved me
more than once when attacked by dogs in Abyssinia. (It
checks their onslaught invariably, but the victim is obliged
to remain on all fours until some one, the dog's owner, or
a Samaritan with a gun, comes to his rescue!) The lighthouse keeper, aroused by the tumult, delivered me from
my undignified position. A Greek, Tselatis by name, lived
there with his young wife, completely isolated; obtaining
provisions and water from Perim (to avoid being poisoned
—he said), and guarded by five Arabs and the pack of
watchdogs whose diligence I had just put to test. The
coast, he told me, swarmed with pirates; the Turks remained on good terms with the Arabs only because they
never interfered in local affairs.

"Fortunate for you you came when you did. My men
have orders to fire on any one who approaches after
dark."

That evening I ate my first European meal in months.
As we sat over our coffee, I related my recent experience
in Moka.

"It seems only natural that the Turks should object
to my visit at Sheik Said," I concluded. "But what I cannot comprehend is how the news traveled to Moka."

Tselatis, his eyes half closed, drew meditatively on his
cigar.

"When you have navigated longer in these waters," he
remarked after a silence, "you will be asking that question
a good many times. Bear only this in mind: here in the
Near East there is only one 'intelligence service' that
functions. Not always efficiently, and certainly not always
wisely. *But it functions.* It isn't a Turkish service; I don't
need to tell you that! So whenever you run against a
mystery. . . ." He paused significantly. "In France, you

say '*cherchez la femme.*' In this part of the world we play differently on the expression. . . . '*Cherchez l'anglais.*' Always we say, '*cherchez l'anglais.*' "

That angle of the question had not occurred to me. Across the table, the round face of the Greek beamed through a cloud of blue smoke.

"It would not be the first time they got the Turks to do what they did not care to do themselves. The cat's-paw way. . . ." He paused with a grin. "I am sorry for you," he continued seriously, "if they have you already on their black list. For you can count on it—they will not forget you."

I remembered Sheik Mâki and his warning. Something in it, then. At the outset as a navigator in the Red Sea, I had run afoul of the Grand Nation. O miracle of "intelligence" that foresaw the effect of wind and weather, and divined my intentions before I was conscious of them myself!

"They are everywhere, *ces gens,*" the Greek murmured.

Everywhere. . . . But on the sea, a man is master of his ship. Blacklisted or not, I would let no adversary, not even the Lion of Perim, prevent me from going where and when I pleased. So I resolved as we lay off the Moka light, waiting for the monsoon to drop, and watching the *zarougs* of the tobacco, arms, and slave smugglers slip north unhindered along the coast.

A puny challenge—but Allah will bear witness—maintained until the end.

VII

The Honorable Arms Trade

Grown men are not supposed to slam doors. Though to
certain conversations, that gesture represents the only
logical conclusion. Had the marble archway leading out
of the governor's study been provided with panels, I would
have been sorely tempted to send them crashing to behind
me. As it was, I clattered down the grand staircase and
across the courtyard at a pace that startled the uniformed
Somalis who mounted a languid guard at the entrance of
the Residence. They stared at me stupidly as I stood there
in the street, looking up at the white façade.

Straight before me stretched the wharf, a white line
cutting into the water that lay level and green in the
afternoon light. To the right, I made out the mass of
my boat riding at anchor. I longed to head her fine nose
out into the swell of the Gulf without waiting for morning; but of my crew, only the boy Moussa remained on
board. I had given the others shore leave for the night,
and they had disappeared in the Bender-Djedid, the native
quarter of Djibouti.

I turned my back resolutely on the sea, tramping west
across town, towards the desert. I felt the need of space and
silence to collect my thoughts and recover my composure.
In the square a gang of Somali prisoners guarded by askari
with bayonets, were busy paving or unpaving according
to the latest whim of a municipal engineer. Beneath the
arcades of the cafés, my countrymen had gathered for

the afternoon *apéritif*. In the light of my recent conversation with the governor, I tried to picture myself sipping
an iced *quinina*—that gastric abomination—giving my
opinion on the stale news of Europe, listening to the gossip
about somebody's wife, somebody's husband, somebody's
"boy," the state of somebody's liver, the latest stupidity
of the Abyssinians, or the financial possibilities of a scheme
for exploiting something or some one— "A sure thing,
I tell you, with every political guarantee. . . ."

"You cannot always stay on the outside," the governor said.

"But perhaps I belong outside," I suggested.

"Impossible!" the governor snorted from the depths of
his armchair. "Unless you are a criminal or an anarchist!"

I wished the white clad colonials no ill, but they and
their *apéritifs*, their stuffy, café-office-salon existence, with
an occasional sniff at a forbidden alcove, belonged to a
distasteful type of life with which I had long since definitely broken. But perhaps what separated us more than
all else was that they were of the land, while I belonged
to the sea. How could men whose every instinct held them
to the warmth and motion of the herd, understand that
just as instinctively I preferred solitude—solitude peopled with the ever-changing moods of the elements? And
that even with the narrow limits of my boutre, however
close and constant the contact with my Somali crew, I
could still indulge my taste for seclusion as isolated among
those men of another race and civilization as if I navigated
alone!

Leaving the arcades and the whitewashed plaster of
the European quarter, I skirted the native town, its
crowded huts of branch and earth, its goats, its flies, its
minarets, and always somewhere the repeated rhythms of

a Somali chant and the thud of a drum. Beyond the town, the smoke-blackened *gourgi* of the nomads, and still beyond lay the desert, a rust colored plain lifting gradually towards the distant mountains. I crossed files of women bent double under bundles of firewood from the distant bush, and Issas from the hunger districts, their flesh shrunken and leathery, feeling their way with tottering precision like men in a nightmare.

Night came swiftly, bringing a soft breeze from the sea. I stretched myself on the sand, hands beneath my head, and face to the sky. Overhead the stars hung polished and bright, immeasurably big, and so close it seemed only normal that a child should cry for them. By that time, my anger had fallen. I could think over my interview with the governor with grim philosophy.

I had gone to the Residence that afternoon: first of all to make my report on the unlucky visit to Sheik Said, which, according to Tselatis, had jeopardized my future with the Masters of the Red Sea; and second, to ask for permission to settle on Mascali Island and install there an oyster-park for cultivating pearls. My trip to Massawa and Dahalak had convinced me it would take many years and considerable capital before I could hope to compete with Saïd Ali or even Chouchan as a pearl expert or merchant. For the time being, I decided to continue my pearl cultivating and to take up pearl fishing in a modest fashion on my own account. Mascali seemed a good enough place to install an oyster-park. It was surrounded by reefs and shoals that sheltered it from the wind and provided shallow water for my plantations of *sadafs*. There I would be my own master and could go and come at will without the formalities of the port.

The governor thanked me for the photographs of Sheik

Said, remarked again that though "interesting" they were of no great importance, and tossed the package on the table with an air of discarding the subject in the same casual fashion. But I had not finished with Sheik Said. I related in detail my experience at Moka. The governor deplored the incident, laying it to what he termed some "layman's" imprudence on my part, and trusted it would have no diplomatic consequences. I resented the word "imprudence," but I thought it useless and somewhat ridiculous to protest. However, I put the question frankly: did he really think the English . . . ?

The governor shrugged his shoulders. Did one ever really know . . . ? There was a chance that my visit, quite unofficial and personal, had been misinterpreted. At Perim, they were very watchful and rightly so. The passage to the Orient. . . . Imperial dominions. . . . A great responsibility. He seemed to have forgotten the photographs and indeed his whole connection with the matter. I half expected to see him hand me back the package with a *"Monsieur vous vous êtes trompé d'adresse."* But his disavowal of any part of responsibility in my visit to Sheik Said did not extend to anything so concrete. As he spoke, the conviction dawned within me that no point in my story had surprised the governor, that in fact he had foreseen every phase of it. He had warned me against the Turks but he had left me in ignorance of the other danger, by far the more important. I began to understand why he had sent a "layman." My annoyance at my own density far surpassed any irritation I might have felt against the official who had acted according to the famous A B C of diplomacy: "Get some one else to do what you may not care to do yourself." Well, the milk was spilt. If indeed my name

figured on the mysterious black list of Perim, manifestly
nothing could be done about it. It was my turn to direct
the conversation. I embarked on my project concerning
Mascali.

The governor listened, his brows puckered in an
Olympian frown. I finished. He offered me a cigar.

"There are several things I have wanted to talk over
with you for some time," he began, clearing his throat.
"A word or two of criticism and advice. I trust you will
accept it as it is meant. Personally and as an official, I
am interested in your welfare. And I dislike to see you
running into difficulty through . . . hm . . . youthful
heedlessness and lack of . . . consideration."

"Lack of consideration?" I repeated stupidly.

"Consideration for others. . . . The way you go about
things. Always an air of mystery. Taking no one into your
confidence. As if . . . now personally I am convinced you
have nothing to conceal . . . and yet already in Djibouti
people are remarking a tendency on your part to secrecy."

"Secrecy," I broke in hotly. "Minding my own business
and letting others attend to theirs!"

"Quite right, quite right," the governor hastened to
agree. "But it all depends on how you do it. At times,
you actually seem to shun your countrymen; and naturally they resent it. In all Djibouti—"

"But, my dear governor, I do not give a damn for the
whole population of Djibouti!"

"That is just the point I was coming to." The speaker's tone grew ponderous. "You know as well as I, that no
man can live independent of his fellows. Even more true,
here in the colony, where we white men must stand together,
unified and fraternal, each engaged in an honorable
calling. . . ."

Here I suppose I gave something not unlike a snort. For no one knew better than I, unless the governor himself, what *honorable calling* had been responsible for a large share of the prosperity of the Somali coast. The speaker chose to ignore my ill-mannered interruption.

"Your way of living, your . . . er . . . exclusiveness while in Abyssinia, was no concern of mine. But now you have come down to the coast. You spend your time with Somalis along the docks—doing no one knows what. You buy a boutre—no one knows why. And you start off on mysterious voyages. . . ."

"To Sheik Said," I supplemented shortly.

"To Sheik Said," the governor conceded imperturbably. "And to Moka. You neglected to mention, if I remember, what took you to Moka. Something quite avowable, I am sure. And now—" he continued hastily, for he saw that I was about to break in again. "And now you plan to settle down on Mascali with a handful of natives, removed from all contact with your countrymen—removed from the control of the port! . . ."

"And from the control of the Customs," I suggested flippantly.

"From the control of the Customs," the governor repeated impassively, "and all that to what end? To raise pearls. Hm. . . . To raise pearls."

For a moment we sat staring at each other as across a chasm, the governor in his leather chair and I speechless, the picture no doubt of confounded guilt. At that point, I was treated to the phrase about criminals and anarchists, and I experienced that overpowering impulse to slam a door.

As I lay on my back in the sand, I might have smiled at the absurdity of it all. For my resentment was not that

of injured innocence. At bottom it was quite one to me
whether the governor thought I was raising pearls or
dragon's teeth in my plantations on Mascali. But I found
myself repeating as a grown man the same phrase I had
uttered so often as a child, on my face among the fragrant
herbs of the Cape, "Why can't they leave me alone?"

To be alone—was it so abnormal, so unnatural a desire? Was my society indispensable to others? Or was
it merely in another form, the same nagging insistence of
my relatives and schoolmates; bent on making all men over
after the same pattern? As if that were possible! For
thirty years I had tried to compromise. That was over
and done with. Between the governor's world and mine
there could be none. We did not even speak a common
tongue. To me that other world, its confused objectives,
its preoccupations, its stifling proximities, its "honorable
callings" that permitted so many interpretations—seemed
purposeless. My world—the clean world of the sea, was
to the governor a secret garden, remote, shadowy, poisonous. The individual and the group: must that necessarily
mean the individual *against* the group . . . or the group
against the individual?

Of one thing I was certain. With the other world I had
broken. No difficulties, real or imaginary, no amount of
persuasion could bring me back. I had chosen to be alone;
alone I would remain. I would follow my destiny—every
man's right—to the end.

I have made no secret of my life during the past years.
To-day I do not attempt to explain nor excuse, to call
this or that black or white. For eighteen years I followed
the sea, took what it offered. It has brought me shipwreck
and success, sorrow, danger, and unutterable happiness.
For eighteen years of my life, I lived completely.

Does this seem a roundabout way of explaining how I became a smuggler of arms? It is not entirely truthful to say that my interview with the governor suggested the idea. It had been simmering in the back of my mind ever since my meeting with Sheik Mâki. And yet that phrase about "honorable callings," the implied opposition to my own secret schemes, brought it upmost at once.

For fifteen years, or more accurately ever since the colony was founded, and when the capital of French Somaliland was still situated at Obok, the arms trade represented the most flourishing commerce of the coast; a trade that brought in millions of gold francs to the merchants of the colony. And to the colonial government as well, for the imported arms paid a heavy duty: 50 per cent for every rifle, and 55 per cent for every thousand cartridges.

Arms and munitions came principally from Belgium. Most of the material consisted in arms of an abandoned pattern,—former government stock (Gras, Lebel, and Mauser rifles) which the Belgian firms bought for a small sum. (A Liège manufacturer purchased the Lebels for one franc apiece.) After adapting the rifles for colonial use, shortening the barrels, and overhauling them generally, they were sold to the importing firm at Djibouti for from twelve to sixteen francs each. The ultimate buyer paid for the same rifle thirty-five to fifty francs if purchased *legally*. If it reached him in contraband, the price was considerably higher.

The Djibouti merchants sold the imported arms to Arab middlemen who carried the merchandise to Arabia. As the sale of arms was prohibited in those parts of the peninsula under British and Turkish control, the French colony obliged the Arab buyers to declare that they

destined all arms for Mascatte, a port at the entrance of
the Persian gulf, where there was an independent Sultan
and a French trading station. On the surface, the trade
appeared legitimate. In reality, most of the arms purchased at Djibouti never reached Mascatte. They were
landed in contraband throughout the whole length of the
Arab coast. That, however, was no concern of the Djibouti merchants. Each year they exported thousands of
cases containing rifles and cartridges all bearing the
label: "destination, Mascatte."

The arms trade at that period was not limited to
Arabia. There was also trade with Abyssinia. Ato Josef
still lived in Djibouti. His had been a strange history: the
son of an Abyssinian and a Chancalla slave-girl, he had
spent his childhood in a Catholic Foundling Home. Later
he became the personal servant of a Russian adventurer,
Leontieff, who for a time had considerably annoyed the
French by attempting, with thirty of his countrymen, to
establish a settlement on the shore of the Gulf of Tajura.
To further his interests in Abyssinia (which at the time
were none too brilliant), Leontieff evolved a magnificent
scheme. He would accompany to Russia an ambassador
from Menelik II, *Negus negusti*, King of Kings, to his
imperial cousin at St. Petersburg. The "ambassador" was
no other than Leontieff's boy, Josef, to whose name the
Russian prefixed the Abyssinian title *Ato* (Sir). Having
announced his voyage by courier, Leontieff was distinctly
annoyed to receive an answer requesting him to dissuade
the "ambassador" from making the journey. But the wily
Russian arranged with the local telegraph agent to return
the telegram to its imperial author stating that the envoy
extraordinary and his suite had already left for Europe.

The court of St. Petersburg perforce received Leontieff

and his companion with appropriate pomp—balls, banquets, and gifts. Leontieff returned to Abyssinia to acquaint Menelik II (whom he had neglected to inform in advance) with the success of his brilliant mission at St. Petersburg. The *negus*, in his ignorance of European diplomacy, saw nothing out of the way in the situation. Leontieff received the reward he coveted (a solidly established position in Abyssinia), and Ato Josef, as recompense for his services, was appointed commercial agent for the *negus* at Djibouti.

When I first came to the Somali coast, Ato Josef occupied a privileged and singular position. There being no Ethiopian representative in Djibouti, Ato Josef styled himself "consul"—which carried with it certain definite, material advantages. It was the presence of Ato Josef which gave the arms trade its chance of penetrating Abyssinia. Ato Josef furnished the façade. For the sum of one pound sterling, *per rifle,* he issued permits adorned with impressive stamps and seals—specifying that a stated quantity of arms and munitions had been purchased *by the Ethiopian government,* for shipment, either by rail from Djibouti to Diré Daoua, or by caravan inland from the port of Tajura.

What went by rail represented *bona fide* orders from the Ethiopian government and was in due time delivered to the army of the *negus.* But the arms that left for Tajura—by far the greater quantity—rarely if ever reached the frontier. Those that did (and imperial Menelik was kept in pious ignorance of the fact) went to arm certain of his subordinates—local chiefs who had ideas of their own in the matter of "independent" allegiance. The rest disappeared into the Dankali country—no one could say how nor where. Nor was any one in French Somaliland sufficiently interested to inquire. Ato Josef's bank account grew larger every month; the five merchants of the arms syndicate credited additional millions to their Abyssinian trade.

Such was the heyday of the arms trade in Djibouti— a legal, "honorable," commerce if ever there was one. Arms for "free" Arabia; arms for "free" Ethiopia— everything open, everything aboveboard.

Constantinople grumbled to no purpose. But from London came sounds more ominous. And suddenly without warning, arrived the news of an agreement between the Foreign Office and the Quai d'Orsay, prohibiting the export of all arms whatsoever to Arabia, however "free." The trading station at Mascatte was closed; its owner, a certain Monsieur Dieu, received a generous indemnity for the rifles and cartridges in his warehouse. The arms trade with Arabia was officially declared at an end.

The news struck the arms syndicate of Djibouti dumb, but not for long. Three months later, the honorable trade was in full swing again, lacking its Arabian façade.

Since the loaded boutres could no longer declare Mascatte as destination, they were given papers for Obok (the abandoned French port on the opposite side of the Gulf of Tajura). There their papers were confiscated; they were permitted to leave Obok, *with no papers whatsoever*, for an unknown destination. Where they went, what happened after they were abandoned by the government *doueri* —which escorted them to the limit of French waters—no one inquired. Djibouti washed its hands of the matter. Destination unknown; *shipping port unknown.* Before loading at Djibouti, an Arab carpenter in the employ of the Customs carefully obliterated with a plane the telltale

word "Djibouti" from each of the heavy cases. The trade
went on as before.

There was one peculiarity about it. It drew the color
line. That is to say, the white men of the colony—the
syndicate of five—imported arms and munitions and paid
the import duty. There their responsibility ended. The
middlemen who bought the arms and transported them
to their unknown destination in Arabia were, without exception, Arabs. (Arabs, likewise, had charge of the Ethiopian shipments that left by way of Tajura.) In the
colony, that phase of the trade—the actual "contraband"
—was considered less "honorable."

When I decided to try my hand at smuggling arms (for
I came to that decision as I lay in the sand watching the
lights of Djibouti trying ineffectually to drown out the
starlight overhead), I determined then and there to pay
no heed to the conventions of the trade. I saw no difference in "honorability" between the sun-helmeted importer and the Arab *nakhoda* with his boutre. (Unless,
perhaps, I had greater respect for the Arab who ran all
the actual risks.) For myself, I would be both importer
and *nakhoda*. I was the first European to overstep the
color line.

The next day, before hoisting sail for Mascali, I ordered by telegraph from the Maison Lalou at Liège 200
rifles and 12,000 cartridges.

I anticipated trouble with the Arms Trust, organized to
monopolize and shut out all competition. The Five—all
were informed of my order even before the Belgian firm
had heard of it—considered my initiative with an unfriendly eye; but I was still too petty a competitor to take
seriously. Presently I discovered how to offset their an-

tagonism. Serious opposition came from quite another quarter. . . .

Having sent my order, I left for Mascali to install my oyster-parks. On the island, the ruins of an abandoned pesthouse was the only trace of human habitation. Fishers camped there from time to time. One of the tumble-down buildings I had planned to restore for my own use; but when I applied for the permission I was refused—no surprise in view of my conversation at the Residence. So with the aid of my Somalis, I set about building shelters for my "settlement"—a central hall of branches and earth, and a group of huts for men and supplies.

In due time, the shipment of arms arrived from Belgium and was deposited at the Customs. I was busy at the moment, gathering pearl-oysters in the Gulf of Tajura, operating *sadafs*, and sinking them in colonies on the reefs about the island. I had made no preparations for the sale of arms; I had scarcely given the matter a thought. Time enough for that, I reasoned, when I have finished planting my crop of pearls.

One morning, a Somali whom I had sent to Djibouti on an errand, brought back a letter from the Customs. It informed me in no uncertain terms that if within forty-eight hours I had not removed my "merchandise," the shipment would be seized for duty.

I had entirely overlooked the fact that there might be a time limit for goods deposited at the Customs. Forty-eight hours, I realized, was far too short a time to prepare an initial trip as arms smuggler. I could sell the arms at auction, but that meant losing a thousand dollars (a sum which, once I had paid the duty, represented most of my capital). On the other hand, if I could sell the shipment in contraband I could count on gaining more than that. The first solution was not to be considered.

Rapidly I thought. That night, about nine o'clock, the *Sahala* slipped from its moorings and skirting the western end of the island, headed north in the open sea. Three hours later we sighted the main island of the Sowaba group, an uninhabited stretch of sand between two rocky peaks. We anchored a cable length from shore. Landing with four Somalis, I set to work digging a series of trenches at different points on the island. By daybreak we had finished. As a precaution, I stretched a network of fine black threads breast-high, in close proximity to each trench; a device to inform us on our return whether any one had visited the scene in our absence (a possibility that seemed, however, most unlikely). We were back at headquarters in Mascali by noon. Neither outward bound nor on our return had we sighted a boutre. We had every reason to believe that our absence from Mascali had passed unnoticed.

The next morning I paid the import duty and was authorized to take rifles and cartridges out of the customs —twenty-two heavy cases, which I loaded on board the *Sahala*, under the watchful supervision of a Customs' clerk. On two Arab boutres that lay alongside us in the harbor, gangs of Somalis were stowing a similar cargo below decks. That same night a government boat was to accompany the three of us—all bound ostensibly for Arabia—first to Obok, and afterwards as far as Roheita, the limit of French waters. This to make sure that no boutre touched anywhere in French Somaliland. Except for the quasi-official shipments of arms through Tajura, boutres carrying this type of cargo were strictly forbidden to land along the African coast.

I thought it prudent—particularly on the initial trip— not to attract undue attention to the *Sahala* by my presence aboard (as I said before, this part of the trade had always been reserved exclusively to Arabs). Abdi was ostensibly in charge (our papers bore his name as *nakhoda*), and as soon as the cases were safely stowed, I abandoned the boutre, and strolling back to the town, spent my afternoon making purchases for Mascali, and ate an early dinner at the hotel on the square.

When night came, I walked east of town to a deserted spot on the beach. There I undressed, and having buried my clothes in the sand, I struck out through the water towards a buoy anchored in the middle of the harbor, about a half mile off the jetty. I had given Abdi instructions to run the *Sahala* as close to the buoy as possible, with a rope trailing from the stern. I reached the buoy without difficulty, but I discovered that it offered little or no support to a man in the water. A cone with a rounded base fixed to the bottom by a chain, it bobbed gently in the swell. I swam around it, from time to time, scraping my finger tips over the shells that coated the submerged half of the buoy (they were sharp as knife-blades) until the buoy, rolling on its side, threw me off again. As I swam, the movement of my arms and legs made circles of phosphorescence in the black water. The chain, too, as the buoy lifted and fell, traced a streak of green fire that plunged down, down, into invisible black depths. I thought of sharks . . . and having heard somewhere that their inherent cowardice makes them wary of the vigorous swimmer, I splashed mightily from time to time, sending up a rain of green sparks. An hour passed before I saw the government *doueri* glide out from the

docks and heard its *nakhoda* hail the three boutres, ordering them to hoist sail.

Slowly the four sails bore down. The *Sahala* headed
for the buoy, passing so close that Abdi and another
Somali, reaching down, hauled me aboard before I could
grasp the rope. In the darkness no one noticed the *Sahala*
take on a passenger.

Outside the harbor we made fair speed, for the breeze
had freshened; the three boutres in the lead, and the
doueri following behind, all lights extinguished. The *Sahala*
was carrying only medium sail (I had seen to that), which
reduced its speed and gave to my swift darling the air of
a respectable and somewhat clumsy merchantman.

At dawn we reached Obok, where our cargoes were
visited by the Customs, and our ships papers confiscated.
The *commissaire*, a young French sergeant, lonely as
Crusoe on his island, invited me to lunch. During the day,
I made myself useful to my host, repairing a shotgun and
showing him how to run an ice machine he had just received from Europe, so that when I told him in confidence
that to pass by Roheita would take me far out of my
course to Arabia, he was only too willing to oblige by per-
mitting us to leave that night unescorted, without waiting
for the others, who were to hoist sail in the morning.

By sunset the *Kamsin* was blowing steadily from the
west. I fretted to be off, but could not with decency refuse
an invitation to dinner. I knew the moon would rise at
eight—which meant we would be sighted from the land
unless we got under weigh at an early hour. The meal
dragged interminably. We were not able to lift anchor
until moonrise—which obliged us to head northeast twenty
miles out of our course, before we could veer unseen to
the southwest. Towards two in the morning we sighted

Sowaba—a pale strip in the moonlight, three miles distant. We hauled in the sail, and with four men at the oars, pulled towards the island.

Straight before us lay a long shoal of sand and coral marked by a buoy. Abdi assured me that the tide being full, we could cross in safety. With a man on the bowsprit we pushed forward, feeling our way through a labyrinth of channels between sharp blocks of coral that broke the surface all about us. A few inches less water, and passage would have been impossible. Half an hour's blind steering convinced me our short cut was scarcely worth the risk. I feared low tide might overtake us, blocking us in broad daylight with all retreat cut off. I swung the *Sahala* about and we picked our way back towards the open sea. Towards four o'clock, with the end of the shoal in sight, our stern grated on the reef and struck fast. Up to their necks in water, my Somalis tugged desperately—to no avail. As a last resort, I ordered the heavy munition cases piled in the bow—the stratagem worked; we floated free. But the east had whitened when the water grew black again beneath us.

Nothing to do but hoist our mainsail and make for the open sea, to spend the day hidden below the horizon. Out of sight of land, I rigged a floating anchor and lowered the sail. All day long we rolled and pitched in the swell; the deck like hot metal under the torrid sun—not even a stretched sailcloth would I permit for fear it might render us visible.

Towards evening we made for the island again, mooring within the shoal, half a mile from the beach. First I swam ashore to inspect our trenches. All was as we had left it. I signaled my men to bring the boutre in as close to land as possible.

The next step was to carry the cases to shore. We began

with the cartridges. One by one, the men struggled through the surf, each carrying on his back 140 pounds. Next came the long boxes of rifles; as each weighed 200 pounds, it took two men apiece to bring them to land. The Somalis carried the cases on their heads, a marvel of balance. I watched the process fascinated, expecting at any moment to see a man make a false step and stumble among the breakers. But all went well; the long, coffin-like boxes advanced steadily without a tremor above the foam.

By ten o'clock, our entire cargo was safe on shore. Transferring it to the trenches came next. As we tugged and shoveled, one might have taken us for a band of fantastic grave-diggers, naked and diabolic in the moonlight. Five hours passed before the last trench was filled and the sand smoothed over to obliterate all traces of our labor.

Not a man of us but sighed with relief when we clambered on board the boutre again. Remember we had been two nights without sleep, and the day we had spent tossing and broiling beneath the equatorial sun.

Outside the bar, we found a choppy sea and a fair breeze that freshened towards dawn, carrying us far from the island which by sunup disappeared below the horizon. Insufficiently ballasted, the *Sahala* behaved badly, waddling through the seas with shortened sails; I had all I could do to keep her headed east, for I planned to kill time for a couple of days in order to give an appearance of likelihood to our trip to the Arab coast.

Towards noon, a vicious roll of the boutre sent everything below decks crashing to starboard. As she righted herself staggering, the boy Moussa came aft with the news that the water barrel had upset; barely two quarts remained in the bottom. That *was* a calamity, though preoccupied as I was with my efforts to keep the *Sahala* on her course, I scarcely realized its gravity.

"We will have to go thirsty," I told the boy shortly. At the moment I felt equal to any hardship (novice that I was, I included thirst along with the rest). I had no intention of compromising the success of my first venture by a premature return. To demonstrate my powers of endurance I gave over the water that was left to the crew.

By four o'clock the barrel had been emptied to the last drop. I began myself to feel a nagging craving for water. Nervous suggestion, I reasoned, and set my lips tight together—they were already parched and dry—and my throat ached with rawness. Two hours more and the craving had become torture; my whole body was on fire. In vain I summoned all my resistance, my stoicism steadily ebbed. At ten o'clock I threw all caution to the winds and headed the *Sahala* for Obok.

We beat our way through the darkness in a nightmare of fever and vertigo. I could think of nothing but water —fountains, cascades, the deep black spring beneath the pines of Leucate, water holes in the desert after a day's march, where you throw yourself face down and drink among the grunting camels; thunderstorms on the Tcher Tcher—O the unmitigated joy of drowning in the rain! Day brought another blazing sun. Crouched on the steering bench, I gripped the helm. Dozens of black spots danced before my eyes; in my ears I had the noise of a thousand locusts. At eight o'clock, as we sighted Obok, the wind turned. The *Kamsin* blew straight from the land, compelling us to tack about for hours before making the port. In desperation, I gulped down a dipperful of sea water. It gave me an instant of relief—but immediately afterwards, throat and stomach burned like fire, and the craving for water became so intense, I would have drunk blood or urine, anything to slake the intolerable fire.

It was noon when we reached Obok. I sent a Dankali on the run to the oasis to fill a goatskin at the well. We lay collapsed on the sand waiting for his return—it seemed an eternity. And then we drank like beasts or madmen, I have no idea how many quarts. The goatskin was emptied in a trice. Our Dankali journeyed back and forth to the oasis. As for me, I drank all day and during the night I awoke to drink again.

VIII

A Trade Less Honorable: Slaves

Tajura, the Dankali capital, lies at the base of the black wall of the Mabla range, jagged volcanic peaks like petrified storm-waves, with the cone of Djebbel Gudda towering 6,000 feet in the air. From the palms of a little oasis, the town stretches east along the blue gulf—Arab houses of whitewashed stucco and hundreds of native huts clustered about the minarets of four mosques, crowding the narrow strip of shore to the water's edge. At evening, the soft air smelling of incense and sheep dung, vibrates with the cries of children splashing along the beach, singing monotonous game songs to the rhythmic beating of hands. The slow cadence of the surf rolling its even ribbons over the sand, is like the measured breathing of the landscape at rest after the burning heat of day.

The *Sahala* dropped anchor a few rods from the beach along which lay fishing boutres and dugouts, with here and there the slender pointed hull of a *zaroug*. I sent Abdi ashore with a message for Sheik Mâki. In a few minutes he was back again accompanied by a Dankali who waited at the water's edge.

At the time of which I write, Tajura did not count a single white inhabitant. Because of their opposition to the slave trade—a time-honored and respectable commerce from the native point of view—Europeans were not welcome at the Dankali capital, whose position at the end of the caravan trail from Ethiopia made it one of the principal shipping ports for slaves en route to the markets of Arabia and Persia. The government at Djibouti rigorously refused to authorize any white man to visit the town, alleging his risk of being shot on sight. (The risk was perhaps exaggerated. During my stay in Abyssinia I had come down over the caravan trail to Tajura several times, though not in the traditional European fashion!)

I adjusted my turban, fastened to my belt a curved Dankali knife, its leather hilt wound with silver wire, and handing Abdi a gift of tobacco for the Sheik, swung myself into the waiting dugout.

A little group had gathered on the beach to watch us land. Children of all ages; some mere babies with a "scalp lock" on the crown of their shaven heads, naked but for their leather amulets. Boys of six and over, each with a poignard at his belt. One lad of ten shouldered with pride an old Gras rifle, much taller than himself. The whole band fell in behind us, chattering and giggling. There was no trace of animosity in the reception; merely curiosity at the arrival of a stranger. Remember my appearance offered nothing shocking to Moslem eyes; for I, too, wore *fohta* and turban, and the short Arab vest, or *siderea*.

Our guide led us back from the beach through a street bordered by peaked-roofed huts of branch and palm-fiber, each with its *zeriba*, a fence of reeds or thorns enclosing a court. Over every roof hung a blue film of smoke that filtered slowly up through the thatch from a fire built on the earth floor. The streets echoed with the voices of children, the bleating of goats, and from time to time a rhythmic thump-thump. Within the courtyards, Dankali women were pounding grain in mortars made from a hollowed tree-trunk set up vertically; or kneeling on the earth, ground *durra* between two stones. Here and there through a doorway we glimpsed a shapeless form wrapped in ample folds of white—the wife of some Abyssinian merchant emigrated to the coast. For the most part, we met only Danakils—dark skinned men with fine straight features, wearing costumes like my own; and slender women, bare of breast and shoulder, carrying goatskins of water from the wells in the oasis—their only garment, a leather *fohta* wrapped tight about the hips, and on their head a folded rectangle of dark blue cotton cloth, held in place by some miracle of balance.

When we reached the northern end of the town looking towards the mountains, the Dankali whom we followed led the way into a large *zeriba* strewn with shells, on which fronted half a dozen native huts. He ushered me into one of these—the traditional "guest house," and motioned me to a raised platform of earth carpeted with rugs. A pot of incense smoked by the entrance, and—equally smoky but less fragrant—a chimneyless oil lamp burned in a niche in the wall. Two Soudanese slaves brought refreshments—dates, pancakes of fried *durra*, an earthen bottle of *keshir;* and the inevitable water pipe; after which my guide left me.

"Sheik Mâki will come," he announced in parting. I settled myself contentedly among the rugs; ate and drank and took an occasional pull at the water pipe, while I prepared the coming conversation.

Hours passed. Through the doorway of the guest room, I caught glimpses of the life of the household—the return of the goats from pasture, and the evening meal of the slaves, about the fire, boiling *durra* in a tin *tanika*. From beyond my range of vision came the sound of women's voices, the falsetto of young children, laughter, and snatches of song. Gradually the sounds grew less; silence fell, as if the household had settled for the night. Dozing on my rug, I speculated on what business it might be that retarded Sheik Mâki's homecoming and regretted not having postponed my visit until morning. Of Abdi and the second Somali who accompanied me on land, I had seen no sign since my arrival. Doubtless they, too, dozed somewhere in some sheltered corner.

At eleven o'clock or thereabouts, the Dankali servant returned alone and beckoned me to follow him. I found my two men—Abdi and Kassim—squatting beside a fire in the courtyard. In the glow of the flame, the Dankali glanced down at my feet.

"You will need sandals. We are going into the bush."

Not even a native ventures barefooted into the bush at night because of the mimosa thorns. I offered to send one of my men to the *Sahala* for our sandals, but the Dankali, after considerable rummaging in one of the dark huts, managed to provide us with three pairs—thick leather soles curved up on either side of the foot and held in place by thongs across the instep, behind the heel and between the toes.

Wet set out, walking single file, on a trail that led to the foothills of the Mabla range. For the first few miles, it followed a stony river bed between banks overgrown with cactus and mimosa. As we mounted, the valley grew narrower and steeper. Our path twisted among blocks of basalt, up through a black cañon, between whose walls, high overhead, we glimpsed a slender ribbon of stars. Leaving the river bed, we climbed in dizzy zigzags up the face of the rock. I followed close on the heels of our guide, thankful for the half-moon that just when we needed it most, showed its white crescent above the rim of the gorge.

We reached the top of a narrow "hog's back" that widened to a plateau, spotted with scrub mimosa trees like black parasols askew. From the height, we could look down on the Gulf of Tajura, glistening in the moonlight, bordered on the farther side by the Issa mountains. Not a cricket's chirp broke the dead silence. Only from time to time, the groaning cry of a hyena; and the answering call, lugubrious in the distance.

Suddenly, as we advanced, two shadows stepped out from the darker shadow of a mimosa. Two Danakils, each carrying a rifle, exchanged a few words with our guide, then fell into step behind us. The six of us trotted ahead in the moonlight, down a gentle grade towards the bottom of a shallow depression cut diagonally by the river bed. Another half hour's march, and the Dankali stopped, gave a sharp whistling cry, which an instant later was repeated a hundred yards below. The foot of the slope was strewn with rocks of a peculiar shape. I stumbled against one of them; it moved and grunted, and suddenly, like a turtle, grew arms and legs and a head. The "rocks" were men sleeping, wrapped in their *fohtas.* I could make out little else in the dark pocket surrounded on all sides by the shadow of the mountains. Picking their way among the sleeping shapes, the three Danakils led me towards a mimosa tree taller than its fellows. In the darkness beneath its thorny foliage a little ring of coals glowed red. A voice spoke out of the shadow.

"Salaam Alaicum, Abd el Hai." It was Sheik Mâki himself, alert and wakeful, seated on a rug with the water pipe glowing at his elbow. I returned the salaam and was motioned to a seat beside him. We exchanged the usual inquiries as to our respective healths and that of our immediate families.

"I regret to have brought you so far into the Mabla, but I shall not go down to Tajura until another night," the Sheik excused. By that time my curiosity was thoroughly aroused. The climb through the night, the armed sentinels, the sleeping camp high in the mountains. . . . I peered discreetly to right and left but could distinguish nothing, only confused patches of black and gray, chaotic in the moonlight.

A few yards away, some one built a fire. A Dankali squatted beside it heating an earthen bottle over the blaze. An odor, spicy and aromatic, spread through the air. Then he brought us cups of *keshir* steaming hot. I sipped the hot drink gratefully, for the temperature of the air had dropped. A chilly breeze swept down from the peaks, and I could scarcely believe that Tajura lay sweltering in the heat barely ten miles below.

After the *keshir*, I was asked whether I cared to rest after the long walk. While I felt no fatigue, I judged the hour ill chosen for a discussion of my affairs. Rolling myself in a rug, I lay pretending to sleep, waiting for the moon to set and dawn to whiten the east. When the first pale halo showed above the peaks, I propped myself on an elbow and looked around. All about me lay sleeping shapes —fifty or more gray bundles, and beside each one, a slender black bar—a Gras rifle. A few rods distant, a *zeriba* of thorns inclosed a typical Bedouin camp—a herd of goats, a dozen camels, and five or six round huts covered with mats of palm-fiber. Beside me, Sheik Mâki still sat beneath the mimosa, the long tube of the water pipe held to his lips. I pointed to the huts.

"Who camps there?"

The Sheik lowered the bone mouthpiece.

"Twenty-four *bogul* (mules)," he replied with a meaning smile.

"May one see them?"

"*Marhaba*, in a moment they will all come out."

The camp was waking. The fire of mimosa boughs crackled briskly. A group of Danakils sat about it, some mixing their day's ration of tobacco and ashes, and others heating earthen bowls of *keshir*. Behind the thorns of the *zeriba*, the "mules" crept from their huts: well-built young women and little boys, who set to work milking the goats and gathering *kabit* (the tiniest of mimosa leaves that fall in a powdery rain when the branches are beaten vigorously with a stick. *Kabit* makes excellent fodder for milk-giving animals).

As they wandered freely about the camp, I noticed that the *bogul* all were of a pronounced negro type. They were Wallamos or Chancallas from the Abyssinian plateau. Of the caravan it was they who seemed to receive the most consideration: the huts were for them, the goats' milk also, and the provisions of dates and rice the camel carried, while the Dankali escort ate parched *durra* and slept in the open.

During my stay in Ethiopia I had occasionally met slave-traders. But this was my first meeting with a caravan of slaves on the march. (I had no longer any doubts as to the nature of Sheik Mâki's camp.) But the group of black women and boys camping in that high valley of the Mabla range in no way corresponded to my preconception of a slave train. They sang and laughed as they moved about. One not in the secret might easily have mistaken the camp for a normal Bedouin village. Yet women and boys were on their way to the Arab slave market. . . . It required a conscious effort to pity them; nothing in their appearance or manner called for it.

In Abyssinia, it was rumored that the slave traffic, in spite of the opposition of Europeans on the coast, still actively continued between the Ethiopian plateau and Arabia. Sheik Mâki gave me my first definite picture of the trade which for centuries had furnished the Dankali tribe with an important revenue. Even before white men attempted to check the export of slaves from Africa, the trade had been carried on in contraband. Abyssinian law, while tolerating slavery as an institution, frowned on the traffic as a means of gain, and expressly forbade the export of slaves. Considered an integral part of the family, a slave might not be sold for money. To dispose of a slave, the owner could only offer him as a gift. That was the law. But the condition of the country, its vast extent, the immense stretches of desert, and above all the lack of a powerful centralized authority rendered the law's enforcement not only difficult, but practically impossible.

In secret, nearly all the local chiefs took part in it. From certain tribes—the Chancallas, Wallamos, and Gouragays, in particular—inhabitants of desert regions, living constantly on the verge of famine,—little could be extracted in the way of taxes or levies. They cultivated hardly any grain and owned few cattle. But these tribes were prolific and vigorous—excellent material for the slave market. The Abyssinian chieftain had no objection— *au contraire*—to collecting the equivalent of his taxes in flesh and blood. A method of payment which the tribes themselves accepted only too willingly, since they too derived certain profits from the arrangement.

A commission sent by the local chief visited the Chan-

calla and Wallamo villages. In each village the head man
brought to the visitors young men and girls who offered
themselves spontaneously or were presented by their parents. These declared themselves ready to abandon their
barren country for rich foreign lands. The choice was
considered an honor almost—a premium for youth and
good looks. The families of the future slaves, the head-
man likewise, received a minimum payment for the lot.
Then began the long march to the coast.

At first the band headed for the nearest Aragouba village. The Aragouba tribe, whose fortified stone towns lie
scattered along the frontiers of the desert region, had
been for generations the principal slave merchants of
Abyssinia. Aragouba traders purchased the young Chancallas, Wallamos or Gouragays from their Abyssinian
escort and shut them up temporarily in underground
rooms built especially for that purpose, until a caravan
could be formed for the coast.

The Aragouba merchants then escorted their willing
captives to the Dankali frontier, paying a tax to every
petty chieftain whose territory they crossed. At the frontier the caravan passed into the hands of the Danakils
who accompanied the slaves to villages scattered through
the Dankali country—Bati, Daoui, Goubay and Casera.
There Arab traders came with cotton goods and copper-
leaf to exchange for the slaves whom they took down to
one of the coast towns: Tajura, Roheita, Eid, Medhr, and
Zeila where they embarked the human cargo on swift
zarougs for Arabia. Only occasionally the Danakils themselves transported slaves to the Arab coast.

On his arrival in Arabia the slave-merchant would rent
a house and settle down with his merchandise to receive
prospective buyers. He offered for sale three categories

of slaves. The majority would be laborers who in Arabia could learn trades: iron working, carpentry, weaving, basket and rope-making, etc. . . . Many, too, would be sold to work in the gardens or to serve in Arab or Persian households.

Others, women selected for their beauty, were reserved for the harem. As wives or concubines, they would bear their master not slaves, but legitimate sons and daughters.

Castrated boys formed the third group, by far the smallest. These were not intended to serve as future guardians of the harem as is popularly supposed. They became their owner's responsible servant; managers of his household, his property; keepers of his treasure. As Sheik Mâki explained, they could be counted on never to betray their master's confidence; none of them risked being tempted by a woman! Many of the young castrates were sent to Mecca to guard the holy ground about the Kahba, the tomb of the Prophet.

These boy eunuchs or *towashi* represented the darkest chapter of the slave traffic. Between nine and fifteen years of age, they were castrated by their parents or more exactly by the village sorcerer in anticipation of their sale. During a heavy sleep produced by the smoke of burning leaves of a poisonous plant (the *datura stramonium*) and infusions of certain other plants (probably the poppy) the genital organs were completely removed. On the wound, after a preliminary application of butter, boiling hot, the operator placed a poultice of crushed plant-leaves. The sorcerer alone knew the secret of its composition. If an infection of the bladder did not carry off the victim within six days after the operation, he was considered out of danger, and for a month was fed on raw meat and honey. At the end of the month, his recovery was pronounced complete. As may be expected, the rate of mortality was high; fully sixty per cent of those operated on died within twenty-four hours. Eunuchs, therefore, brought high prices on the market; from eight hundred to two thousand dollars. The average male slave rarely exceeded in price four hundred dollars. A handsome young girl brought three hundred dollars. Children rarely sold for more than one hundred and fifty dollars.[1]

All this Sheik Mâki told me as we sat by the fire in his camp high in the Mabla, eating a breakfast of Dankali "sausage": the chopped heart, liver, and kidneys of a freshly killed goat, broiled on the embers.

The time had come for me to tell the Sheik of what had brought me to Tajura. I explained that contrary to custom, I planned to deliver the arms myself. Saving the commission of the Arab middleman—and in particular the onerous *backsheesh* to Ato Joseph,—I was prepared to furnish arms at a price considerably lower than the Arabs in charge of the Ethiopian shipments. The Sheik listened intently, his eyes fixed on mine.

"*Tayib*," he nodded, and laid a hand lightly on my knee. "Here in Tajura, there are those who will buy. To-night I myself will bring you customers. But after-

[1] Previous to the war, the efforts of the English, French and Italians to stamp out the slave trade along the Somali coast were only partially successful. After the war, when Ethiopia became a member of the League of Nations, the Abyssinians themselves undertook to do away with the traffic, having first declared slavery abolished within the limits of the state. Severe penalties threatened the border-chiefs who permitted slave caravans to cross their territory. But the task has been difficult. To-day the trade still goes on, greatly diminished, it is true, and practiced with utmost discretion. Small groups of slaves, two or three at a time, pass from English Soudan and are embarked on small *zarougs* from ports south of Suakin. They form part of the crew of supposed fishers, which makes it particularly difficult to detect their presence. In fact, the attitude of the slaves themselves constitutes one of the chief obstacles to stamping out the trade; since they coöperate with the slavers as willing victims.

Descent from the Abysinnian Plateau

wards," he smiled with malice, "beware of Ato Joseph—
He is like the snake who hides to strike. . . ."

As Sheik Mâki was not to return to Tajura until evening, and I disliked abandoning my boutre with neither
Abdi nor myself on board for another twelve hours, I
took leave of the Sheik, and set off with the two Somalis
over the trail we had climbed in the night. That afternoon as I lay dozing on the deck, three Danakils paddled
out to the *Sahala*. From the amount of silver on their
dagger-hilts I took them to be persons of importance.
They brought us salt fish and dates; in return we offered tea. As they sat meditatively chewing the inevitable
mixture of tobacco and ashes, I learned the object of
their visit.

"Abd el Hai, do you know how make bad water
good?" one of the trio inquired. In the oasis to the west
of the town, he explained, were several wells that furnished
water to Tajura. The Dankali women went daily to the
oasis, filling their goatskins with the aid of a leather pail.
In the dry season the water level of the wells was nearly
thirty feet below ground.

Several weeks before my visit, an old woman who had
hobbled out to the oasis towards evening, failed to return. As she was a *very old* woman, one of my guests explained, no one took the trouble to discover why. Perhaps she had been eaten by a leopard. They let it go at
that. . . . As time went on, however, the water from the
oasis, it was observed, developed a strange unpleasant
taste. . . . "Like a water hole in September when there
are many camels. . . ." On the eve of my arrival, an
enterprising soul had investigated the wells at the end
of a rope. He discovered the reason for the polluted
water—she was very decayed indeed.

Secretly thankful that the *Sahala's* water barrels had needed no replenishing, I handed over my entire stock of permanganate, instructing the three to close the well for twenty-four hours after they had thrown in the chemical. The measure may have preserved Tajura from intestinal disaster—though so far as I could learn, no one had experienced more than a very comprehensible repugnance to drinking the water of the contaminated well.

As payment for my gift, I was invited to the "Koran" of the unfortunate old lady, whose disappearance, while it had caused little emotion originally, was used as pretext for a banquet. From the deck of the *Sahala* we heard the drum calling the faithful to feast and pray. I declined; I had other preoccupations more important than *krambo* (durra bread) and roasted mutton. It was nearing the hour set by Sheik Mâki for our meeting. When I arrived at the house on the edge of the town, the Sheik was already there. He was seated in the guest house flanked by two Danakils—one a Bedouin from the Mabla, Dîni by name, with bare torso glistening with butter, and his thick hair held back from his forehead with a fork-like wooden pin. The second, an older man, draped like a Roman senator in the folds of an Abyssinian *chamma* he presented as Bourham Bey, a title that dated from the Turkish occupation. Both, he explained, were Dankali chiefs whose family from father to son for generations were merchants in arms and slaves.

The pot of incense sent up fragrant spirals of smoke, the *medaha* gurgled companionably, and while the tea circulated in handleless Arab cups, we discussed business. The two Danakils agreed to take over all the arms and cartridges I had buried at Sowaba. I was to deliver the cases, the third night following our conversation, in the

inlet of Khor Ali. During the day preceding my arrival,
a sentinel stationed on the mountain would keep watch
over the gulf. If he spotted the approach of a government
doucri, he would send up a smoke signal visible easily
twenty-five miles at sea. If the way be clear and no danger
in sight, at night a bonfire would be lighted on the plateau
above the inlet. Before crossing the reef I, too, was to give
a fire signal, a handful of tow soaked in oil. On landing,
I would find men on the beach to receive the cargo. If
bad weather or any accident prevented me from reaching the coast on the given night, the sentinel would be
posted daily and the signals repeated until my arrival.
To seal the pact, two slaves brought in from the courtyard a sack that clinked heavily as they set it down on
the raised earth platform on which we sat. With grave
deliberation my two customers counted out in Abyssinian
thalers the sum we had agreed upon as a fair price for
the arms; it being the custom in such transactions to make
all payments in advance.

That night as I walked back to the beach, with Ahmed
and Kassim swinging the sack of coins between them, I
felt excited as a schoolboy at the success of my first
smuggling venture. The cases of arms buried on Sowaba
island, however, had still to be delivered.

With my rendezvous in prospect, I thought it prudent
to take another look at the inlet of Khor Ali. It was an
ideal spot for purposes like mine—enclosed on two sides
by high cliffs and masked towards the far end by a dense
tangle of brush and mangroves. From the sea a boutre
anchored there was invisible—and the reef, navigable only
at high tide, shut off all access to the gulf. That fact, to
my own discomfiture, I discovered during our visit. The
tide was already dropping when we entered the Khor,

and within half an hour only a few inches of water covered the reef. The *Sahala* was prisoner until the tide came in.

Another boutre beside the *Sahala* lay in Khor Ali that evening. At the far end of the inlet, a *zaroug* rested on its side in the sand. A heap of fish nets lay beside it, and a solitary Dankali was busy grinding *durra* on a hollow stone. Later on, as we ate our supper, I saw two Danakils come out of the brush and approach the *zaroug*. After exchanging a word with the solitary fisher, they continued along the beach until they were opposite the *Sahala*. They hailed us, asking for the dugout. I sent the boy Moussa ashore with the houri to bring them aboard. To my surprise I recognized one of the Danakils I had seen that morning at Sheik Mâki's camp in the Mabla.

He approached me with a salaam.

"Why are you here, Abd el Hai?" he inquired.

I explained that I was waiting for the rising tide.

"You need fear nothing," I added on a venture, "I am Sheik Mâki's friend. You may pass in peace."

He assured me no, I was quite mistaken. They were only fishermen, he and his comrades, put in to Khor Ali to gather wood to sell at Tajura. But Abdi, who paddled them back to the *zaroug*, told me on returning that the men had hastened to inform their companion that our boutre did not represent a danger. . . .

Shortly afterwards, a bonfire crackled on the sand by the *zaroug*, and a moment later I noticed, high on the mountainside, a red spark that glowed for an instant and then vanished. The bonfire on the beach, too, went out as suddenly.

Later—it must have been ten o'clock, for the tide was running in and the moon had not yet risen, muffled noises filtered to us across the water: the grunting of camels, and subdued voices—a caravan had come down to the beach. With my night glasses I made out a sail, gray-white in the darkness. And discreetly, silently, the *zaroug* slid past us towards the mouth of the inlet. It seemed empty, save for three or four dark figures silhouetted against the canvas. Another slaver had left for Arabia.

IX

Pirates and Coast-Guards: An Eventful
First Venture

From Khor Ali, we made directly for Djibouti. I thought it wise to spend the day in town, ostensibly purchasing supplies, while my men spread discreetly through the native quarter news of my successful trip to the Arab coast. Late in the afternoon we hoisted sail, presumably for Mascali. I counted on reaching Sowaba Island, where we had buried the arms, under cover of the night.

During the day I was disquieted by the news Abdi picked up along the docks that the sea turtle season had opened. A boutre had arrived in Djibouti the day before with the first catch of the year. Catching sea turtles (which furnish the tortoise shell of commerce) was almost exclusively the work of Arabs who trapped the creatures on moonlit nights when the females left the water to lay their eggs. According to Abdi, the little Archipelago of Sowaba furnished a high percentage of all tortoise shell in the Djibouti market.

This unforeseen complication disturbed me considerably. It did not seem improbable that an Arab crew, spending the day in idleness on the islands, might have discovered traces of our excavations. Even if the secret of the buried arms was still safe, I had no intention of digging them up again under the eyes of spectators.

We left Djibouti that same afternoon at four, a land

breeze carrying us briskly across the gulf. By eleven we
had weathered the Ras Bir, and towards two in the morning we sighted the peaked silhouette of the largest of the
islands. As we approached, a spark glowed in the shadow
of the base. Some one had landed on Sowaba. Steering
straight for the island, I kept my night binoculars fixed
on the point of light. Suddenly it disappeared—a bad
sign—for it looked as if our sail, visible in the moonlight,
had disturbed the campers on the beach.

When we were half a mile from shore, the black triangle
of a sail detached itself from the dark mass of the island,
gliding west towards the open sea. My gloomiest forebodings seemed justified. Under normal circumstances, no
native boutre hoists sail at three in the morning. I was
convinced that our cache had been discovered and looted.
Abdi, wiser than I in the customs of the coast, shared the
conviction.

Veering away from Sowaba, I headed straight for the
boutre, a *zaroug*, carrying more canvas than the *Sahala*.
In the open sea, we could not hope to overtake it. But
I calculated that to avoid the reef, the *zaroug* would be
obliged to haul close to the wind—a manœuvre which
would give me a chance to cover part of the distance that
lay between us.

Casting about for an effective means of overhauling
the fugitive, I remembered a length of fine steel chain
fastened about a sea chest belonging to one of my men.
I had on board a 12-caliber shotgun. With a knife I
ripped the charge of shot from two cartridges which I
then placed in the chambers. In each of the gun barrels I
inserted a segment of the chain, about twenty-four inches
long. With that charge, I counted on tearing the sail of
the *zaroug*, provided I could get near enough to fire.

As foreseen, the *zaroug* was forced to tack about to avoid the reef. The breeze freshened—the eastern monsoon was rising as dawn approached. The *Sahala* gained rapidly, for we could sail large while the *zaroug* hugged the wind. Its crew was invisible; evidently they feared I might fire—and had no weapons. As the distance shrunk between us, I heard the sound of muffled blows in the hold of the *zaroug*, a sound which removed my last floating doubt as to the theft of the buried arms.

The Arabs were trying to open the rifle cases. If they succeeded, we were assured of a reception! I comforted myself with the thought that native boats carry no tools of any sort; and I remembered the solid planks of the rifle-cases, reënforced by iron bands. All the same, I had my men build a barricade of rice and *durra* sacks around the helm.

When still a cable's length away, hammer-blows in the *zaroug* growing more vigorous, I ordered my Somalis to open fire with the Gras rifles, aiming at the water line to demoralize the amateur carpenters in the hold. The blows ceased instantly. But like ourselves, the *zaroug* was sailing large. Had it passed the end of the reef? To my despair, I saw the stretch of water widen between us. We were still too far behind to risk sending the shot of steel chain through their mainsail. That trick could not be counted on to succeed at more than 150 yards.

Suddenly I saw the *zaroug* veer to the wind again; the helmsman must have sighted the reef. In his haste, he brought to; the sail slapped emptily in the wind. Fear of our gun shots made the *zaroug* crew work sail with prudence; so prudently indeed, that we gained half a cable length before the Arab boat got under weigh again. We pushed even closer; but just as I prepared to try out my double charge of chain, the *zaroug* veered large—it had made the end of the reef.

At that, I emptied the two barrels of the shotgun— our last chance. A miracle kept the arm from bursting (the charge weighed fully three times as much as the shot I had removed). One barrel twisted slightly, but that was all.

At the same instant, the *zaroug's* taut sail split as if by magic through its entire length. A minute later, the wind had torn the light canvas to ribbons. The crew hastened to lower the sail-yard; too late—the wind had pushed the *zaroug* on the reef. It struck while we were still a few yards away. To avoid a like fate, we accosted them on the side towards the open sea. Only then the *nakhoda* of the *zaroug* seemed to find his voice.

"What do you want with us?" he shouted angrily. I looked him square in the eyes.

"Give back the arms you stole on Sowaba—or I will shoot every man of you." His crew did not wait for the command. With a chorus of terrified yells, "Yahallah! O Yahallah!" they emptied the hold: four cases of rifles and five of cartridges. They had not uncovered all our trenches.

"We did not know they were yours," the *nakhoda* muttered by way of excuse when the last case had been carried aboard the *Sahala;* "Awad Omar is no thief."

"You thought the turtles had laid them?" Abdi inquired jocularly.

Meantime, the deck of the *zaroug* was awash and it was rapidly settling on the reef. To avoid the rock ourselves—for with the morning wind the sea had grown rougher—I ordered the Arabs on board the *Sahala*, and took the *zaroug* in tow (it still floated though full of water; it had run afoul of the very point), and made for the open sea.

Afraid lest I hand them over to the authorities in Djibouti, the *nakhoda* begged me to let him and his crew return to their boat.

"Do you want to drown?" I inquired. "You have a hole in the border as big as my two fists." The *nakhoda* shook his head.

"*Mafisch ghof!* (no fear!) Give me rice."

From Awad Omar, pirate, arms-smuggler, and in his leisure moments, fisher of sea turtles, I learned a trick for stopping leaks, which stood me in good stead less than twenty-four hours later. He took about six pounds of rice, rolling it in a piece of sailcloth like a sausage. This he introduced in the hole the reef had dug in the port side of the *zaroug*. In a few minutes the rice swelled, blocking the aperture completely. In fair weather, according to the Arab, you could count on the patch resisting safely for forty-eight hours. As soon as the leak was stopped, the crew of the *zaroug* started bailing. Half an hour later I set them adrift, and hoisting a jib they made off in the direction of the Arab coast. I kept as hostage, the *nakhoda's* son, a fifteen-year-old boy of great beauty, to assure the discretion of his father and his father's sailors. When my cargo had been safely delivered, they could talk as they pleased—but for another twenty-four hours I did not care to have our adventure noised abroad. In three days, I told the *nakhoda*, he could send for the young Ibrahim Awad at Djibouti.

The *nakhoda* did not protest. Arabs are good losers; the fortunes of war they accept as a matter of course— as a rule they bear no grudge against the victor. Drive a shrewd bargain with an Arab, he will respect you and become your friend; but let him get the better of you through incapacity, weakness, or even amiability—he will never forgive you. "*Ghashim!* (imbecile)" he dubs you disdainfully, as one who cannot see beyond his own nose!

Awad Omar and his crew, I observed, found something mysterious and inexplicable in our arrival at Sowaba while they were still loading the *zaroug* with the stolen arms. What had been mere coincidence, they prefered to interpret as second sight on my part. Nor had they been able to explain—except as evidence of divine intervention —the "miraculous" destruction of their sail. Even had I taken no hostage, chances were that not one of them would have risked mentioning our encounter, for fear of occult and supernatural reprisals. . . .

After this episode, we returned to the island without further incident. I did not like to lie at anchor there in broad daylight, but for me it was a point of honor to arrive on time at Khor Ali that evening. We loaded the remaining cases as rapidly as possible, and at noon when all were safely on board, I headed the *Sahala* southwest towards the entrance of the gulf.

As we neared the Dankali coast, I saw on the horizon sails leaving Tajura for Djibouti. To escape recognition I ran as close to land as I dared and anchored there, lowering the sail. I kept my glasses fixed on the heights above Khor Ali, but seeing no smoke signal anywhere, I concluded the coast was clear.

Though it was not yet dark, I decided to enter and wait there for the signal, for I thought I ran a greater risk of being seen out in the gulf. Besides, I wanted to be sure of landing my cargo before the tide ran out. We had barely dropped anchor when a Dankali swam out to us from shore.

"Abd el Hai," he called guardedly from the water. "A message from Sheik Mâki. There was no time to bring the camels here. Go first to Ambabo."

Ambabo, a little beach with an oasis of date palms, lies ten miles west of Tajura. We reached it at nightfall. Sighting what I took to be a fire signal, I replied with a flare. We dropped anchor 500 yards from the coast, and as nothing stirred along the beach, I swam ashore to find out if arrangements had been made for unloading the arms. I found Bourham Bey, alone on the edge of the oasis. Rapidly he explained.

I was to land half my cargo at Ambabo and deliver the rest twenty-four hours later to Dîni, my second customer, at Khor Ali. A storm on the Mabla had held up the camels. Bourham Bey's own caravan would not reach the coast for another hour or two. In my impatience at the delay, I volunteered to bring the arms to shore myself. The transport proved even more difficult than at Sowaba Island; we carried the heavy cases through 500 yards of shallow water and surf and across a beach strewn with sharp stones. I worked with my Somalis until the last case had been brought to land. On the final trip to the beach, I split the sole of my left foot on a shell, and smashed a great toe as we lowered the last box of rifles to the sand. But these were the only accidents, and long before the moon rose, we were already under sail for Mascali, for I preferred a flying visit to the island to a day tacking in the gulf under the torrid sun, or risking anchorage in full view of the coast.

Morning had not yet come when the island loomed dark ahead—a welcome sight, for all of us showed signs of fatigue. The tide was not yet full; skirting the southern end of Mascali I found barely enough water to carry us over the reef. I hastened ashore, for my feet pained badly. I had had nothing on board to bandage them with and had washed my wounds with sea water and let it go at that.

As we approached the camp, I hailed Ahmed Baket, a Soudanese whom I had left in charge.

"Ahmed—O," I called cheerily, "wake up and make us coffee." To my surprise, I received no answer, but in the dark I collided smartly with the Soudanese who at the call had rushed out to meet me.

"*Yallah roh! Fissa Fissa* (leave at once)!" he chattered in great excitement. "The government *doueri* is moored on the other side of the island!"

I waited for no explanations; wheeling in my tracks, I limped in all haste back to the beach. There was nothing to do but leave by the route over which we had come. I adjusted the antiquated out-motor purchased second-hand at Djibouti some weeks before and the unruly machine on a rare streak of good behavior, propelled us soberly along the reef. Black water was in sight, when I felt a slight shock. A point of rock had torn the rudder from its sockets; a moment later the *Sahala* grounded. At the jolt the entire crew dived overboard. I succeeded, presently, in fishing up the rudder intact, which was luck, but the boutre, caught mid-keel, turned like a top on its axis, and refused to budge. In the east, the horizon paled; I had visions of our being caught like flies in glue. As we tugged and hauled, the breeze freshened, blocking the channel; not even the out-motor, I feared, would push against it, and the motor, besides, seemed to have gone dead. . . .

I ordered my men to hoist the mainsail. As the yard climbed the mast, the *Sahala* leaned far to starboard. The

keel cleared the rock. Throwing all my weight against
the bar, I headed her straight southwest, across the reef,
trusting to luck alone the rocks would spare us. Three
times we hit a block of coral—the shock checked us, but
each time, after an endless second, the boutre lunged
forward. In five minutes we reached deep water and I
drew a deep long breath. We had sprung a leak—not a
bad one—the *Sahala* was a solid boat. Like nearly all the
boutres of the coast, it was built of Indian teak. The men
worked at the pumps, emptying water from the hold as
fast as it came in. There was no time to examine our
damages; the sun had reached the horizon. We must be out
of sight at once.

To my annoyance, looking back towards Mascali—flat
as a table, like all the islands of the region—I saw across
the island, a white triangle of canvas moving slowly
towards the west. The *doueri* was passing through the
channel that separated Mascali from Moucha. Our route
to the open sea was cut off. No choice was ours but to continue southwest into the Gulf of Tajura.

In half an hour, the *doueri* rounded the western point
of Mascali, and veering southwest, headed straight towards us. At the distance, it would have been impossible
to identify the *Sahala* with any certainty. If the *doueri*
gave chase, it was probably only because of our proximity
to Mascali at that early hour.

We continued southwest into the gulf, skirting the
Issa coast—a desolate wall of black rock overgrown with
a burnt vegetation of thorns. Two hours and the government boat had gained three miles of the nine that lay
between us. If the wind held, it was bound to overtake us.
In which case, what was there to do but throw overboard
the remaining cases of arms? Which still left us to account

for our presence in the gulf, and headlong flight from
Mascali with a leaky boat. The idea of failure on that
first arms venture of mine was intolerable. Rather stake
all on a last card, however improbable success.

A mile ahead, Ras Debeleba stretched its long black
cape into the gulf. I resolved, past the cape, to sink—
not the cases of arms, but the *Sahala* itself in the Marsa
Debeleba, and let the *doueri* continue its phantom pursuit
to the end of the gulf. A mad scheme, at the time nothing looked too desperate.

We rounded the cape and I prepared to put the plan
into execution. But a surprise awaited us—close to the
beach, a boutre lay at anchor and half a dozen Arabs
were busy loading it with fagots. My heart sank. Adieu
my self-imposed shipwreck! . . . no longer feasible with
six curious Arabs as spectators . . . and eventual in-
formers. The game was up. And yet, as often in my life
—when reason has demonstrated that defeat is inevitable
and imminent, something stirs. An inner voice cries: "You
cannot fail, *you cannot*. All this is mere appearance. Carry
on!"

There, in the anchorage of Marsa Debeleba—after an
instant of dejection, I had a sudden inspiration. Arabs
who gathered firewood on the Issa coast, had first to
obtain permission at Djibouti, which entailed the payment
of a fee. Most likely that boutre behind Debeleba was
there illegally. Heading towards shore I hailed the *nakhoda*.

"The *doueri* is behind the point. *Yallah roh!*" The words
produced a magic effect. Hurling the fagots aboard pell-
mell, the Arabs scrambled into their craft, and hoisting
sail, made all speed out of the bay. On the *Sahala*, too,
things moved quickly. Everything water could spoil was

tossed into the dugout. Everything that could float went overboard for the waves to carry ashore, even the mast and yard. With a gimlet, I drilled two rows of holes through her side, and with a mallet struck out the plank between the rows. The water rushed in; in less than a quarter of an hour the *Sahala* filled and sank. Only the bowsprit and the stern rail showed at the surface—so slightly as to be invisible a few hundred yards away. Freed of its ballast—all but the cases of cartridges which I had left intentionally in the hold—the boutre did not go to the bottom, but floated "between waters," as the French say, kept from drifting by the two anchors.

Leaving the crew to keep watch, Abdi and I climbed to the top of the cape to follow through binoculars the progress of the *doueri*. To my astonishment, I saw that it had altered its course; it was hot on the trail of the Arab boutre, apparently mistaken for mine! What remorse I might have felt for a sorry trick on a humble smuggler of firewood, was forgotten. The Arabs relying on the speed of their craft had obliqued towards the Dankali coast and the entrance to the gulf. While Abdi watched the chase, I hurried back to salvage the *Sahala*, sunk to no purpose.

The rice trick learned from Awad Omar came in handy. We stopped the leak with a poultice of rice (as an additional precaution we covered the holes on the outside with squares of tin *tanika* nailed fast), my men pumped and bailed. In a couple of hours the boutre was above water again, none the worse for its bath, though it still leaked from its morning blow on the reef. The cases of arms, being waterproof, suffered not at all.

When all was ready again, the whole crew except the boy Moussa, and Abdi still at his post of observation,

Bay of Tajura where Abd el Hai sunk his boutre on his first arms trip

The *Altair II* anchored in Khor Ali

went ashore—stretched in the shade of the bushes to sleep. Towards nightfall, Abdi woke me with the news that the *doueri* had given up the chase, and headed off towards Djibouti. Cheered, I roused the Somalis, and we hoisted sail for Khor Ali, where four hours later I deposited my contraband in the hands of Dîni, the Dankali, who was waiting there with the Bedouins and camels.

What had provoked the visit of the government boat to Mascali—and the ensuing chase in the waters of Tajura —I could only guess. But I thought it wise to run the *Sahala*, its wounds still plastered with rice, over to Djibouti the next day for repairs. While I worked with Arab carpenters on the beach, my men spread through the port a story of how we had run aground while fishing and been obliged to take shelter on the Issa coast—a good enough alibi in view of the obvious damage to the *Sahala's* hull to explain our absence from Mascali Island.

X

Little Wars and Big; Prison

Time went on. My trips to the Dankali coast were secrets to no one. Ato Joseph's spies saw to that. Rumor said, too, that after every trip of mine, he would appear at the customs wringing his hands and whining:

"*Ti ne sais pas*—Abd el Hai carried 200 guns yesterday to Tajura! Can't anything be done to stop him?"

To Ato Joseph, every rifle I sold in the Dankali country meant one pound sterling deducted from what he considered his legitimate income. To my countrymen at Djibouti, the arms trade as I practiced it, with no redeeming façade of any sort, could only be construed as flagrant contraband, of a type that official eyes could not afford to wink at.

Ato Joseph's daily visits made life unendurable for the clerks of the customs; his complaints received due notice from the officers of the port. My activity would not be tolerated; measures would be taken for my prompt suppression.

But it is one thing to give an order in Africa; another to put it into execution. To suppress me, as the chief of the customs put it, I had to be caught red-handed, in the very act of landing arms on the French Somali coast. No one could prevent me from purchasing arms or clearing the port of Djibouti for Obok. To interfere with me at that point meant putting an embargo on the entire arms trade—and too many important citizens of Djibouti

134

dealt in contraband with Arabia. I became vulnerable only after leaving Obok.

Like the other boutres, I always left Obok escorted by a government *doueri* to the limit of French waters. From there on, the game was how to prevent my turning back and landing my cargo on the Somali coast. A simple matter, surely, if one failed to take into consideration wind and tide, and the difficult navigation among the reefs down the vast stretch of uninhabited coast.

One *nakhoda* of a government boat chose to give a personal interpretation to the orders he had received concerning me. Abdi always insisted that the interpretation had been suggested . . . perhaps by Ato Joseph himself; but as the *nakhoda* was the same fellow we had led on that fruitless chase through the gulf I believe his zeal was in pursuit of personal vengeance.

Not long after that eventful first trip of mine, I left Djibouti one July night with a cargo of arms, purchased from the local Trust-of-Five. I tried to make some of my purchases at Djibouti conciliate the local syndicate. Also, by buying arms on the spot, at a price slightly over that of the Belgium manufacturers, I could date my trips when I chose and unbound by the time limit fixed for deposit at the customs. I had no mind to increase the ordinary hazards of the trade by repeating the Sowaba episode!

That particular trip, mine was the only boutre to leave Djibouti. Escorted by the *doueri*, we made a tedious crossing to Obok, after hanging half the night in a dead calm. At Obok, the friendly sergeant told me that the government launch had left for the north near the Italian frontier—a piece of news that made me decide to run for the Gulf of Tajura without delay. Some time previously the customs had purchased a motor boat, the *Djibouti*, to patrol the Dankali coast—the direct effect, according to Abdi, of Ato Joseph's campaign.

As I anticipated, Sergeant D. had received orders not to permit me to leave without escort, and to keep a watchful eye on all my movements. Accompanied by the *doueri*, I left Obok early in the afternoon. Towards five o'clock the *Kamsin* rose in the north, blowing with great violence; beyond the Ras Bir we met a heavy sea that swept the deck at every wave. We took in the mainsail, replacing it with a stormsail. The *doueri* did likewise. I had hoped that given the bad weather, the government craft would not venture far into the open sea; but it continued to follow steadily two miles astern. At sunset we were still heading northeast, while my true course lay southwest into the Gulf of Tajura. As the night grew black, I lowered the sail, trusting the *doueri* would slip past in the darkness. Not at all. It noticed the move and approached rapidly. Hailing the *nakhoda* I imparted the news that we were repairing our canvas. Instead of remaining at a distance, the *doueri* continued towards us, aiming straight for our starboard beam. A few minutes later, in spite of our shouts, it was upon us. For a second I saw its stem poised above us like a huge ax. Then, as by a miracle, a wave swept us aside. The bow of the *doueri* crashed down astern, sweeping the after deck bare. I had no doubt the *doueri* had meant to run afoul of us. I called to the *nakhoda* to withdraw or I would fire. In haste he complied. With that I hoisted sail and we took our course northeast again. We saw no more of the *doueri* and half an hour later we veered south towards the gulf.

On our return to Djibouti to have the *Sahala* repaired, I learned from one of the *doueri's* crew, that the *nakhoda* had filed a report that I had threatened to kill him if he continued to follow us, and that when he persisted, we had opened fire. Such an accusation, I was only too aware, might have grave consequences. But the *nakhoda* had neglected to mention—for obvious reasons—his unsuccessful attempt to run me down. I hastened to have a sheriff verify the traces of the collision, on the stern of the *Sahala* and the bow of the government boat; after which I too lodged a complaint accusing the *nakhoda* of willful collision on the high sea. That I hoped would quash the matter. Neither the *nakhoda's* plaint nor mine, so it fell out, ever came before the court.

But from then on the hunting season was wide open. The new government 18-knot motor boat had been confided to a young official who announced to all who cared to listen that he was going to get me. To whet his appetite, I kept him supplied with anonymous denunciations that sent him touring through the gulf in all winds and weathers. At the same time, I kept two empty dynamite-cases well in view on the *Sahala's* deck, and spread the word through the native quarter that in case of "trouble" I was resolved on a dramatic suicide—I would blow up my boutre and the motor patrol as well.

One night a mysterious visitor landed in Mascali—a handsome young Arab in *fohta* and turban, whom at first I failed to recognize as the chauffeur of the government motor boat. (I had seen him only in the uniform of an askari.) Uneasy at first, he saluted me with deep respect, and after the usual circumlocution let drop the reason of his call.

"If Abd el Hai will let me know where he does not want the patrol to go, perhaps the motor might fall sick," he murmured, his eyes fixed modestly on the *taffi* mat on

which we both sat, while Abdi, his ears alert, served us
coffee. I could not doubt the boy's sincerity, but I thought
it prudent to suggest *where* rather than *where not* to
conduct the customs launch. I concluded a modest bargain, by virtue of which the motor should develop a mysterious ailment every time the launch showed a tendency
to abandon a route which I was to indicate in advance. (I
suggested glycerine mixed judiciously with the gas as a
mode of innocuous sabotage.) From the evening of that
interview, the motor patrol gave me no more trouble.

Meantime Ato Joseph grew daily more impatient at the
incredible languors of colonial justice. A year had gone
by since my first trip to Tajura, and the Abyssinian
reckoned his "losses" in four figures. The time had come
to take matters into his own hands.

One afternoon in Djibouti two men in Abyssinian dress
approached me—one of whom (he had the broad nose
and prominent jaw of a Wallamo) I took to be a freed
slave. They came to inquire whether I would be willing to
carry twenty cases of cartridges from Djibouti to Ras
Siyan—a point on the Dankali coast about twelve miles
distant across the gulf.

"Whose property are the cartridges?" I inquired.

"They belong to us; we have just bought them from X."
(The speaker named one of the principals of the arms
syndicate.)

"But you are Ethiopians," I objected. "How can you
transport across Dankali country?"

"Dîni has a half-interest in the affair. He will take
over whatever you land at Ras Siyan."

I thought it strange that Dîni, my principal customer
among the Danakils, should be concerned with a little matter of twenty cases. But as the trip was a short one, and

the risk at a minimum (I had no scruples against heaving the shipment overboard in case of danger), I accepted the mission and we agreed on a price, but when it came to making the customary advance payment, the Abyssinians demurred.

"We spent all our money buying the cartridges," they objected, "and have nothing left with which to pay you. But have no fear; Dîni will settle the bill at Ras Siyan. You risk nothing; you will have the goods themselves as guarantee."

That being perfectly true, I agreed to deliver the cartridges two days later. The rendezvous at the cape was fixed for midnight, after moonrise, because of the dangerous reef that bordered the only possible anchorage.

Taking leave of my two customers, I strolled over to the wharf of the customs to take a look at my prospective cargo. I found the twenty cases piled on the dock—a sorry looking lot, with the wood stained black from time and exposure and partially eaten by termites. As I turned about the pile, I noticed that one of the cases bore a fresh splotch as if a plane had been recently passed over the weather-stained wood. On investigation, I discovered that every case had been subjected to the same treatment. A closer scrutiny of one of the splotches revealed what looked like a number—imperfectly obliterated. I whistled with surprise. The effaced number and the condition of the cases as well could mean only one thing—government munitions. But what were they doing there on the wharf of the Customs? Decidedly the whole transaction had a curious flavor. . . . I was sorely tempted to let the two Abyssinians ship their precious cartridges in some other boutre. Before deciding definitely, however, I sent Abdi on a tour of the native quarter to pick up any information that might shed light on the matter. When he returned with the news that one of my two customers had been at one time a servant of Ato Joseph, my last doubt vanished. But in the light of that discovery, I resolved to see the matter through to the end.

That afternoon I loaded the cartridges on board the *Sahala,* and when evening came, I left Djibouti, together with another boutre carrying arms, under the usual escort. We sighted Obok at three in the morning. As we rounded the reef that encircles the harbor, I pretended to run aground. My men shouted, we lighted flares, and Abdi tooted lustily on the conch. Several dugouts put out from shore to bring us aid, but by the time they reached us, the *Sahala* floated free again, though we announced that she had sprung a leak. I beached the boutre on the sand, knowing that her hull bore sufficient scars (traces of the everyday accidents of her adventurous career) to justify the hypothesis of a fresh encounter with the reef.

When morning came, I paid a call on my friend the sergeant, to report our latest mishap and to ask permission to leave my cargo on deposit at the post while I returned to Djibouti for repairs. He agreed readily and gave me a receipt for the twenty cases which my men, aided by a squad af askari stowed away in the local arsenal. That afternoon the *Sahala* limped out of the harbor, hugging the coast. We had the *Kamsin* at our backs; by evening it was blowing a stiff gale. The thought of the motor boat tossing in the heavy seas (on this occasion I had purposely neglected sending a message to the obliging *chauffeur*) filled me with indulgent pity. Some day that band of amateur *navigateurs* was going to meet with serious disaster. Personally, I would confront any weather

with a sailing craft; I have a healthy distrust of motors
except as an auxiliary to canvas.

Towards eleven I made out the Ras Siyan thrusting its
peaked cape like a ship's prow into the sea ahead. Within
the shelter of the point, several hundred yards distant
from the customary anchorage, lies a little inlet, too deep
to permit boutres to moor there, but capable of affording
shelter to a small launch. "That is where they are am-
bushed," I remarked to Abdi, reflecting that while hidden
from me in the shadow of the coast, they could easily make
out the sail of the *Sahala* silhouetted against the night
sky.

We rounded the cape, and slipping across the reef (I
already knew the pass by heart) we dropped anchor in
still water close to shore. Though convinced that the whole
business was a trap—and a pretty crude one at that—I
believed in giving my clients the benefit of the doubt up to
the very last. Since we had agreed on a signal, I ordered
Ali the cook to light a fire on deck and set about preparing tea. (I reflected grimly that had I been the "desperate character" whose reputation I enjoyed in Djibouti,
I would in all likelihood have built the fire on the reef. . . .
But I had no desire to provoke a tragedy. Ridicule suited
my purpose even better.) The "signal" received no answer
from shore, but almost immediately we heard the droning
of a motor. In a few moments the patrol boat shot out of
the night. It accosted us on our starboard beam and a
dozen askari, rifles in hand, clambered aboard. Behind
them mounted more prudently the young brigadier of the
customs, guiding his steps with the aid of an electric torch.
Not an imposing figure, in spite of the martial mustache
that showed above the folds of an immense *chamma;* more

like a small boy playing pirate. I addressed him in my sweetest tones.

"*Tiens,* Puthomme (that being the gentleman's name), what favorable wind brings you here?"

"*Inutile de plaisanter,*" the officer snapped with professional briskness. "This time you are caught. Show me your cargo."

"Unfortunately I haven't it on board," I answered with studied politeness. "If you really care to investigate, you will have to consult your colleague at Obok. We are traveling under ballast."

A few minutes' search convinced my visitor of the truth of that statement. He tried to conceal his discomfiture.

"What are you doing here?" he demanded shortly.

"Is it so unusual for a sailing vessel to run to shelter out of the wind?" I inquired. "I might better ask you how it happens that a government patrol—"

"And the meaning of that signal?" he cut me short, with a wave towards the fire in the bow.

"Ali-o!" I called to the Somali squatting before the blaze. "If tea is ready, bring it here. Perhaps *Monsieur le Brigadier* will honor us. . . ."

A strangled snort was the only answer to my invitation. But before preceding his squad of askari into the waiting launch, the customs officer turned to me again.

"I—we did not come here, you understand, expressly for you," he explained carefully. "Not you, any more than any one else. I am merely doing my duty, patroling the coast."

Having laid my suspicions (!) with that revealing phrase, the visitor tossed the end of his voluminous *chamma* over one shoulder in a dramatic gesture and made a dignified exit over the rail.

The episode had no sequel. I never laid eyes on the two mysterious Abyssinians again. Whether the twenty cases of cartridges belonged in reality to Ato Josef, or whether —as I suspected—"some one" had obligingly lent them, remains a mystery. As no one appeared to claim the cartridges, I sold them myself a few weeks later to a customer of mine in the Mabla.

I had begun by this time to make occasional trips to the Arab coast, carrying goods and arms for an Arab merchant at Djibouti—the commercial agent and banker of many of the rich Arabs of the peninsula. I delivered the arms at Doubaba or Kauka, capital of the Zaramigi— a maritime people, owners of swift *zarougs*, given to fishing, piracy and the contraband of tobacco, arms and slaves.

It was at Kauka that I first heard of Ras el Ara, a point on the coast between Perim and Aden—and one of the principal markets for smuggled arms. M'hamed Moi, a merchant of Doubaba, proposed to send me there to buy munitions for him; but it occurred to me that it would be more interesting to run across to Ras el Ara with a cargo of my own.

Since my brush with the emissaries of Ato Joseph, I had abandoned the Gulf of Tajura and the African coast, to give the talk at Djibouti a chance to simmer down.

My funds were low. My new boutre, the *Fat el Rhaman* (fifteen tons, manned by a crew of eight), a swifter sailer than the *Sahala*, had begun to show signs of fatigue after a year's hard treatment.

Having only a small sum of *thalers* at my disposal, I proposed to the arms syndicate to sell me 200 cases of cartridges on credit—to be paid for when I had disposed of the munitions on the Arab coast. I had no difficulty in obtaining the goods; my reputation as arms trader was solidly established. Rumor had it my sales to the Danakils had already netted me a respectable fortune.

With 200,000 cartridges on board, I set sail for Obok and Ras el Ara in late July, 1914. At that season, the southwestern monsoon brings heavy storms in the Gulf of Aden. We were barely two hours out from Obok when the wind rose, hot as a furnace, churning the sea into a tossing chaos of green fire. The *Fat el Rhaman*, its ears laid back (the yard low on the mast; you cannot reef a lateen sail), drove forward, plunging dizzily between the waves that raced after us, higher than the mast. At dawn with the coast in sight, the sky grew suddenly dark; a rust-colored fog blew across the gulf—showering us with sand and swarms of locusts. In an instant, the deck and the surface of the water as far as we could see was covered with the pinkish-yellow insects. My men selected several dozens of the biggest, and tearing off head, wings and feet, roasted them on a piece of sheet iron. The taste is not unpleasant—a cross between crab and hazel nut. . . .

The wind slackened as the sun mounted; we made Ras el Ara towards noon. To my surprise not a boat lay in the inlet—usually full, if for no other reason than that it is so perfect a shelter from the summer monsoon. Even the beach was deserted. I sent Abdi ashore in the dugout to visit the huts usually lived in by "sentinels" who carry messages from the boutres bringing arms to the Arabs of the interior. He returned with an Arab who informed us that for some time English patrols had been running along the coast. The arms market was completely demoralized. Not a buyer remained at Ras el Ara. If I would wait, he could bring me a purchaser by nightfall. To lie all day at anchor, in view of what I had just heard of the British patrols, was not to my liking. My discovery there without papers meant the confiscation of my boutre and a heavy fine besides. To return to the African coast, meant burying my cargo while I hunted a purchaser—a tedious and risky business. I decided to take the risk.

Dispatching the messenger with promise of a generous *baksheesh* for speed, I went ashore with Abdi to find shelter from the sand storm. The *Fat el Rhaman* radiated heat like the surface of a stove. Our heads wrapped in a *fohta* which we dipped often in the sea, we made our way along the shore through the stinging, blinding dust to a little mosque—the tomb of a Sheik. It was a flat-roofed hut of mortarless stone, its earthen floor swept clean by travelers who like ourselves had taken shelter there. An oven-like niche held a bowl for incense, that the faithful might honor the memory of the holy man as they prayed.

Evening came; no sign of the messenger. The night wore on—still he did not come. At ten o'clock I swam out to the boutre leaving Abdi with the dugout to watch on shore. By midnight I was seriously alarmed. Towards two o'clock I had almost decided to hoist sail, when I heard the splash of a paddle and the houri slid out of the night bringing Abdi and two Arabs. In a moment the bargain was concluded; the newcomer offered to take 120 cases off my hands immediately; he had left two slaves on shore with a sack of *thalers*. As for the rest of the cargo, I would have to trust him—he could not get a larger sum on short notice. The money for the eight remaining cases, he assured me, would be on hand before dawn.

I had no real reason for doubting, but something in the man's attitude displeased me. He had a shifty eye—rare in an Arab—and his manner was servile. Then too, the way he kept repeating: "You must hurry, *fissa fissa*, the

English may come," made me almost certain that he hoped to take some advantage of the situation.

I ordered my men to start unloading the cartridges, resolving privately to call a halt when the hundred and twentieth case had been carried ashore. The transport took more time than I had anticipated; the houri could carry only six cases at a time. The Arab and his slaves stowed the cartridges in the mosque. Their presence could not pollute the holy place (Abdi explained), since Allah himself anticipated the use of arms by inventing fire! When the houri had made its twentieth trip the east had grown white. With the glasses I made out on the horizon the smoke of a steamer.

The promised sum for the eighty remaining cases had not arrived. Should I trust the Arab? I hesitated, reflecting that I myself had not yet paid for the cartridges, and that the loss was a sum far in excess of my profits on the remainder. I decided against the risk—a grave error on my part, since that decision was to cost me far dearer than the mere loss of a few thousand francs. Prudence may be a virtue on land, practiced by shopkeepers on the Square, but there is no place for it in the trade I was following—as I learned to my sorrow!

On leaving Ras el Ara—which we did in all haste—I planned to bury the remaining cartridges at Mascali. I could not return to Djibouti with my cargo; as I had taken it out of French waters, duty would have to be paid again, quite as if newly imported from Belgium. At Mascali, a disagreeable surprise awaited me. For months I had not thought of Europe.

War . . . that put a different face on the situation. There was I with merchandise on my hands, at no time highly acceptable, and more than objectionable in war time. To sell it in Arabia was unthinkable—I did not relish the accusation of commerce with the enemy. Nor could I sell the cartridges in Dankali country—a grave offense, with my country at war. I resolved to bury the munitions in the sand and wait. The war might last a month or two. . . .

In the weeks that followed, while news from Europe filtered through with exasperating slowness, I watched the curious spectacle, not altogether inspiring, of Djibouti in the grip of the war fever. A wave of astonishing energy swept away the lethargy of the "hottest place on the globe." The whole white population mobilized for the defense of the colony. Not a gun nor a cartridge remained in the storehouses of the arms syndicate. Every white citizen had been provided with a rifle. Squads of sweating Somalis dug trenches across the Issa country and strung miles of barbed wire in the desert. This was baptized, by courtesy, the "front." A whole band of European small boys wearing the khaki uniform of boy scouts, was mustered to carry messages from the trenches to the officers in town where the General Staff (in the person of the captain of the native brigade) sat devising new plans for the defense.

The bronze cannon that formerly ornamented the terrace of the governor's house were transferred to secret strategic points, to prevent entry of enemy cruisers in the roads. This in accordance with the theory that "in strategy one must foresee . . . everything." But no cruisers came; no enemy lay in ambush among the blistering Issa hills; and except for one night of terriffic excitement when eight unsuspecting shepherds and a herd of sixty camels set all the boy scouts in motion and all the male population of Djibouti in arms, all lay quiet along the "front." Only the sun continued an offensive, unabated, irresistible, crushing alike amateur and professional warriors, until at last the town subsided to normal—its fervor limited to interminable discussions, at the *apéritif* hour, of the *communiqués* that arrived from Europe with delays increasingly prolonged.

I too, had not escaped the contagion. My contribution to Djibouti's defense was a plan for blowing holes in the eventual enemy cruiser with a ton of dynamite "planted" in a submerged houri. But the success of the plan entailed blowing up two volunteers along with the mine and the captain-commander refused to share with me the prospective glory of the explosion.

Alone I retired to Mascali to survey my pearl-cultures and wait for events.

The eighty cases of cartridges on the island worried me considerably. My class had not yet been called to the colors, but if the war continued, my departure for France was inevitable—a matter of months, at the most. The enmity my success in the arms trade had aroused made it distinctly unwise for me to abandon the cartridges at Mascali. Anything might happen during my absence. There might, I thought, be a chance of selling them to the Warsangalis in English Somaliland, then being warred upon by a bandit chief, Mal Mullah, who burned their villages and spread terror generally along the Somali coast. A brief cruise made during December, 1914, convinced me nothing could be done there, and I returned considerably discouraged to Djibouti.

I have often wondered whether, in what followed, I did not play the scapegoat—my previous career and the reputation I enjoyed in the colony fitted me so admirably for the rôle. For some months before the war, it was an open

secret that the London Foreign Office had complained
from time to time that in spite of the arms convention,
Arabia was still flooded with guns and munitions. London
discreetly intimated that French merchants had a hand
in the trade, and invited the Government of the Colony
to take preventive measures. In Djibouti, there were
plenty to assert that my overstepping of the color line
had spoiled the game and drawn attention to the part
played by French Somaliland in supplying arms to the
Arabs.

Whether fresh protests were made after August, 1914,
I do not know; but in one fashion or another, the war
precipitated the storm long piling up against me. And the
wretched eighty cases of cartridges were the plausible
pretext.

Towards evening on Christmas Day—I remember that
holiday vividly—I walked down to the port to meet Abdi
who was due to arrive with the boutre to sail me back to
the island. (I had spent several days in town winding up
the affairs of a friend, killed several weeks earlier at the
front—the real one—in France.) At the quai, the *Fat el
Rhaman* already lay at anchor, but the entire crew from
Abdi to the boy Moussa, stood enclosed in a circle of
armed askari. I took it all in at a glance. Some one had
betrayed the cache at Mascali.

In a flash, I remembered a Soudanese blacksmith whom
I had dismissed several months earlier for petty thieving.
I had met him only the day before on the streets of Djibouti, resplendent in a new turban and *fohta*, a money-
belt of ornate leather, and—supreme touch of elegance—
a pair of yellow, European shoes! Of the source of his
good fortune . . . I now had no doubts. I also recalled
that yesterday I had encountered Ato Joseph who, con-

trary to his habit, had greeted me with beaming inquiries after my health and well-being.

On my way to the tribunal where I went hoping to obtain the release of the *Fat el Rhaman's* crew, I took stock of the situation. The cost of the confiscated cartridges—not yet paid for—together with the heavy fine (I had no hopes of being let off easily), would cost me every penny I possessed. Still in my life material losses never seem worth despair. Money represents little more than the stamp of success, the conventional crowning of effort, and as such a secondary consideration. "Who can hope to succeed indefinitely . . ." I said to myself.

That Christmas afternoon in no anguish of spirit I reasoned that there was a fair chance that I too might shortly be killed in France, like poor Raymond whose affairs I had just settled. In which case, this last misadventure would ease the task of my executors! I whistled cheerfully over this lugubrious thought, far more uplifted than I would have been had I known my immediate future was no hero's grave but a cell in a colonial jail!

The charge of defrauding the customs—to which the discovery of arms on Mascali made me liable—was punishable by a fine. But a graver accusation was in store for me. Scarcely had my store of cartridges been confiscated, when by an odd coincidence a Somali was arrested with 250 cartridges in his possession. He declared I had sold them to him in Djibouti. Vainly I called attention to the fact that the incriminating cases had never been opened. Twenty-four hours later I found myself locked up in Djibouti prison, charged with inciting natives to revolt!

Even "model" prisons so called in Europe are seldom too "comfortable" from the occupant's point of view. The

Oasis—Tajura

Tajura

Gorges—Tcher Tcher
mountainside

Homes of the Fishermen
—Farsan Islands

Interior of a Dankali hut

Taking on water

Scenes for an Artist's Sketch-book

average colonial prison is designed for natives—and
criminal natives at that—which may explain certain defi-
ciencies in construction and equipment. As a prisoner, my
first reaction was one of thankfulness that the month was
December. I defy any European to resist for ten days the
temperature of the Djibouti prison in summer! As it was,
I spent my days in utter nakedness; discarding even the
fohta; the contact of even that most primitive of garments
was intolerable in my stifling cell. At first, I suffered from
the lack of light, which filtered stingily through a shut-
tered opening twenty-two inches square, high up the wall.
In time, my eyes grew accustomed to the semidarkness. I
found light to write by, even to paint by.

Those first water colors of mine represented no ama-
teurish playing with colors (though I am only a "Sunday"
painter). They were born of necessity. One might say that
for months, unconsciously, my eye had registered and
stored away essential fragments of familiar landscapes,
preserving them, simplified of all detail, in their vividness
of line—and color. Assal Lake with its circle of purple
peaks and the blazing crystals of its salt beach; white
strips of table-islands in a sea of ultramarine; volcanic
coasts of black basalt, craters stained with sulphur-yellow
and rust—and the vivid green that marks the submerged
reef and borders the foam line of beaches. . . . I had only
to reproduce the vision. That I was able to do so—to
please myself at least—I have since regarded as my most
precious legacy from my painter father. It gave me an
illusion of freedom and a contact with friendly landscapes
I might never see again; and it helped me preserve a
mental balance during the months in that fetid cell, with
the prospect ever before me of court martial, and firing
squad.

As a prisoner I had been placed *au secret*, seeing no one, not even a lawyer. Fortunately for me, the prison guards were Somalis—I acquainted my few friends with what had happened, and procured writing materials and colors. I even discovered a means of communicating with my crew—prisoners like myself. Every day we held brief conversations through the pipe that served as drain for the two waterclosets of the prison, white and black. Except Abdi and Kassim, who as my "men of confidence" received special attention, the crew seemed fairly comfortable in their crowded quarters. Abdi was *au secret*, shut up in a windowless cell, on half rations; while Kassim had been given the "sun cure," locked all day long in a blistering, shadowless court.

Remember this was wartime. I could expect no miracle of clemency from those who for months had bent every effort to bring me where I was. That the testimony of the Somali was manifestly perjured made little difference. Every one knew that for months I had carried arms to the Dankali coast. In addition, my friendship with the natives and, above all, the fact that I had become a Moslem, counted against me. It was only too easy to spread the story that I had intended to appeal to the "fanaticism" of Islam to wipe out the white intruders. My war-fevered countrymen were willing to believe it.

In March, the case was up. I was brought blinking into the courtroom to hear the Somali repeat his story; in three months the prosecution had gathered no additional evidence against me. For that reason I escaped shooting.

My sentence was a six-month prison sentence plus a fine of 12,000 francs. The figure shrank to 9,000, my entire capital at the time; and the six months reduced to three—the three I had already spent in Djibouti jail, provided I made no appeal and took myself off to France with all possible speed—at the time my one definite ambition.

When I found myself free again, even the sight of the *Fat el Rhaman* waiting in the harbor, Abdi's tears and the affectionate greetings of my faithful blacks, released on the same day, failed to rouse me from the prison torpor. I arranged to leave the boutres in Abdi's charge. The crews—for whose material existence I still felt responsible, were to continue fishing for mother-of-pearl, dividing their gains among themselves. "Until my return," I told them, though I considered my departure final. The war was the end.

It took another jolt of misfortune to shake the apathy from me, and galvanize into reaction all that was left of my energy. I engaged a fourth-class passage for Marseilles. Ironic commentary on my four years of East Africa; I was returning poor as I had come. The morning of my departure, I learned—along with the rest of Djibouti—that a safe of the *Banque d'Indo-Chine* had been cracked during the night. So daring a burglary could scarcely be laid to natives; suspicion led to a band of Greeks, arrived in Djibouti several days earlier and off on the morning train for Abyssinia. I heard the news with no emotion, having no personal interest in the fortunes of the bank.

At three o'clock I went aboard the liner. I had no sooner settled myself with the bundle that was my baggage near the rail with a crowd of soldiers on their way home from Madagascar, when I heard my name spoken. It was the *commissaire de police.*

"I—I regret extremely. I have come to search your baggage," he announced, with a certain embarrassment.

"? ? ? ? ?"

"The burglary of the bank," he explained, biting his lips nervously. "They found a linen cap like the one you sometimes wear, and they thought. . . ."

In the rush of cold anger that choked me, I could find no words to reply. I gave a gesture that included the bundle on the deck and the cap lying beside it and turned away to the rail. I felt sick and weak; my eyelids stung as I stared out on the blazing harbor that danced with the sky and the white line of the town in dizzy waves of fire.

The police officer cleared his throat. He made no move to investigate the roll of linen at his feet.

"Would you mind showing me your bill folder—as—as a pure formality?"

I handed it over in silence; it contained six hundred-franc notes. He returned it without comment; his arm remained outstretched.

"*Bon voyage*," he said briskly, and shook my hand with unusual warmth. A moment later his stout figure stumped down the gangplank to the waiting launch.

Leaning against the rail I watched the white wake of the receding motor boat, while the steam-windlass thumped behind me, and the anchor chains ground in their sockets. Grimly I reflected that if, as certain of my countrymen had evidently suspected, I had secreted a portion of the "fortune" the arms trade had brought me, to carry back to France, I would be seated in the launch riding back to Djibouti to face a more shameful charge than any that had ever been brought against me.

Jailbird and safe-cracker! The ignominy was complete.

As I watched the coast of French Somaliland sink into the water of the gulf, I swore to myself, addressing the dazzling point of horizon below which lay Djibouti, "If human will can avail—I promise you, I am coming back! I am coming back, I promise you!"

XI

Piraeus, Djibouti, Suez

Another liner, outward bound, but this time not for Marseilles. Barely two months had passed since my dramatic farewell to Djibouti, and here was I by the rail of the *entrepont*, a deck-passenger, traveling east once more, on the trail of my elusive fortune.

The army had rejected me. On my return journey to France I contracted what I thought bronchitis. The regimental doctor who examined me in Marseilles took a different view.

"Where do you come from?" he demanded shortly, laying down his instruments to eye me with professional severity through his gold-rimmed glasses. "The Somali coast? Where is that?"

I explained.

"You've had malaria, I suppose?"

"A touch now and then," I admitted. Like most colonials I had come to consider the "equatorial twins"—fever and quinine—inevitable and unimportant.

Again a professional "Hm."

"You have already been declared unfit for service, I see," he continued, tapping a page of my *livret militaire*, that dated from the time of my military service. "Well, this time, my boy, you may consider yourself disqualified for good."

"Disqualified?" I repeated incredulously. The idea seemed preposterous and highly ludicrous as well. I thought of the past four years—the hard life in the desert and on the sea. Surely no physical wreck (for that was what the physician intimated) could have survived. . . . I found myself protesting with considerable heat. My examiner cut me short with gold-braided authority.

"Man, with your lungs, you would not last a week in the trenches!"

A few days later a *conseil de réforme* repeated the verdict. I was turned away with the new title of "invalid" and given the benevolent advice to retire to the hills and look after my health. "Milk and eggs, and above all things, my boy, complete rest!" So convincing was the diagnosis that for twenty-four hours, I almost believed it myself.

But a week spent on the Cape above the silvery salt marshes of my boyhood drove all thought of physical handicap out of my head. As I lay on my back among the aromatic herbs, already powdery and gray beneath the April sun, I found myself launching on new plans with the enthusiasm of a boy.

One scheme in particular pleased me. Its success would quite offset my exclusion from the army. Briefly, it was a plan to acquire new territory for France. But its execution demanded funds. I had none. Nor did I care to ask a loan for that particular enterprise. Success was too uncertain. The money returns were too doubtful and in any event, not immediate. I preferred to risk my own capital— as soon as I had capital to risk. . . .

I reviewed the possibilities of making money rapidly on the Somali coast. The arms trade was dead, killed by the war. Pearl fishing depended too much on chance. As I racked my brains for an expedient, a phrase heard weeks before flashed across my mind.

The evening before my departure for France I had spent

with one of my rare friends among the Europeans of Djibouti: a retired sea captain who led a comfortable existence on the coast, rounding out his lean pension by fishing for sharks in the Gulf of Tajura. Like many a navy man, he had smoked opium for years, though by no means an inveterate smoker. It would have been as absurd to confuse Captain Chambord with the drug fiends of literature as to condemn as drunkard the man who drinks claret with his dinner. Three pipes a day—never more, and often less. He used often to chide me gently for my own abuse of nicotine. On that particular evening, my cigar and his after dinner pipe (alas for the oriental luxury Westerners associate with opium-smoking . . . it was a porcelain mustard-pot with a joint of bamboo inserted in the opening) had brought the conversation to a discussion of the national "poisons."

"Alcohol for the Anglo-Saxon; absinthe for the Frenchman, *kif* for the Algerian, Abyssinian *kat*, Egyptian hashish, opium for the East and now nicotine staining the fingers and speeding up the hearts of the whole world! It isn't the drug, my boy, but the way you use it. And all the laws in the world are not going to teach men moderation. Take Egypt," he continued, holding a black bead of opium sputtering above the flame of the lamp. "It is an open question whether the drug laws have profited any one but smugglers and government employees who have built up a fortune out of *baksheesh*. By the way," he added laying aside his improvised pipe after a long inhalation, "they say there are tremendous profits in hashish. It might be worth looking into, for one of your age and energy."

That was the phrase I recalled, lying among the fragrant grasses of the Cape, watching the sails of the fishing fleet skim towards the horizon in a series of winding zigzags that made me homesick for the *Fat el Rahman.* My acquaintance with hashish was limited to the vague notion that you obtained it from hemp. I had no idea whether you smoked or ate it. Another snack of information came to my mind later that same afternoon as I strolled along the wharf of Port Vendres. A steamer lay along the dock unloading *carobs.* My eye caught the name painted in gold letters on the stern: "*Zenobie:* Piraeus." Piraeus . . . hashish, I seemed to remember, came from Greece.

A sudden impulse carried me up the gangplank. I asked for the captain. From the depths of the engine-room, a voice shouted in French that the captain was not on board, and a stout man in an oil-stained shirt edged through a narrow door out on the greasy deck. He introduced himself: the chief engineer. He would take any message I might leave.

I hastened to explain that my business did not concern the captain alone. If the chief engineer could spare time to accompany me to one of the cafés facing the dock, while drinking a *bock,* we might have a moment's talk. The *bock,* interpreted as four or five cognacs, gave me the opportunity I wanted. I stated boldly that I expected to buy hashish in Greece and would be glad of any information he might be able to furnish. I could not have fallen into better hands.

The engineer's own family, it appeared, raised and prepared the drug for market. A brother-in-law, a priest of the Greek church at Piraeus, to whom he would give me a letter, knew all the details of the trade. If I desired, he could telegraph the priest to meet me at the dock and help me with my purchases.

And that is how, a week later, I took passage on an east-bound steamer, a substantial loan from a friend buckled fast in my money-belt, en route once more for a new country and uncertain fortune.

Below decks, the third and fourth classes were jammed with deported emigrants that half a dozen nations were sending home to their eastern European birthplaces. I found myself sighing for the cleanly Moslems; these "brother whites" were even more primitive than the Somalis. After one night passed in a welter of filth, rags and vermin, I offered my services as steward. That arrangement permitted me to eat with the waiters of first class and sleep on the floor of the dining room. And the head waiter was so delighted with my performance (he could see at a glance, he told me, that I had been in service before!) that he offered me the return trip under the same conditions. I accepted with alacrity.

Four days later we sighted the Greek coast and entered the Gulf of Athens, an immense blue lake encircled by mountains, stained rose and blue in the morning light and spotted over with paler patches like flowers: the tinted plaster of villas. Then Piraeus, a cluster of red roofs against orange hills, swept by a warm wind that spread over the bay the fragrance of heated pine woods and fields of lavender.

I found my priest, Papa Nikopoulos, waiting on the dock. A handsome man of forty, with a long dark beard and a stately profile; carefully dressed, almost elegant in his robe of black broadcloth. Unfortunately he spoke no French, so our conversation was limited to smiles and gestures until an interpreter with a handful of Italian words succeeded in establishing a hyphen between us.

The "honey" (Papa Nikopoulos employed that charming euphuism for the benefit of the interpreter) could be purchased, he told me, in Morea, the district where it was

grown, eight hours by train from Piraeus. The priest himself would accompany me. In exporting the "honey," it
was advisable and in fact customary not to pass through
the customs, in order to avoid a heavy export tariff. My
majestic companion, greeted on the street with every mark
of respect and consideration, led me to a café where I arranged with a specialist of the appropriate name of Caravan, to carry the "honey" aboard a boat for Marseilles
for the reasonable sum of fifty centimes the pound.

That detail out of the way, I was taken to the house of
one of Papa Nikopoulos's parishioners, a worthy lady
with a precise knowledge of my native tongue. There we
settled the question of commissions in a definite and busi-
nesslike fashion. That night, I confess, I slept little. I had
no illusions as to the risks of the business in which I had
embarked. In my lack of knowledge of the language and
my total ignorance of everything concerning the product
I had come to buy, I had only intuition to guide me. That
and a certain natural flair for detecting flaws and wormy
corners in agreements and the men who proposed them.
Like the rat of the fable I had already left a fair number
of tails on the battlefield; but I flattered myself that I
could generally distinguish a floured brick from the edible
loaf. But at bottom I felt far from reassured as I tossed
and turned in Papa Nikopoulos's comfortable bed. I was
still courting sleep when the priest knocked at my door
an hour before train time.

All day long we jolted over an uneven roadbed at an
average speed, I calculated, of fifteen miles an hour. First
the plain of Athens, a garden overgrown with roses and
planted with oranges, lemons and grenadines. Then slopes
with vineyards and olive trees, overlooking the gulf like
a still pond. Beyond the Canal of Corinth the train

plunged south into mountains overgrown with heather and wild olive, peopled with flocks of goats and shepherds in their abbreviated white petticoats and pomponned slippers. At the rare stations, we climbed down from our box-like compartment to drink *rezina*, the white wine of the country, somewhat unpalatable to a Western taste because of the strong tang of rosin.

Towards five o'clock we reached Steno, where we left the train and struck across country towards the village of Tripolis, a dozen houses situated on a plateau barred by a chain of mountains whose summits still showed traces of snow.

Papa Nikopoulos's cousin, the hashish grower and manufacturer, lived a mile from town in a farmhouse that from the outside differed in no respect from those we had passed on our walk from the station: a low granite building like a small fortress, enclosing a paved courtyard.

But once across the threshold, an abundance of rugs, armchairs, lamps and *bibelots,* unexpected in so rustic a setting, testified to the wealth of the proprietor. Cousin Nikopoulos and his wife, an energetic young couple dressed in European costume, received us with hospitable volubility. A niece, who had been to school in Athens, served us as interpreter. After the traditional coffee (served by a young peasant to all appearances as uncivilized as a Dankali from the Mabla, for she stared at me with the terrified fascination of a wild thing from the bush), we were taken to inspect the hashish.

It was stored in an outbuilding—a dozen sacks pressed beneath heavy stones. Cousin Nikopoulos opened one of the sacks, and for the first time I laid eyes on the merchandise I had traveled so many miles to purchase: a dark brown waxy solid that gave off a faintly resinous odor.

Determined not to betray my ignorance by injudicious remarks, I examined the fragment tendered me, and passed it without comment to the priest. Cousin Nikopoulos misinterpreted my silence.

"But I have much better," he hastened to protest.

"Then show it," I declared firmly (through the translator), "we have no time to waste on inferior grades."

After a careful scrutiny of other samples, we discussed prices. (At the time, I could detect no difference in the grades, but later I learned that first-class hashish is distinguished by a more strongly defined odor and by an increased content in resinous matter.) We fixed on the sum of nineteen francs the *ocque* (about 1,200 grams) for 400 *ocques* of hashish, to be delivered in zinc-lined boxes containing fifty packages of one *ocque* each. Whereupon Cousin Nikopoulos left to engage a force of women workers to prepare the hashish for shipment—a lengthy process, it appeared. And we had only two nights and a day before us, if I and my merchandise were to embark for Marseilles on the ship I had planned to take.

Hashish growing and manufacture, I gathered, represented one of the principal industries of the province of Tripolis. Nearly all the peasants of the region raised hemp, selling the leaves to specialists who prepared the drug for market. The chief secret of hashish growing, I was told, consisted in the removal of all male plants from the hemp field. Subsequently a resinous coating forms on the upper surfaces of the leaves of the female plant. The leaves are gathered, dried, and rubbed to powder on a fine screen. The powder so obtained is collected in sacks and stored for sale. In time it amalgamates and hardens. Before selling the drug, however, it must be broken up again and resifted.

For thirty-six hours, Cousin Nikopoulos's barn hummed like a factory. The process took much longer than I had imagined, though every one worked at top speed with an enthusiasm that reminded me vividly of a vintage in my native Roussillon. In one corner a carpenter and a plumber hammered away making the zinc-lined cases. Ten women and four men occupied the center of the floor. One group broke up the hardened cakes of hashish by beating the sacks with heavy sticks. Another emptied the contents of the sacks on a huge sieve, rubbing the powder through the screen to collect below in a sheet stretched to receive it. It was then stirred vigorously in an iron cylinder (generally hashish from two successive crops is mixed together) and shoveled into the sacks that Mrs. Nikopoulos stitched busily on her sewing machine. The sacks of powder were then run through a press from which they emerged in the form of hard, flat bricks—ten inches by five, and one and one-half inches thick. Each brick weighed one *ocque*. When night came, the work went on without interruption in the smoky light of beeswax candles and little pottery lamps filled with olive oil. At six o'clock on the morning of our departure, the last case was nailed shut. I took hurried leave of Cousin Nikopoulos, who kissed the priest and myself on both cheeks, inviting me heartily to come again and "bring all the family."

Again the long ride down through the foothills to Corinth with its cypresses and yellow roofs against an incredibly blue sea, and the steep shores of the Gulf of Athens smelling of pine woods heated in the sun. But neither the beauty of the morning nor the lyric quality of the landscape let me forget my precious merchandise, which had a freight car to itself at the end of the train. At every stop, I climbed down to assure myself that it was

still there—a useful precaution as it turned out, for at
one of the stations the car was uncoupled to be attached
to a freight train scheduled to pass later in the day. It
took all Papa Nikopoulos's persuasion to get the local
station master to annul the order. At Athens, the car was
held up again; no amount of persuasion availed to get it
out of the freight yards before the following morning.
Luckily I got the captain of the steamer to postpone for
twelve hours his departure from Piraeus, and the next
morning I accompanied the hashish from Athens to the
port. Scarcely had we pulled into the station when Caravan and his men invaded the freight car. Loading the cases
on a couple of pushcarts, they hustled them across the
pier to a motor boat that shot away instantly, lost to
sight in a moment among the steamers anchored in the
harbor. An hour later, I received notification that my
merchandise had arrived on board, together with the insurance contract.

Piraeus—Marseilles—Djibouti. On the first day of
July, 1915, the liner, Madagascar-bound, on which I and
my cases of hashish had taken passage, dropped anchor
off the dock of Port Said. Papa Nikopoulos had given me
a letter to another of his innumerable cousins, an employee of the Canal (it appeared that many Canal employees were interested more or less directly in the hashish
trade) who, he assured me, would furnish all the necessary
introductions. . . . I found Cousin Petro as indicated, living
with a large and noisy family in one of the houses of the
Canal Company. In spite of the priest's letter, he received
me with a certain air of mistrust, but promised to be at
Suez in six weeks to receive me and my cargo.

Five days later, I saw the sun drop behind the Issa
Mountains as we steamed into the outer harbor of Dji-

bouti. Scarcely had the throb of the engines ceased when a sail showed white alongside—the *Fat el Rhaman*, with Abdi at the helm. As I showed my face above the rail, a chorus of voices shouted confused greetings in Arab and Somali. And so I came "home," three months to a day from the time I had said what I thought to be a long if not a final farewell to the Somali coast.

It took a week to remove my possessions from Mascali to an old house by the shore at Obok (I had decided to abandon the unlucky island) and fit out my boat for its long journey north. On the eleventh of July the *Fat el Rhaman* was ready to leave the port, freighted, so its papers read, with a "cargo of hashish for (O souvenir of the defunct arms trade!) Mascatte in Arabia."

I spent the night on board, alone except for the boy Fara (in Somali, little mouse), for it was Thursday, the weekly Moslem feast; I had given the crew shore-leave to eat the holiday meal with their families and perform their last devotions at the mosque. A dead calm lay on the harbor; from time to time a damp, warm breeze stirred the surface of the water, heavy and black like liquid metal, spattering it with phosphorescence, or a fish passed below in a streak of green fire.

At dawn, the crew came aboard—ten in all, from Abdi the mate, to Ali the cook—and at nine o'clock the morning wind carried us under full sail into the waters of the gulf. With the deck of the *Fat el Rhaman* underfoot and the feel of the bar in my fingers as the boutre cut through the swell, the strain of the past months slid off me like a cloak. Prison and the contact with civilized Europe were alike forgotten; I drank in the sun and wind, and felt

Abd el Hai's house on the water's edge at Obok

Ship carpenters

exhilarated and young again, skittish as a colt turned out
to grass.

A big Arab boutre lumbered over the horizon, changing
its course abruptly as it caught sight of our swift advance. To the astonishment of my men, I headed straight
for it. When we had overtaken the boutre, I hailed the
nakhoda, ordering him to stand by—following the command with a gunshot in the air. Powerless to flee, the
Arabs obeyed and I ran the *Fat el Rhaman* alongside.
I had hoped that the boutre was a smuggler whom I
planned to send on his way with our blessings; but it turned
out to be an honest merchantman on the way from Moka
to Aden with a load of salt fish. After a pretense of in-
spenting the cargo, I gave the *nakhoda* a parting salaam
and returned to the *Fat el Rhaman;* to the disappointment
of my men, who had begun to take the prank in earnest.
A modest levy of salt fish or chickens, Abdi declared,
would have done no one any harm! I explained gravely
that we were still too close to Djibouti to indulge in piracy
of that sort . . . and swung my boat into her course again.

Bab el Mandeb let us through its black gate in a choppy
sea that set the steady *Fat el Rhaman* bobbing like a cork.
We left the reefs of Assab on our left; I had no intention
of mooring for the night while the weather held. Three
days out from Djibouti, we sighted the jagged outline of
Great Hanish Island. To approach it, we rounded Parkins
Reef, its black rocks like a succession of coal heaps, in-
habited only by a population of birds that swooped about
us at arm's-length, or poised suspended overhead, their
bodies motionless, their bright bead-like eyes following our
movements. The sun slid down behind the Great Hanish
in an orange sky against which the island stood, a fabulous
construction of velvet, black and garnet, streaked with

broad white stripes. Rivers of sand dropped fan-like to a beach strewn with dark rocks that in the evening light looked like a feast of old wrecks half eaten by the sea.

As it grew dark, the wind freshened. In the opaque blackness, the waves broke behind us in cascades of starry phosphorescence, shining eyes of thousands of strange beasts creeping after us through the night. Towards midnight a violent shock astern brought us all to our feet.

"*Lokhum*" (a shark), Abdi, who stood at the helm, called reassuringly, pointing to the fiery trail left by the monster as it fled plunging into deep water. It had struck our rudder but the heavy teak had resisted the blow.

At daybreak the wind fell, and by noon we lay in a dead calm. The heat grew intolerable, 105 degrees by the thermometer hung in the shadow of the sail. The men emptied *tanikas* of water constantly on the deck to keep us from blistering our feet. All of us had broken out with the *bourbouille*—the heat rash of the tropics accompanied by intolerable itching, which comes when the temperature of the air is superior to blood heat. Towards evening a feeble breeze permitted us to make slight headway. By midnight we were becalmed again. All night long lightning flashed in the west. Towards morning we saw the western horizon red with sand clouds. I needed no further warning. We had scarcely lowered the mainsail, hoisting a storm jib in its place, when the sand storm was upon us. The sea flattened out like a table, white as if snow covered. Blinded with sand and spray, we could not see twenty feet ahead in the wind that tore past, fiery hot as if it blew from an immense bonfire. From the forecastle deck came a rumble of voices: my Somali were reciting the *fata*—sure sign of trouble to come.

Five minutes later the surface of the sea had broken up

in short waves that beat against our stern like the blows of a huge battering ram. At each impact the sail-yard bent as if to break.

A bigger wave crashed astern. There was a sinister cracking overhead, a report like a revolver shot, and the yard banged to the deck. The sail ripped in two, flapping like a whip in the wind, and as the sea poured over the stern, I had a flashing glimpse of Nur, one of my seamen, swept overboard in the foam, his head crushed and bloody.

No time for lamenting. The waves struck us amidships, flinging the *Fat el Rhaman* from beam to beam in a mad tangle of ropes. Half the broken yard still held to the mast and at every roll swept through the air, battering against the mast like a tremendous club. With Abdi's help, I tried to seize the spar and finally grasped the end of it, but at that moment Abdi received a double-sheaved block full in the face, laying open his forehead and nose. Staggered by the blow, he let go the yard, clutching at a shroud which kept him from being swept overboard. I still clung. A sudden lunge of the boutre lifted me fifteen feet in the air and as I came down, I caught my left arm between yard and mast. A sharp pain shot from wrist to shoulder; the bone had snapped, five inches above the wrist. The crew rushed up and all hands working together, we brought the broken sail-yard to the deck.

While half my men worked at the pumps, the others roped together two spars and we rigged our spare storm jib. Two hours' frantic effort and we were again masters of the boutre.

Time then to take an inventory of the damage. Nur missing; Abdi's head swollen beyond human proportions, and my arm broken; the rest unharmed. I bandaged Abdi as best I could and tied up my arm in an improvised splint.

Twenty-four hours later we crept into Massawa. Ordinarily I would have hesitated to visit the port, but battered as we were, there was no choice. To the customs inspector, I declared carelessly that the eight precious cases heaped unceremoniously among sacks of rice, *durra,* and sugar, contained sea biscuit. Even our destination— Mascatte—aroused no suspicion. To his limited geography, it was quite normal to travel from Djibouti to the Persian Gulf via the Red Sea!

To replace poor Nur, we took on a young Somali, Abdulleh Ghassim (who had shipped with me before), an expert seaman though hideous to look at, as the result of an extraordinary accident. Like all Somali children from eight to fourteen, Abdulleh had been a shepherd. Every day he took a flock of goats and camels into the bush, leading his charges from one water hole to another, driving them home at sunset to a *zeriba* within which a fire burned all night long to frighten away leopards and hyenas. One afternoon, when the boy was returning with his flock, a river swollen by a sudden storm barred the route. Night came before the flood swept past. The animals, huddled in groups, refused to stir. The boy tore branches from the mimosa bushes, building a *zeriba* as best he could. Unable to light a fire with wood sodden with rain, he marched round and round the *zeriba,* singing at the top of his lungs, hoping the sound would keep hungry beasts at a distance, and signal his presence to the men of his tribe who would in time set out to find him.

He heard the groaning yelp of hyenas all about him in the bush, but it was not the hyena he feared most. He knew that the leopard, silent as a shadow, all but invisible in the moonlight, was turning like himself round about the *zeriba.* Now and then, he caught the gleam of a pair of eyes that flashed and went out, to appear again farther away like a twin will o' the wisp. Then suddenly the leopard was upon him, stifling the child's song in its terrible jaws. I would not have believed had any but a Somali told me the rest of the story. (A Somali will lie to get out of trouble, but I have never known one of them to invent an adventure.) His face caught between the leopard's jaws, Abdulleh set his teeth in the animal's tongue! With a snarl of pain, the great cat released him and fled. The men of Abdulleh's tribe, who arrived shortly after, found the boy lying on the ground, his face a mass of blood, but still alive, and fast between his teeth a piece of leopard tongue.

From Abdulleh's scars, one could easily imagine the original wound. The left half of his face had shrunk to a cavity, and a furrow half an inch deep ran from the left eye to the back of his neck. The wounds were treated in the Somali fashion: application of fresh urine and leopard fat, boiling hot, applied daily with a brush. (As the teeth of the leopard are considered poisonous, the grease of the animal is regarded as the one efficacious antidote.) To that adventure, the boy owed his nickname: Abdulleh-the-Leopard.

For three days after leaving Massawa, we had fair weather. But on the afternoon of the fourth, a second sand storm drove us to take shelter behind the island of Said Bahar, in a broad bay which from a distance offered ideal shelter, but proved to be crisscrossed by ridges of coral reaching almost to the surface of the water. With a man in the rigging, we picked a zigzag path above a garden of madrepores, and anchored close to shore, not far from a boutre that had preceded us into the bay.

In the meantime, a reddish fog had formed on the western horizon, behind which black clouds shot with lightning

were climbing the sky. Flocks of birds swooped in from
the open sea, returning to their nests. Not a breath of
air stirred and the thunder rumbled ceaselessly. Then the
wind came, drowning out all sound. We savored to the
utmost the joy of lying safe at anchor, while the hot blast
roared overhead, pelting us with sand and insects—
locusts, flies and beetles, but particularly sand. We lay
on the deck, wrapped in our damp *fohtas*, like caterpillars
in a cocoon. Abdi risked his battered nose outside long
enough to shout:

"*Al Ham dull illah* (Allah be praised) we are not out
there." In an hour, the worst over, I paddled across to
the neighboring boutre to ask where we might find water.
In the terrific heat I had to count on a minimum of five
quarts a day per man—in reality ten, in case of accident.
The crew of the boutre, Soudanese from Port Sudan, were
fishers of a curious sea product—the hinge-like cartilage
which closes the mouth of certain sea snails. These they
gathered at low tide on the coral reef. The merchants of
Port Sudan bought the strange cargo for two francs a
pound, selling it to Arabs to be ground up with aromatic
herbs for perfume.

The nearest water supply, the *nakhoda* told us, was
to be found on a nearby island, which I took to be that
of Er Reh, noted on the chart as containing "ruins." The
following morning, when my men had collected a provision
of firewood from the mangrove forests that lined the bay,
we hoisted sail for Er Reh, a three hours' journey, and
anchored in a lagoon paved with corals like the one we
had just left.

The island, sandy and flat, bare at one end, had three
conical mounds fifty feet high. We noticed sections of
ruined walls—traces of an Egyptian city founded, ac-

cording to legend, by one of the Ptolemys. But the amazing feature of the island was a series of ancient cisterns that honeycombed the mounds. Some, built of baked clay, had the form of amphorae, with an opening three feet square at the mouth of the great jar. Others were vaulted galleries, twelve feet wide and from 150 to 200 yards in length. I counted twenty cisterns in all, their masonry still intact. For our purposes they offered little interest, as they contained only sand and dried grass. Nowhere on the island did we find traces of modern inhabitants.

Leaving that vision of a dead world (one could imagine it had died of thirst with its cisterns empty) we headed north towards the Hadjar Islands. On Badhar I made out huts that in the hot air seemed to dance above the sand. These huts, built like sea birds' nests of twigs and branches gathered along the beach, sheltered Soudanese fishers, thirty families in all, who added to their scanty income by selling water to passing boutres.

A young woman wearing the full black robe of the Soudanese, led Abdi and myself towards a rocky hill on which, she told us, were located the cisterns that supplied the island with fresh water. Gaining the summit, we stood on the rim of a crater-like depression, twenty-five feet deep and about 800 feet in diameter. At the base of the inner wall, a row of stone piles blocked the entrance of a long row of underground reservoirs. Two women were watering a herd of sheep and goats from an open cistern, carrying out the water in leather sacks and emptying it in an earthen trough.

Our guide indicated an old Arab woman, black and dry as a stick of driftwood, whom the colony had chosen to preside over the distribution of water. After half an hour's haggling, she agreed to let us fill our barrels for the sum of one *thaler* and a half (about sixty cents). I tasted the water that the goats were drinking and found it brackish, but the *agouza* (old woman) hastened to assure me that all the cisterns were not of the same quality. She would open us a better one.

We followed her along the wall of limestone that radiated heat like a stove. Before one of the rock piles, she bent down and with infinite precautions removed the stones, one by one. Behind them, a curtain of branches masked a cave that extended twenty feet into the rock. Within lay the water, clear and cool, precious as an elixir of life. The ritual gestures of the old woman, opening the cistern as one uncovers a treasure and our own silence during the operation, testified to the virtue of the humble liquid in a land of sand and sun. The origin of those cisterns, cut in the solid rock, is unknown. There are more than 150 of the artificial basins, which seem to communicate with each other or with a common reservoir, for the water level in all cisterns is the same. Towards the end of August, we were told, their content dwindles, but all the balance of the year is abundant.

While the crew of the *Fat el Rhaman* carried *tanikas* of water from the cisterns to the boutre, I lay on deck in the shade. Abdi, cross-legged beside me, whittled a fork-like Somali comb, and filled the tedium of the long afternoon by telling me such stories as the Bedoui relate about their brush fires in the evening: humorous tales of Soudanese stupidity—classic among the tribes of the coast; or the practical jokes of Soliman the Vagabond, which every Somali knows by heart.

"One day," Abdi began, his wad of tobacco forming a tumor-like lump beneath his lower lip, "Awad Salim brought home a bull he had bought at market—a beautiful

bull with horns like a crescent moon. Awad Salim filled a
jar with water, for the bull was thirsty after the long
walk through the bush. It drank . . . *katir, katir, katir*
(much). Till at last the jar was empty. But when the
bull tried to lift his head from the jar, his horns stuck fast.
Awad Salim tugged and pulled; his family tugged and
pulled; the neighbors tugged and pulled but the crescent
horns stuck fast. Then Awad Salim called Soliman.

" 'Soliman, what shall we do? My beautiful bull with
crescent horns is fast in the jar.' Soliman scratched his
head until the inspiration came.

" 'First,' he ordered, 'you must burn down the hut.'
Awad Salim hastened to obey. 'Then set fire to the *zeriba*.'
In an instant it was done. 'Then take your *gembia* and cut
off the bull's head. And now smash the jar—and see, the
head of the bull is free!' 'But the bull is dead,' Awad Salim
protested, staring ruefully at the ruins of the hut, the
zeriba, and the body of the bull with the crescent horns.
But Soliman did not heed him. Seated on the ground, he
was weeping bitterly. 'To think,' he sobbed, 'like all men
I am only mortal and must die! And who, alas, will have
genius such as mine!' "

That evening I bought the crew a young goat to cele-
brate the weekly holiday, and they feasted and sang until
late into the night. As I lay on the steering bench, listening
to the dragging rhythm of Somali songs and the thud of
dancing feet, suddenly the melody broke off short. The
dancing ceased. In the silence, a voice uttered strange,
animal-like cries. Abdulleh-the-Leopard lay in a fit upon
the deck.

"A *jinn* has seized him," Abdi called. "We must drive
it away." He filled a large earthen dish with burning embers from the cook's fire, scattering over it crystals of

incense; for the smoke of incense has power to drive away not only mosquitoes and flies, but *chaëtans* and *jinns* as well. He set the basin of coals close by the prostrate Abdulleh and seated himself with the rest of the crew in a circle about him. I lay watching the ring of dark faces in the glow of the embers, bodies swaying and hands clapping to the rhythm of a wild chant. I found it easy to believe in devils. . . .

As the song rose, Abdulleh's limbs ceased their violent twitching. The boy sat upright, his head sagging forward above the platter of red coals. His body weaving from right to left, kept tune to the beat of the clapping hands. Faster and faster; his head bobbed violently in all directions, as if his neck were broken. At last the paroxysm reached a climax. Abdulleh bent over the brazier, and seizing a glowing ember in his teeth, crunched and swallowed it as if it were a nut. Four times he repeated the feat, while the wild song went on, uninterrupted.

Sometimes, according to Abdi, a specialist in performances of this order, it takes as many as twenty to thirty hot coals before the evil *jinn* consents to abandon its victim. But on this particular occasion, Abdulleh, after swallowing the fourth coal, got the better of his tormentor. Sinking to the deck, he fell into a deep sleep. Throughout the episode, the boy's eyes were fixed, and his gestures automatic as those of a victim of hypnotic suggestion. On the following morning, when I examined his lips and mouth, I did not find the slightest trace of burn nor blister. The boy himself maintained that he remembered nothing of what had taken place the evening before.

On leaving Badhar Island, a week of fair weather brought us to Koseir. After some hesitation, I decided to halt for a day in the port. Our supplies were running low,

but more important still, I thought it wise before reaching
Suez, to have the *Fat el Rhaman* inspected by the Egyptian customs. The inspection might be less severe here than
in one of the larger ports. Some days before, we had picked
up an empty box which, like a floating aquarium, contained several dozens of little fish. The cook fried them
for lunch, but my great interest was in the box itself,
which had the same dimensions as the cases of hashish.
When it had dried, I filled it half full of sea biscuits, in
anticipation of our meeting with the customs.

Late one afternoon, we sighted the stack of the Koseir
distillery (not of alcohol, but sea water) against a background of bare hills, and before sunset we dropped anchor
in the harbor. The quarantine came aboard to sprinkle the
deck of the *Fat el Rhaman* with a solution of carbolic
acid; the customs inspector followed, a fat Egyptian in
uniform, smoking a superb meerschaum pipe, and accompanied by two helpers who to my annoyance rummaged
zealously through everything on board. When they had
burst two sacks of rice with the end of a bayonet the chief
called a halt. I had tactfully dropped the hint that I had
several pearls to sell. . . . The stout inspector intimated
that he would be glad to purchase one or two. I understood what "purchase" meant. I would be only too happy
to comply with his request.

When I went on shore to call on the commander of the
port—a white-haired Englishman from Malta, judging
by the deep copper of his weather-beaten features—a devo-
tee of the whisky-and-soda cult. He welcomed me heartily
and invited me to dinner, glad, he said, to air his rusty
French. I did my best in courteous return with the gift of
a couple of white sapphires. The Englishman was boyishly
delighted.

"May I say they are diamonds?" he demanded. "No objection," I replied, "provided you don't try to sell them as such!"

Later in the evening, the customs inspector came on board to choose his pearls. If I cared to bring a cargo of contraband tobacco and coffee to Koseir, we might, he murmured, make an excellent business arrangement! The salaries of government employees were so meager, customs duties so high, what more natural than to increase the one by cutting down the other! We parted on excellent terms, and before we left port several dozens of fresh eggs were sent aboard with the inspector's compliments.

From Koseir on we had the wind against us, the northwest wind which at all seasons sweeps the upper half of the Red Sea. It blew with tempest strength, belaboring us with short, vertical seas. One would have said as much water passed over the deck as under the keel. We beat our way painfully day and night, in interminable zigzags; soaked in our wet cottons, and suffering from cold as a few days earlier we had suffered from the sun. Each tack gained barely one-fourth of its length in the wind. In twenty-four hours we made only nine miles. If the wind held, I calculated that instead of 200 miles to Suez, we had fully 800 miles before us. And we had already been a month at sea.

I decided as we neared the entrance of the Gulf of Suez, to touch at the mining concession of Ras Abu Mingarh, to stock up on food and water—our last chance before Suez. In the narrow channel, we tacked fifteen times before making anchorage off a beach dotted with oil reservoirs. Everything aboard was drenched: the sugar reduced to sirup and the rice a pasty mass which had to be spread in the sun to dry before we went ashore. I was dizzy with fatigue; two of the crew were down with fever. Paddling to the beach, I hailed a uniformed Egyptian. He assured me I would find water and provisions at the mines, an hour's walk inland. A baby locomotive that stood steaming on a track would take me there in a few minutes. As we talked, two Europeans in khaki and sun helmets strolled towards us. To my inquiry whether either spoke French, one nodded. I explained our situation. The Englishman listened, eyeing disdainfully the while my bare feet and wrinkled *fohta*. When I finished, he declared crisply that the concession was closed to "foreigners," and bade me return to my boat in all speed.

I retraced my steps to the *Fat el Rhaman*, cursing. To refuse water to a sailor is every bit as grave as to deny shelter to a traveler on the mountain. In all my wanderings, this was the first and only time I ever met such a reception; though to be sure, most of my experience has been among black men and brown, the uncivilized of two continents.

Luckily, as we left Abu Mingarh the wind slid over to the north. In three days we sighted Ras el Adabieh and the peaks about Suez.

XII

Hashish

Hashish in Egypt is not a distinguished drug. It is distinctly a popular poison. To the fellah who consumes it (his wealthy countrymen show a snobbish preference for European narcotics: cocaine, heroin, morphine), hashish smoking is a daily habit, as customary and essential as the very food he eats! Since the drug cannot be purchased legally, he no longer demands that his employer furnish a given quantity of hashish along with his daily wages, like the Galla of Ethiopia whose ration of *kat* is reckoned as part of his pay. The fellah relies on its stimulating properties to compensate for underfeeding and to combat fatigue. Generally speaking, he uses it with moderation; the "hashish drunkard" with his hallucinations and delirium, is the exception. I have known few men who smoked inordinate quantities of hashish; and these were not Egyptians nor Arabs, but Europeans. . .

In Egypt at that time, the high price of hashish prevented the fellah from consuming large amounts, had he so desired. From the point of view of the merchant, the hashish trade became lucrative only after the drug was declared contraband. When I made that first trip to Suez with a cargo of Greek hashish, practically all the shipments smuggled into Egypt came from Greece and Syria, with only small amounts from Turkey and Roumania. An Indian drug known as charas (which when treated by a special process gives products, one of which resembles the hashish of Egypt) was still unknown except for insignificant quantities brought by employees on liners returning from the Orient.

Practically all the hashish smuggled into Egypt by various underground routes passed through the hands of a powerful syndicate with offices in Alexandria and Cairo. Greeks, Cretans and Egyptians made up the mysterious organization. Englishmen figured as subordinates or as high-placed and consequently anonymous complicities. Among the chiefs of the customs and police, the syndicate counted powerful friends. How else, indeed, account for its immunity? During my whole experience with the hashish trade, I never heard of the Egyptian customs making a single important capture. Its officials never interfered with the widespread activity of the hashish syndicate; their exploits were limited to picking up an occasional little fellow.

Now and again the arrest of a hashish smuggler carried with it a curious flavor of illegality. On one occasion the crew of a coast-guard discovered two pounds of hashish half-buried in the sand by the water's edge several miles south of Suez. The package gave the appearance of having lain there for a long time; the drug itself was dry and brittle and all but odorless. It might even have been washed up by the sea.

The sailors reported their find to the captain of the patrol, who ordered them to put back the drug where they had found it, covering it over carefully with sand, and to hide among the dunes to surprise the "smuggler's boat" when it returned. They had not long to wait, as that strip of shore was frequented by all manner of craft. When a felucca of shrimp-fishers put in towards the beach, the customs men opened fire, killing one of the fishers. His two companions were taken under arrest to Suez where their boat was confiscated and they each received a two-year prison sentence. The local press, as I recall, gave considerable space to the incident, praising the courage of the customs men in their encounter with "desperate bandits." Only the boatmen along the docks knew the inside. . . .

At the time, Port Said was—and still is, I presume—the center for petty hashish smugglers who brought the drug in concealed in vest-pockets, in nutshells, or melons. Rumor had it that certain diplomats even did not disdain to utilize the diplomatic valise for the same purpose. Before the war, one particular scandal gave color to the rumor. A piano, shipped to a representative of a European power, fell crashing to the pier while it was being unloaded. The piano box burst open, revealing not hammers and wires but several hundred neat packages of hashish! The affair was hushed up but not without an amusing sequel. The indiscreet diplomat, requested by his government to hand in a speedy resignation, refused at first. He insisted that the reason for his enforced withdrawal be made public. Confronted by the prospect of so considerable a scandal, the government in question had no course but to pay a fat indemnity by way of purchasing the resignation, and the matter ended there.

As a rule, the Hashish Syndicate never attempted storing the drug or even landing it in large quantities in Alexandria, Port Said, or Suez. The trick was to send the hashish on liners through the Canal and have it dropped overboard in rubber sacks either in the lakes or at given points in the Gulf of Suez. Even to-day, I imagine, passengers on steamers bound for the Orient may often notice fishing boats adrift far from any reef where fish are caught. If the passenger were curious, he might see even more . . . but he can scarcely hope to survey both sides of a liner at once, and a package tossed from a porthole near the water line is not easily visible after nightfall.

The boats which pick up the hashish carry it in all haste to the coast. There they hand it over to Bedouins who transport the drug overland to points in the mountains near Cairo. Several desert tribes made a specialty of the transport as their chief source of revenue. They breed camels for the purpose, splendid beasts, wiry and strong, trained to make no noise when loading or unloading. Such a camel, I was told, could not be bought for less than a thousand English pounds. To avoid pursuit, the Bedouins rode their charges through a waterless region in which, at points known only to themselves, they hid jars of water in the sand. A follower had to reduce the speed of his own camels by loading them with water barrels or risk dying of thirst.

On arrival in Cairo, the hashish was sold to wholesale dealers who purchased fifty *ocques* at a time. They in turn disposed of the drug to retailers who peddled hashish in certain cafés, by the gram. Occasionally the police arrested a peddler, but so far as I was able to discover, no one interfered with the men who bought and sold in large quantities.

All these details of the trade I learned long afterward. When I sighted the searchlights of Suez on my first trip north with my eight cases, I had no inkling how to dispose of my cargo. I knew that simple precaution demanded the removal of the hashish from the hold of the *Fat el Rhaman* before entering the harbor. As our course lay along the east shore of the gulf, the obvious was to land the cases somewhere and bury them in the sand. But at the point I

selected we found a boutre which seemed also to be unloading merchandise of a special nature, for our arrival
created a small panic. We steered west for Ras Adabieh
on the other side of the gulf. By midnight we had reached
the cape, approaching as close as I dared, and anchored
in three fathoms of water. Abdi and I set out to examine
the shore two cable-lengths away. The tide being low, we
were forced to abandon the dugout on a sand bank and
continue on foot, wading through deep pools and bruising
our toes on a strip of sharp pebbles welded together in a
hard matrix of sandy clay.

Beyond the beach, a ragged line of dunes shone pale
through the darkness. An excellent place to bury the
hashish, I decided, as we stepped into the shadow of a
dark little valley between two hillocks. Suddenly it was as
if something tugged violently at my left foot. As I struggled to pull it free, the suction seized on its mate and a
cry from Abdi warned me that he too was caught in the
quicksands. Fortunately at either hand the dunes lifted
a firm wall. We scrambled out of our predicament with
no great effort. Abdi, who began exploring the unstable
ground with a pick, encountered rock bottom twenty-five
inches beneath the surface—a reassuring discovery. Wandering there in the dark, one experienced a distinctly unpleasant thrill on sinking down through the sand, not
knowing whether the bottom lay inches or yards below.
But the proximity of the rock to the surface rendered
the spot impracticable. We picked our way back. When
we reached the boutre, we hoisted sail again for the east
shore of the gulf.

At daybreak we were within two miles of the coast. Not
a boat in sight; the boutre of the night before had vanished. Behind a long beach bordered with rocks and dunes,

a sloping plain rose towards the distant mountains. A preliminary survey revealed a hollow among the rocks, which the wind had filled with drifting sand. We could not have hoped to find a spot better suited for our operations. I ran the *Fat el Rhaman* close to the beach and lowered a raft, loading it with cases of hashish. Their weight pushed the surface of the raft below water; everything received a generous soaking. As the cases had been lined with zinc and were presumably water-tight, I had no cause for worry. But as we heaped the boxes on the sand, I noticed that the water which dripped from them gave off a strongly resinous odor. On examination, I discovered that all the soldered joints of the zinc linings had burst: the result of the heat which must have caused the air within the zinc-lined boxes to expand. My precious cargo was drenched with salt water; we had to dry it instantly or risk having the drug irremediably destroyed. Opening the cases, we laid out four hundred sacks of hashish on the sand. Two of the men kept watch among the dunes. No time this to receive an indiscreet caller! Luckily for us . . . and for him . . . none came. Within three hours we nailed the boxes up and set to burying the hashish in the sand.

I kept out two sample cases. These we buried separately at a point closer to the entrance of the harbor. By midnight we were back on board and early the next morning the *Fat el Rhaman* was anchored with a dozen other boutres in the harbor of Suez.

With a sack of pearls in my pocket as alibi, I left the boat in charge of Abdi and paddled ashore. At that hour, though the daily life of the harbor had already begun, Suez the town—the European part of it—was still abed. The streets lay deserted. Waiters were setting out café tables and small boys in gandouras like elongated night-

shirts swept out the shops—traps for the unwary tourist
—with languid brooms. In the main avenue, I encountered
a sole pedestrian—Cousin Petro, the Canal employee I
had covered so many miles to meet. He seemed more surprised than I at our meeting. He had come to Suez to keep
his promise, but hardly expected to find me there.

We set off together to call on the friend who was to
initiate me into the mysteries. Our route took us into old
Suez, through the streets bordering the inner lagoon that
lies between the town proper and Port Tewfik. Following
a narrow avenue between high houses still sleeping behind
closed shutters, we turned into a dark alley scarcely wider
than a door. A few yards further my guide, who preceded
me, paused to knock—three blows, then two in quick succession—on an oak panel in the wall. With a clatter, a
window opened overhead. A rapid exchange in Greek, and
the blinds banged to again. I heard the patter of footsteps
beyond the door, the click of a lock, and the heavy panel
swung inward. A figure in voluminous drapery flattened
itself against the wall to let us pass, then closed and locked
the door behind us. We were led through a narrow hallway
into a room, the center of which was occupied oddly by
a rowboat on which perched two sleepy hens. A row of
chairs encased in linen covers stood against the wall, a
sideboard draped with ribbons and bearing an impressive
number of little porcelain figures, blocked the end of the
chamber. In one corner an oil lamp burned below an ikon.

All this I had time to take in before a door opened, ad-
mitting a burly figure—a black-haired giant in a broad-
brimmed hat, with wide velvet trousers belted into a generous coral sash. He wore a gray flannel shirt open at the
throat. An immense mustache and a pair of earrings com-

pleted the picture. He reminded me absurdly of a comic opera brigand minus cartridge-belt and daggers.

The giant crushed my hand, roared his delight at making my acquaintance, and the three of us sat down, Petro and I on the linen-covered chairs, and our host sharing the rowboat with the two hens. Nikopoulos (for he was still another cousin of the priest at Piraeus!) spoke excellent French. He had lived in Egypt for thirty years and had learned the language while working for de Lesseps as a boy on the Canal.

"Where have you left the merchandise?" the Greek inquired, not without anxiety.

"In safety," I reassured him.

"Not on board your boat?"

"Naturally, no."

Nikopoulos drew a breath of relief. It was madly imprudent to bring the hashish so close to Suez, said he. Nothing less than a miracle had kept me from being intercepted.

"The finger of fortune surely lies upon you," he asserted. "This very night my wife dreamed of a cupboard full of bread. An excellent omen. In thirty years of the trade I have never neglected dreams, and not once have they deceived me!" The same finger of fate, he went on, had surely led me to his door. I could not have fallen into better hands. "The others," his brows puckered in a terrible frown, "would have flayed you like a rabbit! Sent by Papa Nikopoulos to me, you are one of my own family!" The amiable brigand clapped me on the shoulder and all but sent me reeling.

By my experience so far, the hashish trade seemed decidedly a family affair! It was clear that the hemp-grower of Tripolis and the men with whom I talked belonged to the same organization, but I suspected that Nikopoulos II and Cousin Petro were merely subordinates. I had yet to meet with the "brains" of the trade. Meantime I felt no compunction at entrusting my precious cargo to the giant smuggler. For all his terrible exterior, the man inspired confidence. In my dealings with men, I let myself be guided nearly always by first impressions. Generally they are justified. Often I find myself referring to them to "check up" on a man, when our subsequent relationship tends to obscure that initial opinion.

I confided to Nikopoulos that beside the buried cases I had twenty pounds of hashish concealed on board the *Fat el Rhaman*. The Greek threw up his hands.

"Holy Apostles!" he ejaculated. "If the Customs men were to find so much as a nutshell of hashish, they would seize your boat and send you to prison. You must bring it ashore at once!"

What had preserved us from a minute inspection apparently was the fact that we had come up from the south of the Red Sea. Before returning to the boutre (the Greek assured me I must not abandon it an instant so long as the drug remained on board) a daughter of our host served coffee—a mastodon of a child, built on the same lines as her father. When evening came, Abdi, whose waistline any European might well have envied, hung a garland of hashish sacks about his belly underneath his *fohta* and the two of us walked through the customs gate unhindered, Abdi carrying a coil of rope.

At the house in the alley, Nikopoulos examined the drug, and pronounced it fair quality. An Egypto-Arab present at our interview, a dark-skinned taciturn fellow, was presented by the Greek as his assistant. We agreed that I should fetch the contents of the two cases buried

near the port to a point on the docks, M'hamid, the lieutenant, would point out to me. The Arab went back to the
harbor with me to a modest café at the edge of the wharf,
a shed of planks used as landing place for hashish arriving
by sea. Not a frequent occurrence, M'hamid explained,
since a sentinel stood on guard every hundred yards along
the dock, with orders to fire on anything that stirred after
dark. This was no effort to stamp out smuggling, but part
of the Canal defense against enemy submarines.

To avoid notice, I decided to go for the two cases of
hashish in the houri. Ali, a second Somali, and myself
paddled out of the harbor, a pile of fish-nets well in view
in the middle of the dugout. Towards sunset we reached
the hiding place, ten miles across the bay. I had brought
several goatskins with us to insure the drug against a
second soaking, and into these we emptied the contents of
the cases, tied them securely, carried them aboard our
houri.

The wind had freshened. We had it in our teeth. Though
the two Somalis paddled with all their strength, we made
little headway. In the middle of the bay, three miles from
the nearest shore, we began to ship water. It was clear
that for rough weather, three men and 180 pounds of
hashish on board overloaded the dugout. Either to swamp
or throw half the cargo overboard. Abdi anticipated my
move. Before I could lift one of the goatskin sacks to the
gunwale, he dived into the sea.

"Take the paddle, Abd el Hai," he called from the
water, "I will come to land *on foot!*"

We shipped no more water: the lightened houri made
some sort of speed against the wind, but every half minute
the searchlights at the Canal entrance swept the bay with
their long white beams. I kept the dugout parallel to the

line of light; each time it passed over us, we lay back in the houri while an unpleasant thrill went pricking along my spine. By ten o'clock, we made out the dark mass of the wharf and I aimed for a point where I hoped M'hamid would be waiting, but in spite of the landmarks carefully noted by day, it was difficult to judge accurately in the blackness of the night. At any moment I expected the sentinel's cry: *"Min?"* (Who goes there?) and the crack of a gun. We pulled nearer. I distinguished a white something among the rocks. A sentinel? We slid towards it, both of us prepared to leap overboard at the first suspicious gesture. The figure stood as if frozen; no outcry greeted our approach. It was indeed M'hamid.

Having disposed of the heavy goatskins which the Arab was to deliver by some mysterious means of his own, we paddled to the *Fat el Rhaman*. Abdi had not returned. I had become so accustomed to his feats in the water that I had felt little anxiety at leaving him in the middle of the bay. But as the night wore on and he did not appear, I tormented myself with thoughts of sharks, filled with remorse at the idea that I had sacrificed my mate, my devoted friend—Abdi was that and more—for a few kilograms of hashish and a few hundred English pounds! towards four o'clock, Kassim, as preoccupied as I with the fate of our missing mate, pointed a finger into the blackness, indicating something which my eyes, less keen than his, failed to distinguish.

In a few minutes, Abdi, for it was he, clambered aboard, as fresh as if he had merely taken a bath, though he had been in the water six hours. He had gained the shore, he told us, without difficulty, but had encountered so many askari with guns that he preferred the water again, returning to the boutre by the "long route."

In the morning I received from Nikopoulos the sum we had agreed upon. He was strongly against landing more hashish in Suez.

"Much too great a risk," he insisted. "You cannot expect to slip in and out of the port an indefinite number of times without the customs getting wind of the matter. If they do," he went on with one of his wide smiles, "trouble or . . . more trouble sharing a large part of our profits!" In addition, the Greek had no customers in view for so considerable a quantity and he hesitated to store the drug in Suez.

"A much better plan is for us to go to Cairo and see the boss," he advised. "He will take the cargo off your hands in the usual fashion." Of the "usual fashion" I had no inkling. But I forbore to inquire, preferring to learn as events developed.

We took the afternoon train for Cairo. Before leaving, however, my astonishing host led me into a little room, transformed into a chapel to assure the success of our enterprise! Nikopoulos left me among the ikons while he went personally to buy candles, for he did not permit the women of his household to go unattended into the street. The train for Cairo was filled with the usual crowd of natives—fellahs, Arabs, veiled women, children—surrounded by humming clouds of flies. In the first- and second-class compartments sat impressive effendis, wearing the red *tarbouche*—government employees, officials of the customs and the police. With a few beefy-red exceptions, it was difficult to determine from their outward appearance where they had been born—on the banks of the Nile, or of the Thames.

In the Cairo station, I followed at a distance the huge silhouette of the Greek. (We had made the journey in

separate carriages.) He led me discreetly to a big blue
limousine in which sat an elegant gentleman, ivory-skinned
and dark-mustached, who greeted me with a polite handshake, inquired whether I had found the journey fatiguing,
and when I had taken a seat beside him, began a circum-
spect discussion of the weather. Nikopoulos had disappeared. With a *s-sh* of tires, the car shot off through the
broad streets of the modern quarter. Before an imposing
façade festooned with marble balconies it halted. My companion preceded me past a liveried servant through a
marble entrance into a vast reception hall, carpeted with
dozens of handsome rugs and containing much gilt-legged
furniture, a piano (also gilded), and an enormous phonograph painted with gold and flowers.

There I was presented to the wife of the drug baron,
Madame Sofia Volikis, handsome and affable, resplendent
as the furniture of her salon, wrists and fingers glittering
with diamonds. In a dining room that repeated the style
and furnishings of the reception hall, with a vast amount
of silver plate on exhibition behind glass doors, we sat
down to a meal of Gargantuan proportions. There were
only three of us at the table, but the food served would
have sufficed for thirty. A soup dish of caviar—imported
specially for my host—first made the rounds of the table;
a ham followed, of the identical brand served to King
George; dusty bottles of Marsala accompanied it, "the
very same vintage that the Khedive drinks";—and so on
throughout the meal. I was given every opportunity to
admire the magnificence of my host who thirty years before had come to Egypt with Nikopoulos to work as a
laborer on the Canal. Nikopoulos had not been invited to
dine with us. I inferred that the manners and appearance

of the amiable brigand ill-fitted so much gilt and silver. . . .

After a short siesta on a monumental bed, so festooned with satin and gold lace that an ordinary man felt timid in approaching it, Volikis and I set out on "business." Picking up Nikopoulos at a modest hotel, we drove in the blue limousine through the narrow streets of the native quarter to a big café crowded with Arabs, Greeks, and Egyptians, drinking coffee and smoking water pipes. We zigzagged among the tables to the rear of the hall where a tall Egyptian sat alone, handsome and dignified, dressed in a robe of striped yellow silk and wearing the white fez and turban of the Bedouins from the interior.

We took seats beside him, Volikis explaining in an undertone that the stranger, whom he called Mustapha, was chief of a tribe that smuggled hashish, carrying it from the coast across their territory to Cairo.

"His Bedouins will deliver your cargo," he went on lifting his voice. "You have only to make a little journey south along the shore. . . ." While we discussed the details of the affair, the Greek ordered a light lunch (we had risen from the table barely two hours before) of fried fish, roast lamb, and cheese. Six or seven waiters bustled about, the proprietor himself lending a hand in view of the importance of the client. Mustapha the Bedouin watched with detached interest while tossing off several glasses of whisky. It was finally agreed that I should land the remaining cases of hashish on the west shore of the gulf at a point called the Three Mountains. One of Mustapha's Bedouins would pilot the *Fat el Rhaman* to the place of meeting and serve as go-between with the camel drivers.

On our way to the station (I was taking the night train for Suez) Volikis gave me a brief glimpse into the or-

ganization of the drug trade. He himself did not belong to
the "syndicate." In spite of many overtures on the part
of the drug ring, he had always avoided merging with the
group which comprised many influential persons of the
Egyptian administration.

"I cannot trust men who are capable of betraying the
government that employs them," he told me. "Sooner or
later they are bound to betray you. All is a question of
price!"

Volikis preferred to work alone, with Nikopoulos as his
only European collaborator.

"But at present I am delighted to procure a new one,"
he went on. "That is why I permitted you to purchase
hashish in Greece."

"You permitted . . . ?"

The Greek's smile grew enigmatic.

"Naturally I was informed. Before you left Piraeus for
Tripolis. From what I knew of you I thought we might
be useful to each other. And I took care that the hashish
you bought did not pass out of our hands!"

My discomfiture that I had not been acting as a free
agent seemed to amuse him.

"My dear man, none of us can afford to admit competitors into the field. Not a gram of hashish is sold anywhere
without our hearing of it sooner or later!"

He controlled, Volikis gave me to understand, nearly
all the hemp-farms of Greece, which gave him a practical
monopoly of the entire Greek output. Otherwise he could
never have maintained his prestige with the "syndicate."
As things stood, there was a sort of armed truce between
the rivals.

"Which does not mean that they would not be delighted
to get me," the Greek concluded, setting his firm white

teeth together in a manner which implied that he too had forces which he would not hesitate to use if occasion offered.

Two days later the promised Bedouin from Upper Egypt arrived in Suez, bringing me a message from Mustapha that our expedition was arranged for the following night. After dark, I smuggled the man on board the *Fat el Rhaman* and hid him in the hold. Early in the day, I had changed the anchorage of the boutre to the outer rim of the harbor. All day long the sea rolled heavily; towards sunset the wind was blowing a gale. In the roadstead of Suez, squalls from the south represent a serious danger. At six o'clock red lights from the signal station signified that the harbor was closed and all marine operations suspended.

As soon as night fell, however, we lifted anchor and with sail and motor aiding us, crept out of the harbor. In four hours we lay off Ras Messale, on the south side of which I had buried the hashish. As the wind had shifted west, I dared not risk anchoring; two miles from land I had the sail lowered, and with the motor kept us headed into the wind. Five men went ashore in the dugouts, their bodies naked and greased with butter—a surer method to avoid being chilled than wearing drenched clothes in raw wind. By midnight the six cases were safely on board the *Fat el Rhaman* and we hoisted sail for the African coast twenty miles away.

By three, I made out in the black mass of the shoreline the three peaks of our destination. Sounding continually, we approached within a mile. Taking two of the crew with me, together with the poor Bedouin, half dead from twenty-four hours' seasickness in the hold, I paddled to the first sand bank. There, as the tide was low, we aban-

doned the dugout, picking our way across the shallows
to the beach beyond which a dry river bed twisted among
low hills of black rock streaked with white ribbons of sand.

No one spoke. The only sound, the thud of our bare
feet on the sand. When we had walked some two miles
inland, a rasping note like the vibrating hum of locusts,
brought us to a halt. The signal. . . . Impossible to detect from what direction it came. The strange call was
repeated; this time it came from the lips of our Bedouin
guide. At the sound, a second Bedouin, armed with a rifle,
stepped out of the night.

The two exchanged words in a guttural dialect; our
guide explained that morning was too near to risk bringing the camels to the shore. We would have to postpone
landing our cargo until another night. The Bedouin advised against burying the hashish on the beach, frequented
by day by fishers from Suez. That meant we must cruise
all day in the gulf with the precious cases on board. And
how explain our absence from Suez without papers? I had
counted on slipping into the port before dawn. However,
we had no other choice. . . . Having agreed to return as
soon as night had fallen, we made our way back to the
Fat el Rhaman and headed south in the open sea.

For twelve hours, we tacked about in the gulf. Late in
the afternoon, as I swung the boutre north again, I sighted
a small steamer coming from Suez, and as it drew nearer,
recognized an Egyptian coast-guard. Had it set out to
hunt for us? Hoisting our colors, I altered our course,
steering straight for the approaching gunboat. When
within a cable's length, I dipped the flag. The bluff succeeded. The coast-guard acknowledged our salute and apparently reassured by our good manners (what suspicious

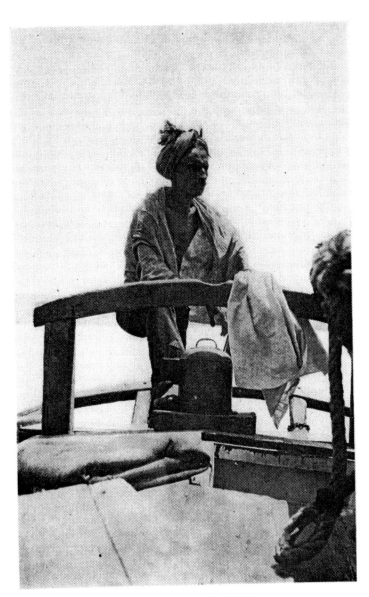

Abd el Hai at the Tiller

boat would have offered itself so readily for inspection?)
continued towards the south.

Shortly after sunset, we returned to our anchorage off
the Three Mountains. During the last hour of daylight
I had carefully examined sea and shoreline with the glasses.
Not a sail nor a human being in sight. By seven o'clock
we had landed the six cases on the beach. No signs of
camels anywhere; I wondered impatiently whether the
Bedouins were again to disappoint us. I had scarcely formulated the thought, when five camels stepped out in single
file from behind the rocks, splendid beasts, hard-muscled
and long of leg. Seven Bedouins accompanied them, five
camel drivers and two men with rifles to cover the retreat
of the caravan. Their rôle, one of the Bedouins explained,
was to bring down any indiscreet stranger who manifested
an interest in the band.

We loaded the drug on the packsaddles; the drivers
mounted their silent beasts; and one by one the tall silhouettes strode off in the darkness on the route to Cairo—
a two nights' trip across desert and mountain. Left alone,
we effaced our tracks by dragging empty sacks over the
sand while we walked crab-fashion back to the dugouts.
As for the camel-tracks, a herd of young camels had been
brought to the coast during the day, so as to leave footprints leading in all directions.

By midnight the *Fat el Rhaman* was back in the harbor
of Suez. In the morning I went ashore with misgivings to
explain our absence of the day before. As I had hoped,
the European port commissioner had not yet arrived at
his office. I found only a stout Egyptian to whom I had
already given a generous *baksheesh* on our arrival. He
greeted me as an old friend. I embarked on a fishy tale
about a dragged anchor, but the employee cut me short.

No need to give myself all that trouble . . . was he not there to arrange everything? I thanked him, an English pound changed hands; the incident was closed.

"How soon may we count on your making another trip?" Volikis inquired when we had finished settling our accounts three days later in Cairo. "This autumn perhaps?"

I shook my head. Not that autumn certainly. Perhaps never. It all depended. . . . That hashish venture had been a means to an end. With a few thousand dollars in my money-belt, I was free to embark on a project of my own, fully as hazardous as smuggling drugs to Egypt, and perhaps even more uncertain of success!

XIII

The Last Adventure in Pearls

The Farsan Islands extend, a necklace of two hundred beads, for over 150 miles along the east coast of the Red Sea, between Jaafere and Hodeida. Like the Dahalak group, they might be called Pearl Islands; all year long, hundreds of boutres fish there for *sadafs* and *bil-bil*. Every season, the pearls of Farsan sell for thousands of pounds at the markets of Massawa, Aden and Bombay.

Farsan Zekir and Farsan Kebir form the center of the archipelago. At the southern end of the islands, ebb tide uncovers an oil bed, for years utilized only by the Arab population who employed the crude oil to grease their boutres. In 1910, a German company sunk several wells which flowed abundantly. At the outbreak of the war, the German engineers abandoned the wells, first strangling them by pouring melted lead into the pipes. A year later the Turkish garrison evacuated the islands.

This was the region I had chosen for my first and only political venture, the project formulated after my military rejection in 1915, and which, thanks to Greek hashish, I now had the means to execute. It had occurred to me that aside from the oil on the Farsan Islands, their strategic importance—their proximity to the coast of Yemen—would make it distinctly worth while to plant the French flag there. The Minister of Colonies, to whom I broached the plan in the spring of 1915, manifested a benevolent interest, but gave me to understand that he viewed the ad-

venture ‚as a purely personal undertaking. I did receive
the assurance, however, that should I succeed in establishing a settlement on the islands, the Quay d'Orsay would
not be slow in "realizing all the advantages to be drawn
from the situation."

Interpreting that ambiguous statement as a promise of
eventual support, I fitted out the expedition for Farsan.
My plan was to win over the local Arab chiefs and secure
permission to install a pearl fishing station on one of the
islands. I equipped a small fleet: the *Fat el Rhaman* and
two smaller sambuks, hired crews and divers, and bought
provisions for a six months' season.

In September we prepared to sail from Massawa. As the
Italian authorities refused to deliver papers for the Farsan Islands (they maintained the region was closed to
navigation owing to the blockade of the Arab coast), I
had to content myself with papers for Djibouti, but once
at sea I was master of my route.

At daybreak, four days out from Massawa we sighted
the northern-most point of Farsan Kebir. Beyond this
opened the channel between the twin islands which I had
planned to follow to the town of Seguid at the southern
end of the Farsan Zekir. But as we rounded the cape into
Katoub Bay the breeze dropped to a breath. The strait
lay like a river, not a ripple between the two stretches of
shore. Above the sand the hot air flowed, a quivering
transparent stream; farther off tufts of date palms seemed
to float in the sky. Dead calm in such channels may last
indefinitely, so I pushed our course further east (to reach
Seguid by the outer passage) then south through shallow
water, navigating at sight with a man in the rigging to
shout directions to the helmsman. The water was so clear
we seemed to be sailing above a forest, a fantastic forest

of sponge and coral, peopled with blue sea slugs and fish like rainbow butterflies.

Dozens of dugouts, fishing for *sadafs* and *bil-bil*, dotted the still water. At sight of us they made off for shore with splashing paddles, in spite of reassuring signs.

Piracy thereabouts was an everyday occurrence, generally the work of *Zaramigi* from the coast between Moka and Hodeida. Ordinarily, they confine their attacks to merchant ships, but often when a *zaroug*, far from its base of supplies, ran short of water or provisions, the *Zaramigi* attacked the first boutre that fell into their hands, singling out by preference a sambuk of pearl fishers, loaded with supplies for several months. No wonder the *Fat el Rhaman*, low in the water and carrying sail like a racer, inspired the peaceful pearl divers with distrust.

When the rapid twilight put an end to our navigation among the reefs, we dropped anchor near the entrance of Seguid Bay. Early the following morning, we poled our way through the tortuous channel. At the far end of the inlet, a grove of date palms masked the village.

In Arab dress I landed with two of my men, one of whom—Salah—had spent several years on a pearl boutre among the islands. The beach was deserted. Our arrival had not reassured the inhabitants of Seguid. Crossing the sand, we entered the pleasant twilight of the palms, in whose shade lay gardens, irregular plots cluttered with low stone walls built to hold in the earth about the tree-roots. Higher walls over which we clambered, marked the limits of each garden and gave the oasis the aspect of a city in ruins. The morning sun filtering through the palm leaves, lay in round patches on the grass, tender and marvelously green. While we feasted an eye on this unexpected Eden, an Arab stepped through a break in the wall. Five black slaves followed him, armed with scimitars and guns.

"Sheik Ibrahim Metaffer," Salah whispered, and hastened forward to kiss the hand of the dignitary. Not very prepossessing at first glance, the Sheik of Seguid—a thick-bodied man with a pair of restless, bead-like eyes in swollen, heavy features. He wore a wrinkled *fohta*, and a tattered, greasy *siderea*, though the silver dagger at his belt was studded with precious stones, and an emerald glittered on one of his fat fingers. He greeted me with ponderous servility, rare in an Arab, and invited me straightway to honor his poor house. We followed the sheik and his black escort through the labyrinth of walls to a flat-roofed stone building, across a succession of enclosed courts, strewn with a layer of white shells. In one of the courts slaves spread rugs in the shade and brought the coiled and snake-like water pipe.

Our host seated himself cross-legged on an *engareb*, with a dozen relatives, servants and slaves about him. I took a seat facing him, while little cups of tea, strongly sugared as always, circulated among the company.

"I have come to buy pearls," I told the sheik, adding that I hoped to pass several months in the islands, while my boutres fished for *sadafs* and *bil-bil*.

Sheik Ibrahim, in a flowery phrase, assured me of his friendship and protection. After an hour he rose, begging me to excuse him until evening. He was leaving, so he said, to inform several pearl merchants of my presence on this island. I knew from Salah that Ibrahim himself owned important collections of pearls. His eagerness to call in competitors was curious, not to say suspicious. When the sheik had left, I decided to send one of my Somalis to

Abdi, telling him to call the members of the three crews back from shore and have the boats ready to leave at a moment's notice. For myself, I had no fear of a direct attack so long as I remained a guest in the house of the sheik.

The day slipped away slowly in Oriental fashion. At noon, I lunched with Ibrahim Metaffer's son and his "man of confidence," a white-haired Ethiopian who hovered about me with the diligence of a custodian.

During the afternoon, a rainstorm broke over the island. In fifteen minutes the oasis was a lake fed by muddy yellow torrents. The whole population rushed madly about, improvising ditches to bring the precious flood to their gardens, the women uttering joyful "you-you-yous," strident and piercing, while hundreds of children splashed noisily in the warm pools.

In the doorway where I had taken refuge, I received many a friendly glance from members of the sheik's household. My arrival on the day of the first rain in six months gave me the prestige of a miracle-worker. On the other hand, if our coming had coincided with locusts or a cattle-plague, better for us to take leave in haste.

At nightfall, Sheik Ibrahim clattered into the courtyard, his white mule streaked with sweat as if his master had ridden hard and long. The "pearl merchants" would arrive the next morning; Ibrahim himself would esteem it an honor to act as my "dallal." And so, after a ceremonious meal, we parted for the night. Early the next morning several Arabs brought insignificant lots of pearls and I made a few expedient purchases. In the meantime, Salah, by discreetly questioning the servants, discovered that all the dealers without exception were from Seguid—

an odd fact after the Sheik's mysterious journey of the day before.

Towards eleven o'clock, a band of Arabs and slaves, all carrying arms, invaded the courtyard. A tall black-bearded man whom I took to be their chief, advanced towards me, salaamed gravely, and retired within doors accompanied by Sheik Ibrahim. His men squatted about the courtyard, eyeing me with frank curiosity. They were a handsome lot, splendidly built, with fine, regular features and long hair hanging about their shoulders. All wore the same uniform—a *fohta* close-wrapped about the loins, a knife and a rifle. Their bodies, the color of pale bronze, glistened with butter.

I lay on an *engareb* in the shade, preserving the attitude of drowsy immobility that is supposed to reflect the tranquillity of an untroubled conscience. At last the two Sheiks sent for me. I took a seat on the divan; a slave brought coffee, and after a long silence, the newcomer, Sheik Nasser Sehel from the north of Farsan Zekir, addressed me, fixing me the while with a severe and penetrating gaze.

"It is said," he articulated slowly, while beside him the silhouette of his fellow Sheik seemed to dissolve into the shadow, "it is said that the Turks have sent you here, to accomplish evil designs."

Undisturbed, I sipped my coffee, letting several long seconds slide past before I troubled to reply.

"If you believe . . . what is said, put me in irons and lead me to Hidris, your Sultan. But you must take with me Sheik Ibrahim also, for he invited me to cross his threshold and he received me as his guest."

Sheik Nasser nodded as if my answer pleased him.

"These are lying rumors, no doubt, spread by spies and cowards," he remarked disdainfully. "But as their breed is plentiful and widespread, it may come to the ears of M'hamid Hidris and those whom he calls his friends that we have taken money to hide a Turkish spy at Farsan. Our Sultan is far from here and not having seen you, he may believe the report. Go to M'hamid Hidris. He will receive you well, I swear it on my head. Afterwards, you may return to Farsan, where, for my part, I will welcome you as a guest and a brother."

Having spoken, Sheik Nasser rose from the *engareb* and took his leave. I remained to dine with Ibrahim Metaffer who had spoken not a word, but sat crouched in the shadow, the stem of the water pipe hidden in his untidy beard. I felt convinced that he and no other was the author of the "spy" legend.

At ten o'clock that evening, I went aboard the *Fat el Rhaman*. The crew sat gorged and content over the remnants of a roasted sheep, a present from the Sheik. The night was clear, but too black to risk the reefs and shallows of the channel. I stretched myself on deck, telling Abdi we would hoist sail at daybreak for Arabia, and fell asleep to the vibrant hum of crickets, chirping after the recent downpour. Clinks and thuds, the muffled noises that betray the approach of a bark, roused me from my doze. I made out the contours of a little *zaroug* which slipped past in the darkness and disappeared in the direction of the channel. No fishing boat would have taken to sea at that hour; it could only be a courier bearing an urgent message from Sheik Ibrahim . . . to whom?

I longed to give chase, but the *Fat el Rhaman* drew too much water to attempt the channel at low tide. The night dragged on interminably. At last through the silence sounded the call to prayer. I woke my men and we lifted anchor. At that very moment a voice hailed me from the land. A slave leading two goats stood at the water's edge, another gift from my generous host. Impatient at the delay (which I had every reason to believe intentional), I made no answer. The three boats poled their way through the channel, the *Fat el Rhaman* in the lead. Beyond the reef, the sea spread like a mirror, its still surface spattered with islands. But not a sail in sight; the *zaroug* had disappeared. I abandoned hope of overtaking it.

Twenty-four hours later, we lay off the Arab port of Medy. In the harbor, a dozen boutres lay at anchor. We gave them the customary hail: a long cry uttered in unison; and one by one they replied, shouting the usual inquiries.

"Men en?" (Where do you come from?) *"Kev al Khabar?"* (What is the news?)

All along the beach bordered with low white dunes, were heaped baskets of dates, and sacks of rice brought from India in big sambuks. Two miles away, the town of Medy lifted a fortress towards which we set off, following a path that zigzagged among the dunes, passing files of camels, ten or fifteen in line, the head of each animal attached to the tail of the one preceding. Arabs of the tribe of Beni M'Zellah, dark skinned and long haired, accompanied them.

As we neared the town I discovered that the "towers" of the fortress were merely the peaked roofs of the grass-thatched huts. In a cloud of dust, a horseman rode towards us on a racing ass, his belt bristling with daggers and a sleeveless vest of green silk streaming back from his bare shoulders. Upon request, I showed him my papers from Massawa. Having scrutinized the document on all sides, he handed it back to me and dismounting, offered me the ass, remarking that he had been sent to escort me to the house of *Omer el Bahar*, the "Commander of the Sea." From that, I gathered that we were expected at Medy; the nocturnal courier had evidently preceded us.

Medy, the "capital" of M'Hamid Hidris, Sultan of half a dozen tribes in the north of Yemen, was of recent growth. Supplied with money and arms by the English, Hidris had warred for years on his less powerful neighbors, forcing the conquered tribes under his leadership. Medy, at the time of our visit, had 10,000 inhabitants. It was literally built of straw—each hut thatched with palm leaves, the walls covered with whitewashed mats of *taffi*, and surrounded by a *zeriba* of thorns or reeds, bound together with palm fiber.

At that early hour the narrow streets were redolent with incense. On awaking, the Arab housewife drives out the evil spirits of the night by thrusting an incense-burner in every corner of her hut. How the evil spirits take it, I do not know, but the flies escape everywhere in humming sticky clouds.

Hundreds of *douhakims*, dark little shops, lined the narrow streets like the cells of a honeycomb. The shop-keeper, adolescent, sickly and greasy, sat in the semi-darkness of the interior, measuring out rice, sugar, pepper, ginger, henna, incense—in paper cornucopias. Though it was not yet eight o'clock the streets were crowded. The all-pervading odor of incense mingled with smells of rancid butter, spices and rat's urine.

At the house of Hamid Taber, the "Commander of the Sea," I stated my intention of calling on M'Hamid Hidris to request his written consent to my presence at Farsan. Taber, a dandified young Arab, eyed me suspiciously as I spoke. When I finished, he left abruptly to notify the Vizir, M'Hamid Yaya, of my visit. He left me alone with

Salah who, according to custom, had deposited his rifle at the door. We noticed that it had disappeared. But I still had my revolver tucked out of sight in the folds of my *fohta*.

A slave brought us lunch—cakes of *durra*, clabbered milk, broiled mutton, and dates. A dozen armed slaves sat on their heels about the courtyard guarding the house in which we were prisoners. Hours passed. I pretended to sleep, while Salah, who made no attempt to conceal his anxiety, paced the dark and stuffy room like a vigilant watchdog.

Early in the afternoon, a tongueless Soudanese armed with a huge scimitar entered the room and signed for us to follow him. The sinister appearance of the mute might have inspired misgivings, had I not known that in the East, even the most complicated situations can generally be "arranged," provided one does not take events too tragically. A few rods distant from the house of the "Commander of the Sea" we halted before a tall doorway opening in a façade blazing white with sun. We followed our guide down a dark corridor, stumbling over a score of recumbent forms—prisoners in ankle-chains. A frequent spectacle in Arabia, for the Arabs consider prisons as expensive luxuries. . . . Moreover, they necessitate the presence of jailors who are always susceptible to being bribed. When behind the walls of a jail the prisoner is invisible, and cannot serve as an example. In chains, he can be turned loose to excite public reprobation, pity, or charity in the matter of food. Another economy.

In a courtyard our guide indicated a closed door. The soldiers guarding it moved aside. I was ushered alone into a room where twenty Arabs sat on divans arranged in a semicircle. I received the not wholly flattering impression

that the council had gathered on my account. A profound
silence greeted my entrance. Tranquilly, I proceeded with
the traditional salutations. When I had finished, the vizir,
a bulky figure with the belly of a Buddha, began the invariable series of questions.

"What is your religion?"

"Moslem."

"Is that the truth?"

I met his gaze squarely, and repeated the profession
of faith:

"*La iloha illa Allah; Muhammid rasul Allah.*"

A murmur of approbation greeted the words.

"But your tongue, it seems, did not drink in the language of the Believers with your mother's milk?"

"My father was a Frenchman."

A long silence. Then a voice at my elbow.

"*Toi parler français?*"

At the words, an electric thrill seemed to animate the
assembly. I felt acutely conscious of the presence of two
armed slaves who stood at either shoulder.

"And you—where did you learn the tongue of my country?" I replied in French.

A ripple of interest—of relief, one might have said,
ran through the council. My interlocutor spoke cate-
gorically—

"This is indeed a Frenchman."

I seemed to have weathered the cape.

Again I repeated the reasons that had brought me to
Medy, and urged to be taken without delay to M'Hamid
Hidris. The request appeared to embarrass the vizir. He
replied M'Hamid Hidris was not in Medy. He had left
that very day for Ghisan twenty miles away. Twenty miles,
I returned, represented a small matter for a traveler like

myself. I was prepared to leave instantly for Ghisan.
That remark troubled the vizir even more. Muttering
hastily that I had only to remain in Medy and that
M'Hamid Hidris would certainly return to the capital
within the next few days, he rose from his seat on the
divan. The audience had ended.

I left the council chamber unhindered, followed by Saïd
Ali, the French-speaking Arab, whom I invited to accompany me to a nearby *mokaya*. Over the thimble-like
cups of *boon* he grew communicative. During the night,
he told me, the vizir had received a message announcing
the arrival of a German spy disguised as an Arab, who
was coming to Medy to assassinate the Sultan! An Indian
merchant converted to Islam had brought the message.
He had been present at the council, it appeared, though
I had not observed him because of his Arab dress. According to the Indian, the spy carried invisible bombs which
by sorcery could annihilate at a distance. The council,
Saïd Ali related, received me in fear and trembling. The
guards had received orders to strike me down at the first
suspicious gesture. A hasty movement on my part might
have cost me dear. As it was, I had produced a favorable
impression. Of that, Saïd Ali was sure. The vizir now felt
he has been misinformed; but under no circumstances
would I be permitted to see Hidris.

The Arab promised to procure me a copy of the incriminating message. He proved as good as his word; two
hours later, I had the paper in my hands. The author was
my host at Seguid.

"Ibrahim Metaffer to Yaya Vizir—" it read. "Greetings
and on thee be Allah's benediction. I send to warn thee
that one who claims to be a Moslem will come to render
visit to M'hamid Hidris. He is sent to carry out criminal

designs against the life of him who is our master. I could not prevent him, as Nasser Sehel refused me aid. I pray thee send word in all haste to the *chief at Kamaran.* Be prudent. May Allah guard thee; but spare nothing to protect thy life."

Kamaran—I began to understand. From the island of Kamaran, held by a British garrison, secret tentacles spread east and north through Yemen. . . . I held the key to Ibrahim Metaffer's "inexplicable" hostility. With Hidris, his master, I still hoped to succeed. Though an avowed ally of the British, his allegiance, as I well knew, went little deeper than the surface. I would waste no more time at Medy. Having ascertained that the Sultan had in reality left for Ghisan, I returned to the house of the vizir to demand my papers and rifle. It was four o'clock, the hour of public audience, which took place in a hut of palm mats, rolled up on three sides to give air. Fifty persons or more sat smoking and drinking coffee, the vizir in their midst.

Clearly my request annoyed the vizir. Though at bottom he may not have been displeased to be rid of me so easily. After brief deliberation he tendered me arms and papers, bidding me leave at once. Without giving him time to change his mind, I hastened on board the *Fat el Rhaman.* I had given Saïd Ali leave to accompany us. The Turks held his family prisoner at Hodeida and I promised to do what I could to effect their escape.

That trip to Medy, I regarded as a mistake. It had drawn too much attention to my presence at Farsan. While I hoped eventually to secure the consent of Hidris, it behooved me first of all to establish a station on the islands—and that without further delay. The authorization could come afterwards.

I had selected as the site of the future station, Dumsuk, a horseshoe-shaped island, lying to the south of Farsan Kebir. Sailing west from Medy, we entered the Bay of Dumsuk at nightfall and dropped anchor behind a point of sand.

In the morning we landed supplies on the beach and the pearl-divers set off in their dugouts to hunt for fishing grounds. I strolled along the sand on the lookout for a sheltered basin in which to install an "oyster park." I found precisely the spot I was looking for—a rock pool one hundred feet long and nine feet deep, at the inner end of the bay. From there, I started out to explore the island. Dumsuk, like the rest of the archipelago, had come into being at no very remote geological period, I estimated, as the result of a marine upheaval. Its surface repeated in stone the sea bottom of to-day. A tangle of madrepores lifted their branches above chalk-white clusters of sponges: enormous *tridacna* yawned half-opened—fossil cousins of the giant shellfish lying beneath the transparent water of the bay.

Deep salt pools spotted the surface of the island, their water curiously red, bordered by a pinkish crust of salt crystals that glistened in the sun. No waterplant, no fish, lived in their depths, still and dark as pools of blood. On the whole island I found no living thing but sea birds that nested on the sand.

Following the western shore of Dumsuk, I discovered two water holes, shallow pockets in the rock, water-tight and filled with sand. We had only to dig there to collect the water fallen during the rains.

In the meantime, my crew of Somalis had built me a "cabin," two walls enclosing a natural hollow in the cliff. For themselves and the Soudanese divers, they threw together shelters of brush and palm mats. In a few days, our station had taken on the aspect of a little village. As a final touch, I set up a flag pole on a hillock behind the settlement, and hoisted the French colors.

Every day we received visitors, Arabs, Somalis and Soudanese, fishers of pearls and *nacre*, who came in dugouts or *zarougs* to drink tea or beg *durra* and tobacco or simply to squat on the sand for hours conversing with my men. The legend of "the man-who-makes-pearls" spread through the islands. At the end of two weeks, I decided the time had come to pay a visit to M'Hamid Hidris at Ghisan. To my surprise, the little tribe of Soudanese opposed my departure energetically. Without me, they insisted, they would not feel in safety on the island. However, I succeeded in persuading them, and early one morning, I sailed the *Fat el Rhaman* out of the harbor, leaving Abdi and Saïd Ali in charge of the station, above which the tricolor floated, whipping in the dawn wind.

At five o'clock we dropped anchor off Ghisan. An old fortress, half in ruins, dominated the little port that straggled down to the water's edge, bordered here and there by the vestiges of an old wall.

Taking Salah with me, I paddled ashore in the houri. On the beach, we were met by two askari of the *Omer el Bahar* and the four of us squatted on the sand to talk. A crowd gathered rapidly about us, handsome fellows, their foreheads bound with palm leaves holding back the long hair that fell in black ringlets to their shoulders. Each man carried a rifle, even to the boys of ten or twelve.

When the conversation had worn itself out, the whole band escorted us to the courtyard of a caravansery. There an old Arab with a beard dyed red with henna came forward to greet me, sent, so he said, by the Sultan, himself. His master, unfortunately, was ill—too ill to receive me. But he had given orders to have me treated as an honored guest. I was led to a whitewashed chamber while slaves hurried about, spreading rugs, burning incense, and stirring up the dust generally. They brought milk in wooden jars, cakes of *durra,* honey and dates. By that time night had come; instead of the evil-smelling oil lamp, candles were lighted, an extraordinary honor.

The next morning, I tried vainly to discover what had happened to the letter for M'Hamid Hidris which I had entrusted to his messenger the evening before. But the little old man with the red beard had disappeared. Through Salah, who had met with friends in the kitchen, I succeeded in learning that the elusive Sultan was not in Ghisan, but at an oasis a day's journey inland. What was more important still, a messenger (an Indian, according to Salah) had left early that morning in great secrecy for Medy, bearing a message to Yaya the vizir. The inevitable Indian . . . an obscure presentiment warned me.

I hastened to the house of the Commander of the Sea to inform the dignitary that my affairs did not permit a prolonged stay at Ghisan. If the Sultan could not receive me at once, I would have to take leave without waiting for a reply to my letter. The *Omer el Bahar* exhorted me to patience. My letter had been dispatched to M'Hamid Hidris by a special courier. I would receive an answer the following morning.

Not one day but two I fretted at Ghisan, drinking sour milk and dining on dates and *durra* in my cockroach-infested hut, preserved from the invading clouds of flies by even denser smoke-clouds which obliged me to spend the day lying or sitting as close to the ground as possible. On the second day, hoping to hurry up matters— for the prolonged delay seemed more and more suspicious —I ordered my men to make ready to sail at nightfall.

My impatience procured the desired result. I received a visit from the Arab with the dyed beard. He had just returned, he stated, from a journey to the camp of M'Hamid Hidris. Plunging his fingers in the belt of his *fohta*, he drew forth a paper folded lengthwise. It bore several lines of Arab characters and an enormous seal stamped with an intricate pattern of arabesques. I read the paper carefully. It was a permit authorizing me to fish for pearls and *nacre* in the waters of Farsan and bore the seal of M'Hamid Hidris. With my document in hand, I made haste to hoist sail for Dumsuk.

A headwind that rose towards sunset obliged us to run for shelter to a little bay where a *varoug* lay half beached on the sand. It belonged to a crew of fishers who had already visited us at Dumsuk. To my amazement, they told me that the preceding day they had encountered at sea the two sambuks I had left at Dumsuk under full sail and headed towards the south!

I was at loss to interpret the strange news. The man must have been mistaken, but I could not keep myself from indulging in the gloomiest of forebodings. All night long I tossed in my bunk. Before daybreak, I gave the signal for departure. At ten o'clock, I made out the silhouette of Dumsuk, but through the glasses I failed to distinguish the flag I had left floating above the station. As we drew nearer, I discovered that not only the flag but the staff as well had disappeared.

After three mortal hours of tacking about, hours that seemed endless to my impatience, we entered the Bay of Dumsuk. It was deserted; no sambuks lay at anchor; the camp, too, was abandoned; not a voice answered our hail. More than abandoned. . . . Of the station there remained not a vestige, nothing but scattered stones and brush; as if a cyclone had passed, strewing the earth with rubbish—empty boxes, broken bottles and torn bits of sacking.

My first thought, that Saïd Ali had engineered the pillage with the aid of my crews, I dismissed as unlikely. My men had wives and children at Obok or Djibouti. They would not dare return home after such an act of piracy. Had they been attacked? massacred? And by whom?

I had barely set foot on shore, when a figure crept from behind a hillock. I gave a cry of joy as I recognized Abdi.

"*Esh fî?*" (What has happened?) I called.

"*Arami*" (Pirates).

Seated on the stone pile that a few days earlier had been my cabin, he gave me the story of the raid. Two days after I left Dumsuk a forty-ton *zaroug* dropped anchor at nightfall off the southern end of the island. Three Arabs paddled ashore, bringing a basket of dried fish to exchange for tobacco. The visit dissipated the fears that the arrival of the strange ship had aroused. As the evening wore on, more Arabs came on shore, twenty or more, each man carrying a rifle. Last of all appeared the *nakhoda*. Approaching the group about the fire, he announced that Hidris had sent him to bring the two sambuks under escort to Ghisan.

At that, Saïd Ali, who until then had remained in the background, drew the *nakhoda* aside. The two men conferred earnestly for several minutes. Then Saïd Ali disappeared in my cabin. Abdi heard the lock of the strongbox tinkle (Arab locks have a system of little bells that tinkle at each turn of the key). The Arab reappeared, holding in his hand a sack of *nacre* balls I had brought to Dumsuk for my pearl plantations. With an air of mystery, he showed the sealed sack to the *nakhoda*, whereupon the two of them joined the group about the fire.

Saïd ordered tea for the crew and their "guests," telling my men they would all break camp the following morning. Hidris had thrown me into prison, he said. He would free me only when the sambuks and their crews had left the island. "I for one did not believe his story," Abdi continued. "I thought him a lying dog and a traitor. As I sat wondering what I could do to prevent the infamy, Saïd Ali came towards me, a cup of tea in his hand.

" 'Do not embark with the others,' he whispered. 'Hide among the dunes, and when Abd el Hai returns, tell him we have gone to Hodeida.' " With that, Saïd Ali rejoined the other Arabs while Abdi crept off through the darkness to warn the Soudanese divers, who had taken to the dunes when the *zaroug* first appeared, fearful of being captured and sold for slaves. When he had explained the situation, they crawled through the brush to where the dugouts were beached, and paddled away in all haste. At dawn, the visitors looted the camp, and with five or six Arabs on each of the sambuks, the three boats sailed off towards the south.

All day long I burned smoke signals at the north of the island. When night had fallen, the missing divers paddled cautiously into the bay. We had not a minute to lose, if we were to recapture the stolen boutres. I wasted no time conjecturing what lay behind the looting of the station; the immediate problem was to recover my stolen property.

I had embarked crew and divers and had given the

orders to hoist sail, when Abdi called to me from his post by the bowsprit:

"Abd el Hai, you have forgotten the most important of all!" He pointed to the beach, where the extra rudders of the stolen sambuks still lay upon the sand. Abdi was right. To keep a boat "prisoner," the first step is to confiscate its rudder. If you possess a second one, you hold the key to its prison.

At first, luck was with us. A brisk land breeze carried us swiftly southward. By morning, we were in sight of Kameran. I planned to anchor the *Fat el Rhaman* in the lee of Ras Katib, a cape that projects six miles into the sea. The southern end of the bay lies eight miles from Hodeida. I planned to pass overland to Hodeida and take possession of the two sambuks by surprise, if possible, and if necessary by force. To avoid being seen, I had to make the bay behind Ras Katib during the night. No easy task, for the Ras Katib is a low point of sand, invisible after dark. An error of a few miles north or south would bring us fatally on the coast reef—it, too, almost invisible at high tide. Unfortunately we had the wind against us. We spent a fatiguing day tacking about in a heavy sea. Night fell; we continued our zigzag course, creeping painfully south, mile by mile.

As the gale gave no sign of abating, I resolved to swing back towards land, hoping to reach the shelter of the cape on a single tack. During two hours we forged ahead, nerves tense, eyes straining through the darkness out of which the white wave-crests rushed towards us, tearing past in cascades of foam.

Suddenly from the bow, faint in the scream of the wind, came the cry: "Surf!"

I could see nothing, but listening intently I made out,

barely audible, a low rumble—the thunder of breakers. The sound came to us, it seemed, off the starboard beam, to windward. I concluded it must be the cape. The noise of the surf grew louder, then—all at once—the sea subsided. We had weathered Ras Katib and entered the bay.

During the night, we lay at anchor. At daybreak, we pushed closer to land, for I feared to be seen by Turkish sentinels posted at the point of the cape. While still two miles from the southern end of the bay, the *Fat el Rhaman* was obliged to drop anchor again. I dared advance no further because of the reefs, hard to detect in the storm-troubled water.

Towards three, we paddled Salah ashore to let Saïd Ali know of our arrival. Tide being at ebb, he had time to cover the route to Hodeida before nightfall, in particular the stretch of quicksands that border the bay. A fire signal was agreed on for the following night.

On board the *Fat el Rhaman*, the night passed without incident. At dawn, we observed several little sails close to shore, harmless fishers, probably, but their presence made me uneasy. I wanted to meet no one. To my annoyance, one of the *zarougs* headed towards us. Two Arabs whom I took to be father and son asked for some tobacco, a good pretext, but curiosity, I knew, was the true motive of their visit. Our callers walked about the deck of the *Fat el Rhaman*, manifesting a keen interest in every detail of its construction. They could observe that my boat had little in common with the ordinary run of coasting vessels, and I was certain that within two hours at most, after the fishers had returned to their village, the Turkish authorities would know that a suspicious ship lay in the lee of Ras Katib. I had to prevent their going ashore. I thought of holding them prisoners, but in case other *zarougs* visited us, their presence would prove embarrassing. Summoning the elder Arab, I asked him to carry a message to the *nakhoda* of a second boutre with which I told him we were sailing "*sangar.*" (Native boutres rarely undertake a long journey alone. Generally they go in couples, sailing "*sangar,*" as the Arabs say.) The boutre, I explained, had anchored at Aucan, an island twenty miles north of Hodeida. We had been separated during the storm.

We fixed on the sum of twenty *thalers* as fair payment for the errand, five *thalers* to be paid in advance; and the rest, by my imaginary colleague. That arrangement, I assured myself, would keep the Arabs away from Hodeida for at least two days. I delayed their departure by inviting them to lunch, and it was past two o'clock before they could set sail. Happily no other visitors came.

At nightfall, we paddled to the tip of the bay to meet Salah. All night long we waited, scanning the black stretch of the lagoon. But no signal showed red in the darkness. Dawn came, and still no sign of Salah. Discouraged, I had already started back to the boutre, when Abdi called my attention to a row of dots, five in all, moving towards us from the direction of Hodeida. Much intrigued by the presence of the little caravan in the lonely landscape, we watched its approach, hands on our rifles. As it drew nearer, I recognized Saïd Ali in the lead, followed by three women and a boy. One of the women carried a baby on her back, the others bore a variety of household utensils, among which I remarked a hideous oil lamp with an ornate silken shade.

The Arab hastened to explain that he had thought it prudent to evacuate his family fearing reprisals in case I should succeed in recovering the stolen sambuks. While

Zaroug at anchor

Repairing a boutre

my Somalis embarked the passengers and their baggage, Saïd Ali gave me his version of the raid.

The *zaroug*, he assured me, had been sent by Yaya, the vizir of Medy, who had learned of my absence from Dumsuk from the same Indian who spread the spy story at Medy two weeks before, and who, as soon as we left Medy, had hastened to Ghisan to await my arrival. The *nakhoda* chosen by the vizir to carry out the raid was a *zaramig*, an ally of the Turks. He had brought the two sambuks to Hodeida, claiming to have captured two "enemy ships" on the high seas.

As Saïd Ali talked on, furnishing one by one the tangled threads of the story, I translated. The vizir Yaya, an ally of the English, warned by the Indian, a British secret agent, had utilized an ally of the Turks (that is to say, an enemy) to wipe out my settlement at Farsan. The same old story: "Get some one else to do for you what you do not care. . . ." I remembered my experience at Sheik Said and Moka. Apparently the war and its alliances had in no way altered the methods of diplomacy in the Near East. And all to what end? To prevent a French flag from floating over the Farsan Islands. The success of my political venture seemed compromised. For the second time in my career, I had run afoul of the "Masters of the Red Sea."

In any event, I meant to recover the stolen sambuks. On their arrival at Hodeida, Saïd Ali had succeeded in bribing the Commander of the Sea. In secret, he showed the official the little sack of *nacre* balls (valuable pearls, he assured him), offering to share the booty, provided the *Omer el Bahar* detained the two sambuks for several days in the harbor of Hodeida. With the same "pearls" Saïd Ali had already won the friendship of the *zaramig* who raided Dumsuk, persuading the *nakhoda* to claim my boats as prizes of war—otherwise the *zaroug's* crew might have looted the two sambuks. They lay undisturbed in the harbor of Hodeida, their rudders locked on land while their crews circulated freely in the town. Salah had remained in Hodeida to collect my men at a point on the beach as soon as it was dark.

At five o'clock, four Soudanese carrying the two extra rudders, I set off with Saïd Ali across the neck of Ras Katib, a treacherous plain of quicksands and lagoons. In two hours, we reached firmer ground west of the cape, the lights of Hodeida twinkling in the distance. From that point, we followed close to the water's edge, the usual procedure of expeditions who wished to avoid encounters. We could always plunge into the sea, and the rising tide would efface our footprints.

When we had covered half the distance that lay between us and the town, a shrill whistle from the darkness ahead stopped us in our tracks. Twice it was repeated. Cautiously we replied. At the sound, a group of dark figures rose out of the night—Salah and the Somali crews. The two sambuks, they told us, had been brought in close to land because of rough weather. The men had taken care, however, to pay out the full length of the anchor chains, which would permit them, when the tide came, to haul away a respectable distance from shore before hoisting sail. The disappearance of Saïd Ali had not passed unnoticed. Since morning, a squad of askari patrolled the beach.

Leaving the others concealed among the dunes, I went cautiously forward, to reconnoiter. I wore only a revolver belt, having discarded my *fohta*—a white splotch in the darkness. Beyond the dunes, the silhouette of a hut was visible. I approached prudently, crawling on all fours. It was empty, and to all appearances, abandoned. Retracing my steps, I told the men to advance as far as the hut, and to wait for me there. Creeping along the beach I came within sixty feet of the askari, placed there, evidently, to guard the sambuks, whose rigging I distinguished barely fifty yards from shore.

I made my plan accordingly. Hurrying back to the hut, I ordered the two crews to swim to the sambuks, taking the rudders with them. Once aboard the boats, they were to make ready the sail and haul away slowly to the limit of the anchor chains. All this, I felt confident, would not be visible from shore. Hoisting sail was another matter; it would undoubtedly draw gunshots from the beach. I instructed the men not to raise the yards until I gave the signal. When they perceived a fire on shore, they were to lift anchor, hoist sail, and make all speed out of the harbor, to join the *Fat el Rhaman* at the point of Ras Katib.

Left with the four Soudanese, I set to work gathering grass and driftwood, which we heaped within the hut. On the pile, I poured the contents of a *tanika* of coal oil, brought along to make fire signals. Before lighting the bonfire, I had the four men run back and forth across the sand making footprints in the direction of Hodeida. When they returned, I touched a match to the pile and the five of us took to our heels.

A flame shot high in the air, scattering sparks in all directions. The hut had caught fire. A yellow glare spread over the sea. In the distance, two sails spread their white triangles against the sky like the wings of a butterfly. In all Hodeida, apparently we were the only ones to notice them. Everybody else was hurrying towards the blaze. In an incredibly short time, a hedge of agitated shapes ringed the burning hut.

We ran along the shore for the better part of an hour before we turned east across the swampy isthmus. There we lost our way. The tide had risen, the lagoons were flooded. We floundered about helplessly, in water to our necks, huddling together for fear of quicksands. Then at a venture, I shouted; to my joy, a voice answered close at hand. It was Abdi with the dugout. He had been told to wait for us at the tip of the bay, but as the tide lifted, he had foreseen our predicament and paddled across to meet us.

By one o'clock we boarded the *Fat el Rhaman,* and as the east grew gray, we made the entrance of the bay to find the missing sambuks lying tranquilly at anchor. Ordering them to follow, I headed the *Fat el Rhaman* towards the west and the open sea.

On the way to Djibouti (the loss of our supplies—aside from other considerations—made a return to Dumsuk out of the question), we met with a minor adventure that capped most neatly our experience at Farsan. Near Perim, we were caught by a dead calm, and as we lay rocking in the swell, the smoke of a steamer rose over the horizon. A British coast-guard was heading straight for my little fleet. When three cable-lengths away, its engines stopped; I hoisted colors and signaled our port of departure in the international code. Suddenly, as I waited for the visitors to lower a dinghy, a funnel-shaped jet of water rose in the air thirty feet from the bow of the *Fat el Rhaman* and two seconds later a heavy report jarred the silence. A cannon shot!

Without waiting for the gunners to correct their aim (!) I sprang into the dugout, paddling with all speed towards the coast-guard. On deck, the officers gathered to receive me; a few yards to their left, some sailors were busy cleaning a six-inch gun.

"That was a pretty big shot for such small game!"

An ensign translated. Laughter from the knot of officers.

"We had no blank shells," the captain returned in excellent French. "Believe me, you ran no serious risk."

"But your whistle would have sufficed," I objected.

"A shell makes a better impression. Besides, good training for the crew!"

I produced my papers. Nothing out of the way there. A steward brought a tray of glasses. The traditional whisky and soda. As if by magic, the soldiers of the "Grand Nation" had disappeared, replaced by members of the vast brotherhood of the sea, jovial, friendly and fraternal. And yet, I reflected, as we exchanged toasts, what guarantee had I that the next time we met, the man behind the six-inch gun might not take a better aim!

As for my dying political venture at Farsan, its deathblow came in the form of a letter from the French Minister of Colonies, some months later.

"You have acted at your own risk and peril with respect to the Farsan Islands," the letter read. "And purely as a private citizen. The Minister of Foreign Affairs begs me to notify you that his department will not let itself be drawn into any action on your behalf with respect to the government of Great Britain."

And the sequel to the story. To-day a flag does fly over Farsan. Not the tricolor, but the Union Jack.

XIV

Running the Blockade

After arms and pearls—freight.

The shadow of the Lion lay over Farsan. Its imponderable paw had just dealt me a resounding cuff. On the Arab coast, the blockade closed the ports of Yemen to all but "home" ships. The humblest freight had become contraband, provided it was not carried in British bottoms. The merchants of Aden, protected by patrolling cruisers, sent cargo after cargo to Loheiya, Medy, Lith; and, guaranteed against all competition, were accumulating fortunes at the expense of their allies on the western side of the gulf.

I owned a boutre and, since Farsan, I had a score to settle, a personal grudge to satisfy. So it was that the *Fat el Rhaman* became a "freighter." A modest one: her fifteen tons represented little more than a water-drop in the stream of commerce flowing to Arabia from Manchester and Calcutta by way of Aden. But her insignificance was quality, when it came to slipping the blockade.

For months I played at cat and mouse with the British coast-guards. Often I ran afoul of them; but always when traveling under ballast, with my papers in order: a fishing permit for Djebbel Zukor, or on my way to Assab or Massawa. Would the gentlemen visit the hold? Or the six-foot cell that served me as cabin? Only too delighted; *"Faites comme chez vous."* Seated in the shadow of the sail, I smoked blond cigarettes with the officer in charge,

226

discussing shark fishing and pearls, while his men rummaged below decks, streaking their uniforms with tar and machine oil. I carried coal oil, flour, cotton, sugar, and occasionally passengers for Doubaba and Kauka. Sometimes I made the trip for the Arab merchants of Djibouti. Sometimes I carried a cargo of my own. It was an exciting game, with all the risks of contraband in war time, and the personal satisfaction of a minor vengeance. At the same time it was profitable; freight rates were high; my Arab customers paid well. In time, I wiped out the losses at Farsan, and saw my way clear to building a better boat than the *Fat el Rhaman*, which now showed signs of wear. Her successor would be a big boutre, big for me, destined to carry freight. Not over 150 to 200 tons, with a draft of no more than six feet—a maximum for that type of navigation, to allow free circulation among the shoals. The new boat was still a dream.

At about that time, journeying up and down the coast of Yemen, I first heard of a certain English colonel. One day in Kauka, an Arab from the desert, Sheik Ahmed Ibrahim, came to me offering a lot of Lee-Metford rifles. I had no use for such merchandise, but my curiosity was aroused.

"Old army models?" I inquired.

"No, all new rifles, fresh manufacture."

"Where did you get them?"

"From the English," came the surprising reply.

"The English? Are Aden merchants selling arms in contraband?"

"Not that," Ahmed Ibrahim assured me. "The English give them away and they are sold to us. There is one *Inglis* who travels about the country, and promises money and guns to any one who will fight the Turks. One who goes by the name of ———."

He spoke a word, it was not the "King-maker" nor anything that resembled it—a highly untranslatable epithet, carrying with it a precise and scandalous . . . context.

"That is not an English name," I objected.

"I know." The Arab's lips twisted in a dry smile. "Still, that is what every one calls him. You have only to tell him how you hate the Turks and he gives you guns, as many as you want. And afterwards you sell them—as you please."

"But if you sell the guns and do no fighting, the *Inglis* will give you no more arms."

The Arab shook his head.

"To have a vine bear fruit, you must trim it many times. The more you trim, the more it produces," he remarked sententiously. From the figure, it was not clear whether the pruning process applied to Arab or Englishmen.

In general, most of the Arabs I knew shared that attitude with respect to the Citizens of the Empire. "Humor the English and you will obtain much," I have heard them declare on more than one occasion. "But never let them get beyond the door. They are like the mange: once you have it between the toes, it spreads over the whole body." Or fully as expressive: "A few locusts are good to eat; but when the swarm arrives, it will eat you and yours." Still they were, I, too, remembered, talking to a Frenchman.

Often, during the months that followed, when news of the "revolt in the desert" filtered down from the north, I heard the question of "United Arabia" discussed and dismissed as a vast Utopian illusion. Whether the speakers belonged to tribes currently supposed to have pro-English or pro-Turkish sympathies, the reaction was the same. "We are all of one faith, brothers. We love each other and we fight each other. By fighting, men are made. If a brave man has no herds, it is just that he takes those of his neighbor who has flocks but no courage to defend them. Riches belong to the brave. Shall we unite to be governed by a coward whom the English have brought?

"We want no foreign masters—be they Turks or English, though the Turks are men like ourselves, Believers. They collect taxes, but they leave us in peace, while the English turn the world upside down."

The "revolt in the desert," at any rate, was not big enough to divert British attention from modest blockade-runners like myself. The men at Perim knew of my trips to Yemen. In spite of the dozens of fruitless searchings of my empty boutre, I suspect that few cargoes landed by night along the coast went unreported to the "intelligence" whose yellow, black, and parti-colored agents swarmed in every port of the peninsula. The Lion sharpened its teeth. I was insignificant prey for so mighty a flesh-eater; but for that very reason preposterous to let me flaunt my immunity indefinitely, dancing scot-free over the blue gulf, under the very nose of Perim. Warnings reached me through my Arab friends, preserving me more than once from disastrous encounters. I realized that the situation could not be endlessly prolonged. The odds against me were too great.

One day in October, 1916, I arranged with Salah Mouti, an Arab of Djibouti, to carry 200 cases of petroleum to Doubaba. In addition, I was to transport twenty passengers, ostensibly to Assab, in reality to the Arab coast.

I ordered the coal oil brought to a warehouse facing the sea, on the eastern side of town, and engaged twenty *Bedanis* to put it on board the boutre after dark. The customs must get no wind of my intentions.

The *Fat el Rhaman* sailed out of the harbor at sunset, presumably for Assab. When night had fallen, we turned back, and as soon as the new moon set, we lowered dugouts and crossing the reef which lay under several feet of water at high tide, we landed on a deserted strip of beach. The coolies crouched by the warehouse wall I separated in two groups—the first to carry the cases from the warehouse to the water's edge, the second to load the dugouts which plied swiftly back and forth between beach and boutre. The men glided back and forth silently through the brush—a procession of shadows, each bent double beneath his burden. Now and then, a thud, as a case slipped to the sand. Close at hand, Abdi, Kassim and myself stood sentinel.

Suddenly Kassim gripped my arm. "Askari," he whispered. Peering through the night, I made out a dark figure fifteen yards away, wearing the cylindric *checchia* of the Customs. I sprang forward. "*Min?*" (Who goes there?) I called sharply. No answer. In an instant, we surrounded the astonished soldier.

"I meant no harm," he muttered. "I came down to the sea to urinate."

I had been flourishing a big revolver, very impressive, a typical "stage gun." At his words, I shifted it over to my left hand and jingled suggestively the rupees always ready for such emergencies.

"Sit down here with us," I commanded. "It will only be for a few minutes; perhaps five rupees will cover the time."

Nothing loath, the askar squatted on his heels between my two men. When the last cases had been piled into the dugouts, I paid off the head coolie and we released our prisoner, who trotted away pleased enough with his *baksheesh*. No danger of his reporting the incident to his superiors!

With Abdi and Kassim, I climbed into the last dugout, loaded to the gunwales; we slid over the black water to the rhythmic dip of the paddles. On deck, the Arab passengers lay like heaps of dirty linen.

We hauled the two houris aboard and hoisted the big sail yard. No wind. The stars danced in the sea polished like metal. Towards two o'clock, a sharp pull on the sheet and the sail burst through the *taffi* cords that held it prisoner. Slowly, without a sound, we glided through the swell, leaving behind us the town and the vigilant Customs officials fast asleep. . . .

When day came, we were far at sea. The plan was to make Bab el Mandeb at sunset; after dark we ran less risk of meeting a British gunboat. The wind freshened as the day wore on, and for a time, the sea threatened to sweep away everything on deck. We took in the mainsail and rigged a storm jib. Towards five o'clock, we slipped past Perim, hugging the African coast.

Night fell. We spun along with the wind astern, piling up huge waves as it met the current from the Red Sea. We crossed liners headed for Aden and the East, majestic black bulks garlanded with lights. I gripped the tiller, holding the *Fat el Rhaman*, tiny thing lost among the black combers, northeast towards the Arab coast. The point where my cargo was expected lay behind a break in the coast reef, several miles east of Doubaba. Kassim knew the channel. A tall sheaf of spray marked the entrance.

By day, we could have made the pass without difficulty. At night, in rough weather, it was nothing short of a feat. If we passed by the gap in the reef, we could not hope to turn back in the teeth of the wind. Miscalculation meant shipwreck on the rocks. The moon had set. The wind still held, blowing like mad. Twice I lost sight of the line of surf that marked the reef—to discover it again abruptly a few rods to starboard. Kassim, flat on his face by the bowsprit, scanned the sea from as low an angle as possible. All at once he cried, "*Djoch*" (Luff). I made out a white column of spray straight before us. I swung over the helm, the *Fat el Rhaman* shot through the rift at top speed, passing between two points of rock that showed black at the surface in a whirlpool of foam. Ten seconds sooner or later, and we would have missed the passage by twenty yards at least. Even to-day, when I recall that blind manœuvre, it gives me the goose-flesh.

Beyond the reef, calm water. I lighted a flare of waste soaked in oil which threw a blot of light on the water, a jade-green disc veined with white. Then a gust carried away the torch, quenching it in the sea. Two gunshots a moment later answered our signal. We put out an houri with two men, to arrange for landing passengers and cargo. They returned, bringing an Arab—the agent of Salah Mouti. He reported that a British gunboat had patrolled back and forth before the anchorage for several days. There was a chance that our signal had been seen. He advised us to leave the shelter before dawn.

To expedite matters, we flung the cases of coal-oil into the sea, and five of my men dived overboard to guide the strange flock safely to the beach. When the Arab had counted the cases I asked him to write me a receipt on one of the pages of my log—a formality which later on I had plenty of reasons to regret! By three o'clock the hold was empty, and we made for the open sea.

Beyond the passage, we found rough weather again. The wind howled and little rags of cloud tore past overhead as I headed for the African coast. I did not dare push too far west because of the great Syntion Reef, a death trap for unwary ships, which at that point lies seven miles from shore. You can run afoul of it on a clear night without having sighted land. No surf reveals its presence: its limits are indefinite. For twenty miles, it is strewn with the wrecks of boutres caught there like flies in syrup. And not a lighthouse anywhere on that strip of coast. Only far to the south, below the horizon, the whirling light of Perim swept the sky with the regular flash of its long pale beam.

All at once the sea subsided, though the wind still blew with undiminished violence. I strained my eyes through the darkness, fancying that all about us lifted menacing crests of rock. It might be, I reflected, that we had entered a zone of currents that ran with the wind. I veered east again, away from the reef. Day brought the explanation of that suspicious calm. We had been caught by a current that was carrying us north. I decided to make for the Arabian coast where the currents have less force. If I met with a British patrol, no matter; they would see that I came from Africa. Besides, we were traveling under ballast.

Towards nine o'clock, when within five or six miles from the land, I sighted a steamer bearing towards us from the north. As it approached, I distinguished the white hull and yellow funnel of a coast-guard. The sea

was still too heavy for me to fear a cannon shot. A mile
away, the gunboat whistled, and obediently we lowered the
sail and drifted. When barely a cable's-length separated
us, our visitors put down a ladder, hailing us with unin-
telligible shouts—in English, doubtless, through a mega-
phone. We lowered a houri, and, carrying my papers, I
paddled over to the gunboat. The captain received me on
the bridge, assisted by an interpreter with whom I conversed in Arab, since no one on board spoke French.

After a hasty examination of my papers, the officer
informed me curtly that the coast-guard would take us to
Perim. We set off accordingly towards the south, the *Fat
el Rhaman* following behind at the end of a towrope. I
had no objections to making the journey in that fashion;
in four hours we would cover a distance which, tacking
about in the wind, would have taken me fully eight. I did
not worry, still I could not help wondering what the
British wanted of me in Perim. Their annoyance was comprehensible. In two months they had met my boutre a
dozen times, always in the same condition, cargoless and
traveling in ballast. Perhaps the governor of Perim desired to see for himself the bizarre sportsman who persisted in piloting an empty boat in the most inhospitable
corner of the Red Sea.

Suddenly I remembered the receipt of the 200 cases of
coal oil, written in Arab on the last page of my log. Ir-
refutable proof that I had been running the blockade. I
racked my brains for a pretext to warn Abdi. But my
hosts detained me, courteous but firm, on the bridge of
the gunboat. That wretched receipt. . . . If Abdi knew
of its existence, he would destroy it. Of that I was confident. But had he seen the Arab write it down?

The interpreter made desperate efforts to engage me

in conversation. Obviously he had received orders to that effect. He was a Somali from Berbera, the product of a mission school. I have often wondered at the effect of those institutions on the mentality of the native. He seems, in most cases, to acquire there a far richer collection of European vices than virtues. In any event, the mission serves as an excellent training school for spies, who, I may add, generally betray the government that employs them with the same ease with which they denounce their own countrymen. Often they die at an early age from a mysterious colic, or a dagger in the back. . . .

I recalled the fate of one such secret agent who in his non-political capacity acted as *nakhoda* of a boutre that smuggled tobacco and slaves to the Arab coast. His mission, rumor asserted, was to keep the Intelligence Service informed of what went on among the tribes of Yemen. He came on board the *Sahala* once to ask for drinking water, when I was carrying a load of flour to Kauka. About that time, he had been charged with a delicate piece of business of inflicting a bloody beating on a tribe supposedly under British protection, while giving the impression that the arms for the purpose had been furnished by the Italians. He succeeded; but some one denounced him to the *Zaramigi* of *Khor Gouleifa* as an English spy. By an odd coincidence, one of his next political missions took him to *Khor Gouleifa*. The *nakhoda* had scarcely run his boat into the Khor—a lagoon-like harbor south of Hodeida—when two *zarougs* came to pay him a call. In less time than it takes to tell, the *Zaramigi* tied Saleh M'Hamoud securely to an eighty-pound grappling iron and "anchored" him in thirty feet of water. I had the story from one of his crew, a Somali from Cape Gardafui, who shipped on the *Fat el Rhaman* the winter following the *nakhoda's* tragic end.

I took malicious pleasure in repeating the story to the interpreter on the gunboat. It had a deadening effect on the Somali's loquacity. Abandoning me by the rail, he plunged down between decks and I saw no more of him.

Three hours later, we steamed into the harbor of Perim. We passed by the commercial end of the port, its docks and pyramids of coal, and dropped anchor at the foot of a steep slope crowned by the buildings of the Residence. To my disappointment, I was given no chance to communicate with my men. Flanked by the captain and a lieutenant, I climbed a blistering path that zigzagged up the incline to the Government House. On the crest of the rock, the Perim light lifted its steel column into the sky. Below, the sea showed white with foam, lashed by the wind, which at all seasons sweeps over Perim as if bent on polishing the worn surface of the lava block, cleansing it of the intruders that cling to the inhospitable island, polluting its crust with their factories, their coal yards, their offal. . . .

Dazed from the wind, we were ushered into the governor's study. There I learned from the governor himself, a red-faced major, who eyed me with uneasy curiosity (as if I represented a new sea monster, fished up from depths!), that I was to remain temporarily at Perim. No further explanations were furnished. Two orderlies escorted me to a little room, a sort of storeroom, encumbered with brooms and paint pots. The men set up a cot for me and brought a chair and a table. The governor sent word that I might wander as I pleased about the grounds of the Residence, providing I would give my word not to attempt to escape. A pure formality, my parole, since even beyond the walls, there would have been little chance of escaping. Every few rods, an armed Sepoy stood guard.

From the window of my room, I scanned the bay for a sight of the *Fat el Rhaman*. I was not long in discovering it, lying at the far end of the harbor beside a massive structure, presumably a barrack or a prison. The boy who carried in my dinner proved to be a Warsangali from the same district as Abdi. He promised to bring me news of my men. I spent an anxious night listening to the wind howl over the rock, wondering whether the boutre had been searched and what had happened to my papers. In the morning, the Warsangali came to tell me he had not been able to approach the boutre. The Sepoys had received orders to isolate the crew from all contact. By day the men remained on board the *Fat el Rhaman*; at night they were locked up in the barracks. Not a reassuring piece of news. The thought of my papers, of the incriminating receipt in particular, became an obsession. If they had been seized, they lay no doubt locked in the governor's safe. I could only hope that chance, a friend in whom one should never lack confidence, might in some miraculous way come to my aid.

That afternoon, the governor sent one of his aides to invite me to tea. I found His Excellency seated before a tray of bottles and glasses. He rose as I entered.

"Fortunes of war," he remarked cordially. "Have a whisky and soda."

I accepted not one but several, drinking like a Scotchman, in an attempt to produce a favorable impression! I had already observed that abstainers are rarely popular with the ruddy-faced soldiers of the Crown. . . .

Heaps of papers littered the governor's desk, but I saw nothing that looked familiar. Behind the desk stood a safe, its heavy door obstinately closed.

As we sat talking, a lieutenant strode through the

doorway, saluted, and handed the major a folded slip of paper. The latter glanced through the message, then, rising from his chair, bent over the safe and whirled the combination lock. The steel door swung outward on its hinges. I, too, had risen, pacing absently through the room, entirely preoccupied with fishing a fly out of my whisky glass. The governor's back hid the safe. But as he stooped lower, I experienced a slight electric shock. On one of the two shelves of the safe lay a red-covered book. The log of the *Fat el Rhaman.* I was right, the papers were there. Perhaps they had not been examined. Perhaps the governor was waiting for some one else more qualified than he for that sort of business. . . . Perhaps. . . . A dozen conjectures shot through my brain.

The governor gave the safe door a shove and turned to speak to the lieutenant. Not more than three yards lay between the safe and the door into the hall. And between me and the safe, the major's desk. These details I noted mentally as I walked back and forth at the far end of the study, for I had withdrawn discreetly to be out of earshot.

The two officers spoke in undertones, moving towards the door, the major with his hand resting affectionately on the younger man's shoulder. I strolled to the desk, picked up a box of matches that lay there, and lighted a cigarette. Out of the tail of my eye, I surveyed the couple by the door. The lieutenant saluted, disappeared. My heart sank. But the governor called him back, and continued speaking, his back turned towards me and his two hands resting on the doorframe.

Every nerve of my body grew tense. Then or never. And suddenly by a form of presentiment, second sight or whatever you may choose to call it—a phenomenon that I have experienced more than once in desperate circumstances—I was certain, *I knew* that the major would not stir. Stooping down, I crept beneath the table, pushed the safe door ajar, sezied the red-covered book, and opened it. The page with the receipt was missing.

Cautiously I replaced the book, crept under the desk, and stood upright. An instant, a bare second, later, Major Holmes with a hearty: "Well, I think that's all, my boy," turned back into the room.

Then, when the danger was past, all the blood seemed suddenly to leave my brain. I dropped into a chair, my heart hammering desperately. Had the officer spoken, I doubt if I should have been capable of replying. Only then, I realized the full extent of the risk I had taken. The safe contained, undoubtedly, military documents. Had I been discovered, my investigations would have cost me dear. . . .

Happily the good major saw nothing. Closing the safe, he lighted his pipe and picked up a copy of the *Times*. Eyes closed, I leaned back in my chair, taking stock mentally of the situation. The page had been torn out. That was clear from the irregular stub which remained. With the receipt out of the way, I had no cause for worry. I could count on the discretion of the crew from Abdi to the boy Fara. But I persisted in tormenting myself with the thought—which my reason dismissed as inconceivable —that other hands than Abdi's had torn the page from the book, and had sent it perhaps to Aden.

The days dragged past. No news, not even a protest, came from Djibouti in reply to a telegram sent on the day of my capture. Had the situation been reversed and I an Englishman, I reflected bitterly, a battleship would already have dropped anchor in the port. Whatever its faults, the Empire stands back of its citizens, the white ones at any rate. I cringed inwardly before the smiling disdain of my captors, as time went by and my telegrams remained unanswered.

Down in the harbor the *Courage*, flying the Union Jack, loaded merchandise for Arabia, with two cruisers standing by. Merchandise for M'hamid Hidris, doubtless, who would eventually resell the cargo to the Turks, or any one else who was willing to pay. Across the harbor, the *Fat el Rhaman* lay prisoner—a humble competitor, victim of the blockade.

I spent hours watching the distant barracks through the glasses. My men boarded the boutre at sunrise. At night it was deserted. Somehow, some way, I had to find a means of communicating with the crew. By land, it was out of the question; I counted a dozen Sepoys stationed between Government House and the barracks. Water—a two-mile swim—offered the only possibility.

Accordingly, one morning before breakfast, I clambered down the rocks, a towel over my arm, and took a bath in the sea. From the shore, a sentinel watched me, indifferent, bathers from the Residence being no new spectacle. At the lunch table, for I shared the officers' mess, Major Holmes warned me good-naturedly about sharks, but made no further reference to my swim. From then on, I repeated the performance daily, often before breakfast.

My plan was to cross the bay during the night, reaching the boutre before sunup. At that hour, the currents swept out to sea; I knew their strength from experience. It would take me fully three hours, I calculated, to swim the two miles to the boutre, and possibly an hour to return. The essential thing was for me to be back at Government House by eight o'clock, when the boy brought my *café au lait*.

Though a good swimmer, I doubted whether my strength would prove equal to the long struggle with the current. I noticed that the soldiers of the Residence cooled their drinking water in canvas bottles with a screw-top. I had no difficulty in procuring such a bottle, which I rendered water-tight with two coats of paint from one of the open tins in my room. I planned to use it as a floater, attached by bands under my arms.

Two weeks had passed since my arrival at Perim. And still no news came from Djibouti; I concluded that the authorities of French Somaliland hesitated to offend their powerful ally. . . .

"So much the better," the governor remarked with irony. "We can enjoy your society until the end of the war!"

The attention was flattering, but scarcely reassuring. If it had not been for my crew whom I hesitated to abandon, I might have attempted a swim to the Arab coast. I resolved in any case, as soon as I had seen my men, to lay plans for a general escape. I began to fear that the Sea Wolf, as the British Officer had christened me, would have to rely on his own wits, if he was not to become a fixture at Perim. And however painless my captivity, I had no intention of remaining indefinitely interned.

One morning as I came up from my swim, I noticed an Arab sail heading into the wind towards the harbor. Painfully it crept into the port. Through the glasses, I made out a French flag; and recognized a *doueri* from Djibouti. Not a European on board, as was comprehensible. No government employee would have risked his life in so fragile a craft on a voyage that lasted two days. I watched the *nakhoda* climb the path to the Gov-

ernment House, bearing an official looking envelope which
I suspected contained news for me.

Shortly afterwards, the burly figure of Major Holmes
appeared in the doorway of my room. His round face
beamed with sincere pleasure.

"Good news," he announced briefly. "I have orders to
release you. Your government has sent a boat to convey
you to Djibouti."

"And my boutre?" I inquired.

"Oh, that is another matter. The orders concerned
only yourself. There are still formalities. . . ."

"What formalities?" I insisted.

The major seemed embarrassed.

"The usual formalities," he repeated vaguely. "It takes
time, you know, to get word back and forth between Perim
and Aden. But don't you worry, we will take good care
of your dhow."

The intention was clear. My captors hoped to demoralize my crew with the report that I had abandoned them,
or had been sent away to prison. My men would doubtless
be told they might buy their release by telling all they
knew; or graver still, things they did *not* know . . . that
I had to prevent at any case.

"When may I leave?" I questioned.

"At once, if you insist."

I replied that probably the *nakhoda* might like a night's
rest after thirty-six hours at sea; that personally I had
no objection to spending another day in the company of
my hosts. I hinted, too, that the formalities might be put
through by wire, which would permit me to leave Perim
on my own boat. The major thought that eventuality
unlikely; but invited me to a farewell dinner with two
of his officers who spoke French. A good fellow, Major

Bedouin huts on the outskirts of Djibouti

Holmes—like nearly all English officers I have met, taken as individuals. At bottom, I was glad to avoid attempting an escape from Perim: I would have disliked to betray his confidence.

Dinner—whisky and soda in abundance, cigars and conversation. The four "exiles" talked of Europe and the war, discussed news brought by the censored *Times* three weeks old. At eleven o'clock I bade my hosts good night and retired to my room, to count the minutes until three o'clock. At that hour the moon set, and the harbor lay black beneath the walls of rock. Climbing through the window, I crept barefoot over the stones to the beach on which the sea broke in phosphorescent crescents of foam. I adjusted the canvas bottle on my back and waded into deep water. The sea was warmer than the night air; I could scarcely feel it against my flesh. As I anticipated, the current pushed steadily seawards; at first I let it carry me slightly out of my course, for I knew I must save my strength.

I was not the only swimmer in the bay. From time to time a "man-eater" made a rapid dart to the surface, and plunged again in a wake of green fire. The water of the bay is deep; big fish from the open sea circulate freely in its depths. But I did not let my mind dwell on sharks. By that time I was swimming with all my strength against the current. It seemed as if I made no headway. An iron band pressed against my temples. In the chill stream of the current, my muscles stiffened and ached. Something brushed against my leg. I kicked energetically and struck out with all my force.

At last—hours later, it seemed—I made out the lines of the *Fat el Rhaman* black against the paler mass of the barracks. A sentinel paced slowly along the dock. Swim-

ming silently, I drew nearer until my palms met the curved
flank of the boutre. I let myself float from bow to stern.
Not a rope; the deck was out of reach. I would have to
climb over the rudder, in full view of the sentinel. I waited
until his beat took him past the boutre. As his footstep
grew fainter, I dragged myself out of the water. When my
feet touched the deck, I felt a distinct thrill, as if at
last I had come home. Swinging myself stiffly into the hold,
I lay wrapped in a sailcloth, for I was naked and shivering, to wait for day.

The clear note of a bugle sounded the reveille in the
near-by barracks. I heard the Sepoys stream out on the
quay, splashing and shouting in the water, barely fifty
feet from the boutre. A warm gold light, as the sun
mounted, streamed through the open hatch. I thought with
considerable anguish of the return swim across the harbor in broad daylight. Would my men never come? At last
bare feet pattered across the deck. Kassim leaped into
the hold, stifling a cry of astonishment as he recognized
me. I sent him to summon Abdi, directing him to keep
the crew busy washing the deck, during the time I remained
on board.

Abdi's joy was comforting to witness. Though he maintained that from the first he had felt no anxiety on my
behalf, he exclaimed with quiet satisfaction at this fresh
proof of my invulnerability. The governor in person, he
related, had come with his men to search the *Fat el Rhaman.* They had rummaged everywhere, sounding even the
mast and the beams in the hopes of finding hidden money,
to prove my participation in the forbidden trade. And
it was Abdi who destroyed the famous receipt; he had
hastened to tear out the page from our log when the boutre was taken in tow. In return, I told him briefly of my

captivity, and announced my departure for Djibouti, urging him to keep the crew in good spirits until my return, however much it might be retarded.

The cabin clock, striking half-past six, put an end to our conversation. It was high time to strike out again for my prison across the bay. Abdi called to the crew to spread out the sail on deck as if to dry. Behind the improvised screen, I slipped into the water, swimming straight out from the boutre, to keep hidden as long as possible from the soldiers on the dock.

My men had orders to stage a noisy quarrel to divert attention. I had gained a hundred yards or so when I heard a burst of voices, angry shouts, and the laughter of the Sepoys who had gathered to watch the fun. I swam rapidly, each stroke carrying me further from the danger point. All at once silence fell; then voices called from the shore. I had been seen.

I made ready to dive, ears strained for the report of a gun and the splash of a bullet cutting the water. But nothing happened. I risked a look over my shoulder. Six hundred yards lay between me and the shore. I was practically out of range. A group of soldiers pointed and gesticulated on the dock, yet no one fired. I wondered at their reticence. Later Abdi gave me the explanation.

"What is that thing floating out there?" one of the Sepoys called to him. Abdi threw a glance in my direction.

"It looks like a *calebash*," he returned carelessly.

"No, it is a man swimming," the Sepoy insisted, lifting his rifle. Abdi stood up for a better view.

"You are right," he agreed. "A white man, an *Inglis*, taking a bath." At the word "*Inglis*" the soldier lowered his rifle. A group formed to watch the swimmer, but prudently refrained from firing.

In less than an hour I reached the beach below the Residence. Five minutes later, I was in my room. Two minutes to eight, by my watch, on the stroke of the hour, the boy brought my breakfast.

Three weeks later, to a day, I sailed the *Fat el Rhaman*, flags flying, out of the harbor. During my absence, as I had foreseen, the boutre had been searched again and the crew narrowly questioned; threatened with prison and the whip, but on the whole, well treated. They had never had so much to eat, they assured me. All were plump and shining. Even Fara, the boy, had stowed away a provision of flour and sea biscuit.

The wind of the strait carried us briskly south. In an hour, the black rock of Perim had shrunk to a dot on the horizon. A holiday atmosphere pervaded the boutre. Abdi stood beside me at the helm, every tooth showing in his dark face. Kassim, perched on the bowsprit, improvised a song in honor of our "marvelous" escape, to which the rest of the crew kept time, marking the rhythm with clapping hands.

We had slipped through the claws of the Lion. But I had still to experience the grip of the Lion's teeth.

XV

Phantom Ships

Aden—docks, reservoirs, coal yards, the zigzag route
to Aden-crater, the blue stretch of the harbor—itself a
crater, shut in by a circle of jagged peaks. Every man
likes to take a pretty girl out walking, if only to flaunt
a fictitious proprietorship in the eyes of envious males.
Taking out a ship on her trial run gives much the same
thrill, its intensity tripled when the man at the helm
is captain, owner, and shipbuilder, all in one. That afternoon in Aden bay I found beauty even in the drab clutter
of the water front, seen from the deck of a 100-ton
schooner that I had built myself and half of which belonged to me.

My dream of a big boat was realized, thanks to the
aid of a countryman of mine, a merchant established for
many years at Aden, who had furnished half the capital.

It had taken me eight months to build the schooner.

At first I had hesitated risking nearly everything I
possessed in that ocean-stronghold of an Empire which
viewed me, as I was only too aware, with no favorable eye.
But my countryman reassured me; he esteemed his credit
with the English sufficient to preserve me from annoyance
in that quarter. In addition Aden represented the one
point in all the region where wood and other material
for shipbuilding could be conveniently procured. I let
myself be persuaded, somewhat against my better judg-
ment.

247

The authorities at Aden gave me no trouble. On the contrary, I obtained a shipbuilding permit without delay; and was given every facility for the rapid construction of the schooner. I built her of Indian teak, ideal wood for ships, being practically indestructible. Teak does not rot; insects and that pest of wooden hulls, the shipworm, find it indigestible. She had the general lines of an Arab boutre, clumsy to a European eye, but assuring rare qualities of sturdiness and speed. Through the blistering summer, while the pest raged at Aden, I worked with a gang of Arab carpenters at Mahalla, a strip of beach lying to the east of Steamer Point. In eight months the schooner was ready for sea.

That November afternoon, I steered my new boat with pride, all canvas set, zigzagging across the harbor of Aden and back and forth beneath the latticed windows of the Club, for the white-clad Britishers to admire and envy. I had applied for my papers and engaged a crew. The following morning we were due to leave for the Somali coast.

I did leave for Africa before another round of the clock, but not precisely as I planned. The afternoon's exhilaration was short-lived. In the evening I received not my clearing papers but two official envelopes. The first contained a document notifying me that my new boat had been requisitioned for government use; the second, a writ expelling me from Aden until the conclusion of hostilities. No explanation whatsoever, merely two bare statements. I was informed that, as was customary in such cases, I had only to present the bills and the cost of construction would be refunded—wood, iron, canvas and labor. Eight months' work obliterated at the stroke of a pen.

Useless to protest. Even my French associate discouraged me.

"You will only waste time and energy," he counseled from long experience. "Be thankful that we get our money back."

What I wanted was my schooner. I never laid eyes on it again.

Months later I learned the pretext given for its seizure: the testimony of four mysterious Somalis who swore I had built the schooner for the arms trade with Arabia. That they had put in their appearance on the very eve of my sailing struck me as a singular coincidence. Why not eight months earlier? One of the men I succeeded in tracing; he retracted before the French consul at Aden (to no effect), all that he was reported to have sworn. Who the three others were, I never knew. And so I lost the big boutre, and was hustled out of Aden on a writ it took four years to have repealed, considerably poorer in purse, but infinitely richer in experience.

Nothing to do but write down another item to the score of the Lion . . . and begin all over. I had turned the *Fat el Rhaman* out to grass, too battered to be seaworthy on long trips, particularly such as I planned, where speed and perfect trim under all circumstances were first requisites. Besides, her fifteen tons had already proved insufficient for carrying freight.

Begin again. That refrain was acquiring a familiar sound. But how? My funds were cut in half. My experience at Aden had chilled my accommodating countryman. I possessed enemies too powerful and too active, he concluded, to risk his capital in any enterprise of mine! There was also the question of timber. I had my heart set on Indian teak. I wanted to build a boat that would last.

Aden had closed its doors. But at Makalla, an Arab port to the east of Aden, I could buy wood of the sort I desired. I gave the *Fat el Rhaman* a thorough going over; and in view of what had happened at Aden and Perim, I took care to provide myself with a letter from the Governor of Djibouti stating the reason for my trip to Makalla and specifying the sum of money in my possession and the purpose for which it was destined.

Ten days after my return from Aden, I cleared Djibouti for Makalla. Under ordinary circumstances, the direct route led across the Gulf of Aden to Ras el Ara and east along the coast to Makalla. But on the coast, the blockade functioned well. Besides, I had been warned to keep away from the neighborhood of Aden, which liberally interpreted meant all the territory "ruled" by the Iman of Sana. I was too keen on the new boat that was to replace the unlucky *Altaïr*, to take the risk. The safest course for me lay due east in the open sea; but there again, two obstacles barred the way. I did not own a chronometer (for Red Sea navigation a sextant had sufficed); I had no means of recognizing the longitude of Makalla, or for that matter of determining in advance any fixed point on the Arab coast. In addition, the Eastern monsoon was sweeping northwest towards the Red Sea; I would have to fight head winds and a strong current, tripling or quadrupling the length of the route. Along the African coast, on the contrary, the monsoon created a counter-current which piled up a heavy sea, but facilitated navigation. On that route, I had no need of a chronometer. I had only to follow the Somali coast to Bender Ghasim which lies directly opposite Makalla, and strike across for Arabia.

That meant skirting British Somaliland, a minimum

risk, since my prescription from British waters applied solely to Aden and its vicinity. With my authorization from Djibouti I felt no qualms about penetrating a zone of British influence, however unwelcome I might be there personally.

To my regret, I had to abandon Abdi at Obok, crippled temporarily by a stingray puncture combined with an attack of dysentery. In years, it was my first trip without my faithful mate. Abdi tried his utmost to have me postpone our departure; failing in that he lavished advice concerning his countrymen, the Warsangalis.

"Accept no invitations from strangers," he warned. "Many will invite you, but only to rob you, if they can. Anchor always at a distance from shore, with the sail ready to leave at a moment's notice."

I tried to reassure him. I had no intention of stopping anywhere on the African coast. He shook his head lugubriously. "Something unpleasant is sure to happen," he prophesied. "If you will only wait a few days longer . . ."

But I was in no mood for delay. I took hasty leave of my disconsolate mate—a gaunt black ghost, his teeth chattering with fever.

For three days, we made little headway, rolling on a sea like oil—a heavy swell and only occasional puffs of wind. All about us, huge jellyfish stirred slowly in the transparent water; so transparent themselves, they seemed more like freaks of light than living matter. Their presence kept us from bathing, as their touch is like the sting of a hundred nettles. Bands of porpoises, dozens at a time, lunged and splashed about us. I shot a couple (my men esteemed their meat a great delicacy), but before we could haul them aboard two sharks, which followed us persistently, made quick work in disposing of the corpses.

Towards morning the third day out, we sighted the Berbera light. I had hoped to pass Berbera during the night, but we slid past at sunrise, the town scarcely visible behind the projecting cape. A few hours later, we were within sight of Ras Karam against a background of black mountains. The swell grew heavier as the wind freshened. The *Fat el Rhaman*, still sturdy for all its battering, beat its way forward in the wind, the deck half under water. We passed Khor Sorech like a still lake surrounded by mangroves, its shallows, so my men told me, dotted with pearl-bearing *sadafs;* and the little port of Ankar in an oasis beneath a wall of purple rock. The wind grew steadily in violence. By the time we reached the Gulf of Raguda, it was blowing a gale. A bad corner, Raguda, with night coming on, and the only shelter behind a labyrinth of reefs; sheer suicide to attempt crossing them at that hour. Our only course was to steer towards the horizon, in a sea rolling as only the Indian ocean can roll in a heavy gale. At each wave, our bow lifted, shot out beyond the crest, poised and dropped. The second or two that elapsed before the crash seemed hours. Happily the ribs of the *Fat el Rhaman* were solid; a lighter boat would have smashed to bits at the impact. Twice a shroud snapped; luckily, only one at a time, which saved the mast from going overboard.

An interminable night, with no Abdi to relieve me at the tiller, and the crew working in relays pumping water from the hold. At dawn, the gale seemed to have blown itself out. I veered towards land again, hoping to reach shelter at Hais before the monsoon set in. By noon, it had risen; on the horizon a white line of foam rushed towards us with the roar of a torrent. The sail strained taut as a drum. I watched it anxiously—would it resist the ter-

rific pull? Then what I feared happened. A tiny rip
started on the windward edge, above the boltrope. It
widened, widened. We brought down the yard to save the
sail from tearing in two, no easy task in a high wind and
heavy sea, for the yard measured fifty-two feet and
weighed 400 pounds.

Hoisting a jib, we managed to reach shelter a mile below the village of Hais, anchoring off a pebbly beach
bordered with rusty hills. Scarcely had we dropped anchor
when a dozen Somalis appeared as if by magic on shore,
and plunging through the breakers, swam towards us
splashing and shouting. As a precaution, I had set up a
billet of firewood on an empty box and covered it over
with sailcloth, trusting that the sight of that improvised
"machine gun" and our display of rifles would have a
salutary effect on our visitors! After the usual questions,
who we were and where we were going, they offered to
bring us firewood and meat in exchange for rice and *durra*.

The next day we made Maït, where I planned to put
in for repairs. Sail and rigging needed attention after
our twenty-four hours' battle with the monsoon. Before
reaching Maït, we passed within sight of the tomb of
Sheik Issak, reputed ancestor of one of the two main
divisions of the Somali tribes. My men threw into the sea
the ritual offering—rice, *durra*, and a cup of water.

Three miles beyond, Maït showed its scattered white
cubes along the shore. Among them, a larger structure
lifted two square towers and a cupola with walls cut in
an openwork of arabesque. On nearer view, we saw that the
town lay half in ruins, the work of Malmullah who was
still sowing terror among the tribes of the coast.

In the market where I went with Kassim to make a

few necessary purchases, I was surprised to hear some one call my name.

"Abd el Hai, salaam." The speaker was an utter stranger, an Indian, who had followed me into an Arab shop, the usual dark cubby-hole smelling of *berberi,* incense, and tobacco. I answered his greeting.

"What brings you here?" he inquired.

"To buy a boutre," I replied shortly.

"So far to buy a . . . boutre?" he commented with an odd smile. "Are there no sambuks to be had in Djibouti?"

On the face of it there was nothing extraordinary in that meeting, for I and my boat were fairly well known up and down the coast. But something in the Indian's manner bothered me. And besides the mere fact of his being an Indian . . . I decided, repairs or no repairs, to leave Maït that night. We lifted anchor at sunset.

For two days we encountered good weather. We rounded Maït Island, a white crest of rock three miles long, shaped like some fantastic sea monster swimming half submerged. From there, we headed east for Bender Laskhorai, the town from which Abdi came, where I planned to make a last stop for water. If the wind held, another forty-eight hours would bring us to the point from which we were to veer north for Makalla.

We had just sighted the cape of Ras Lasmaan, when Kassim, who for some time had been scanning the western horizon, handed me the binoculars.

"*Shoof*" (look), he said shortly, "a steamer."

A steamer traveling east. A freighter, was my first thought; but in a few minutes I made out the yellow funnel of a coast-patrol. I hoped she might deem us unworthy of attention; the *Fat el Rhaman* might easily have passed for an ordinary fishing boat. In that I was disappointed: as the steamer drew closer, it veered in our direction. To remove any further doubts in the matter, a puff of smoke lifted off her bow and the dull report of a cannon thundered across the water. She had fired a blank shell. Obediently, I lowered the sail. While the government boat approached, I took time to shave and dress myself in the white clothes of civilization, before it accosted us with a shock that sent the *Fat el Rhaman* reeling heavily to starboard.

We were boarded by a dapper officer and three sailors who went through the customary formalities of visit and search, after which they invited me to board the patrol with my papers. To my surprise, I was not taken to the bridge. When we reached the deck of the steamer, the young officer confiscated my papers.

"Take this man below," he ordered the two sailors, who led me down the companionway to a dark inner cabin near the engines. A blond engineer came to survey operations.

"You are prisoner of war," he informed me curtly and prepared to lock me in.

The heat in that black cupboard (it would have been exaggeration to call it a cabin), was terrific. I protested energetically.

"Tell the captain to put me in irons, if he wants to, but let me stay on deck," I insisted. The engineer wrinkled his brows in an effort to understand. Apparently my fragmentary English was beyond his comprehension. I scribbled the message in pencil on a sheet of my notebook, and he sent one of the sailors to deliver it.

Then he, too, went away, not without having first offered me a cigarette. To my gratitude, he left the door of my prison open, with a sailor standing guard in the corridor outside.

Seated on the edge of a bunk beneath the yellow glare of an electric bulb, I puffed philosophically at my cigarette, wondering meanwhile where this last "adventure" of mine would take me. . . . A few yards distant the engines had resumed their rhythmic thumping; we were under weigh again presumably with the *Fat el Rhaman* in tow. Was it going to be a repetition of Perim? My arrest was arbitrary; of that there could be no doubt. With my papers in order, and above all—the letter from the governor at Djibouti . . . The English, I knew, were great sticklers for "legality." But in war time, you could never tell . . . Well, nothing could be gained by anticipating trouble. I smoked the fraternal cigarette until it burnt my fingers; after which I sat listening to the throb of the engines, waiting for the captain's reply to my message, while my head grew drowsy from the heat, the lack of air, and the hypnotic thud, thud, of the machines.

I had not long to wait. The same immaculate lieutenant who had boarded the *Fat el Rhaman* appeared in the doorway, and gestured me to follow him.

On deck, I drank in greedily a blaze of sunlight and the sea breeze. A group of white uniforms stood aft under an awning, the captain, a man in his fifties, clean-shaven and long-chinned, with a pair of keen seaman's eyes in a face tanned a deep copper-red. At his elbow, two young officers—one blond, one dark, so incredibly trim and spotless, either might have served as mannequin for the tailor of his Majesty's navy. All three stood surveying me with frank curiosity. I may have imagined it, but I fancied that the curiosity was not wholly unfriendly.

"The captain permits you to remain on deck." It was the dark-haired lieutenant who addressed me in French singularly free from foreign accent. "*Sans les fers*, unless you prefer them," he added, smiling maliciously. "And now, if you don't mind telling us . . ."

I explained with careful details the reasons for my presence in British waters, requesting that a radio be sent to Djibouti to confirm my statements. Also, if the gentlemen had no objection, would they mind telling me where they were taking me?

"The captain has orders to convey you to Berbera." With that remark, the official conversation ended. I found a comfortable seat against the rail from where I could watch the *Fat el Rhaman* dip in the wake of the steamer, the crew huddled in a group forward. Kassim stood apart from the rest, a disconsolate figure against the mast. I would have liked to give him a reassuring wave; but I realized my gesture might be interpreted as a signal. I compromised by making myself as visible as possible by the stern rail, knowing that his keen eyes would soon spy me out.

"Have a cigarette?" The officer who spoke French came to lean conversationally beside me.

"You led us a chase," he began, bending towards me to give me a light in the wind.

"We lost you in the storm," he went on. "They had signaled you from Berbera. Ever since, we have been steering in circles. Until last night at Maït."

"Ah—so it was at Maït?"

Dorset—that was the young officer's name, nodded. "They said you had passed there twenty-four hours before. Though if we had missed you, you would have run into the *Juno*. She is looking for you further east."

The *Juno*—a two-funneled cruiser! I remarked dryly that so much attention was distinctly flattering.

The young Englishman grinned.

"Oh, the Admiralty has you signaled everywhere. Do you know what we call you, by the way? 'The Sea Wolf.' "

I made a wry face.

"In French," I reminded, "by *loup de mer*, generally prefixed by the adjective *vieux*, we mean an antiquated seaman generally found in the cafés along the dock, or seated on a lobster pot telling stories to the young."

Dorset shook his head. "In English, it isn't that at all," he told me gravely. "A 'sea wolf' is a—well, I suppose you might call him—a variety of corsair."

"A pirate? Grateful for the implication."

"Oh, not necessarily," the lieutenant hastened to assure me. "He can be a man who sails around alone, as you do, and has adventures. You must have had fascinating ones!"

"Fascinating" was scarcely the word I would have applied to my latest "adventure." But it had a certain piquant aspect, as I was fast discovering. I looked the speaker straight in the eyes, handsome eyes with long curling lashes.

"You speak excellent French. Do you mind telling where you learned it?" The Englishman flushed to his helmet.

"Oh, I spent two years in a French school. And besides I have a fiancée in Tours—a *Tourangelle*." His English accent reappeared suddenly in the adjective which he articulated shyly as if he had spoken a girl's name. "That's one of the reasons why I am interested in Frenchmen. Though from all I had heard, I thought you would probably wear whiskers and earrings!"

The call to mess interrupted our conversation. Somewhat to my surprise, I was invited to share the officers' table. The *Pinto*, a former yacht, boasted a commodious wardroom, green leather and mahogany, one wall lined with bookshelves, and—amazing detail for a boat of its type—a piano! I had not touched a keyboard for months; it took no urging to get me seated at the piano bench when the captain joined us at coffee. The first lieutenant sat at my elbow; a Scotchman from Inverness, who had promised some one he would shun alcohol in all its forms, which may have contributed to his general melancholy. He was a lugubrious soul, lank and red haired, with a hollow tenor voice that went oddly with his huge frame. He, too, was a musician, he confided. I abandoned the piano long enough for him to give an illustration of his talents: Paderewski's minuet performed with great *brio* and, as he stated proudly, entirely by ear.

Whisky, tobacco and music. I played, as I remember, for hours on end. What they preferred, however, were songs of the old French navy; particularly the chantey of the men of Morlaix with its unequivocal refrain:

C'est la devise de Morlaix:
Si Anglais te mord, mords-les!

They made me teach them the words, my amiable captors, and roared out the chorus accompanied by peals of laughter—"*Si Anglais te mord-d, mord-d-les!*"

Dorset, as his contribution, attempted a French song "*Quand l'amour meurt*" in which his careful accent went back on him totally as he twisted his tongue about the double vowels.

A fraternal evening: its atmosphere far more suggestive of the *entente cordiale* than a prisoner-of-war among his captors. And yet the fact was there. While we played and sang, the *Pinto* steamed on her way to Berbera where the jail of the Grand Nation and perhaps worse—stood ready to receive me.

Late that same evening I took a turn about the deck to fill my lungs with air before going down to my stifling cabin by the engine room. Dorset joined me as I stood in the stern watching the *Fat el Rhaman*, its deck deserted— bobbing behind us in the moonlight. The inevitable cigarette glowed in his finger tips.

"We reach Berbera to-morrow," he remarked. As I was already unpleasantly aware of the fact, I construed the remark as leading up to something.

"Yes, and then what?" I encouraged.

"That's just the point. I don't mind telling you the captain is worried. He's a great stickler for legality, the old man. Point of honor, you know. And he is convinced you are all right. Papers and so on. So long as you stay with us, no one is going to harm you. The orders said hold you, nothing more. But if we hand you over to the chaps at Berbera—Well, there is no telling what may happen."

"You mean—court martial and a firing squad?" I suggested coldly.

"Yes—and perhaps without court martial. They're a nervous lot, those army fellows," Dorset added with true seaman's scorn. "Always dying to shoot some one. And where there is no German handy, a Frenchman will do almost as well." He gave a grewsome chuckle. "Ten to one, some one will want to shoot you merely on the strength of your reputation!"

"A pleasant prospect," I agreed. "Is my reputation so bad?"

"Pretty black," Dorset nodded soberly. "That is, if we believe all the things they tell about you. But the point is that just now there doesn't seem to be any real motive for holding you, much less for shooting you. Then, too, you are an ally, a pretty awkward business all around, in case of a mistake. The old man has sent off a radio to Djibouti—you can count on it, he won't let you out of his hands until he gets an answer."

With that doubtful comfort, we parted for the night. I went below to my airless cabin, but not to sleep. The thought of an eventual firing squad, however problematical, makes a poor lullaby.

Late the next afternoon, the *Pinto* stationed off Berbera. A launch flying British colors put out to meet us, with the governor himself seated in an armchair beneath the awning. A striking contrast to the cordial seamen of the *Pinto*. This was the bureaucrat *à l'anglaise*, long, lined, and gray; rigid in his white linen and so lean one would have said his body had only two dimensions.

He strode up the gangplank, looking neither to left nor right, greeted the captain of the *Pinto* with cool formality, and the two walked aft to the captain's quarters. The conversation that took place within seemed extraordinarily animated. Echoes of it floated up to the deck; Captain Crawford's deep tones, emphatic and heated, and a high-pitched voice uttering saw-like monosyllables. After a long quarter of an hour, the two officials reappeared. The governor icier than before; the captain's face a deep copper above his white coat—and followed by Dorset, his features puckered with consternation.

When the governor's launch put off again, the captain disappeared in his cabin, calling the steward to bring him a whisky and soda. Dorset paced the deck restlessly a half dozen times, hesitated, and came towards me, biting his lip beneath his short mustache.

"It looks pretty bad," he told me, dropping his voice to an undertone. "I ought not to tell you, I suppose. They have found some kind of a native who swears he helped you land rifles and machine guns of German make for Malmullah near Maït three days ago. But the captain won't hear of giving you up until he gets an answer to his radio. When the old man sets his teeth in anything, he never lets go. But, I say, it does sound rather bad."

Dorset strode away abruptly, realizing, I suspected, that his enthusiasm for the "adventurer" had led him to overstep the limits set for the treatment of prisoners-of-war, however allied. He kept out of my way studiously the rest of the day.

A certain constraint lay over the dinner that evening. Outwardly nothing had changed in the attitude of the officers towards me; but it was as if each man had withdrawn behind the façade of the uniform. I resolved to step out on deck immediately after dinner.

When coffee was served, Captain Crawford joined me.

"Surely you are not going to bed without giving us a little music, Captain," he suggested. Obediently, I sat down at the piano and, little by little, the atmosphere thawed. The melancholy Scot took up his position beside me on the piano bench. I accompanied him while he sang ballads of the Campbells, Camerons, and Chisholms. Only Dorset, smoking furiously, remained aloof. And, significant fact, that evening no one asked for the song of the men of Morlaix. . . .

Early next morning I was jolted from a troubled sleep by some one knocking at the door of my cabin. As the pounding on the door jerked me into consciousness, the thought flashed through my head that this was the classic awakening of the prisoner at dawn; and that the firing squad stood ready. . . .

I threw open the door. In the corridor, his hair tumbled and dripping from his bath, stood Dorset.

"Did I wake you? so sorry," he stammered. "I thought you would like to know at once. An answer has come to the captain's radio. Everything's all right." It did not need the uncertain light of the corridor to betray Dorset's delight. The tone was sufficient. I thanked the boy warmly and he went away whistling. In a moment he was back again.

"The old man wants to see you after your breakfast," he called through the crack in the door.

When I had shaved, dressed, and breakfasted, I mounted to the captain's quarters. With a gruff "I imagine this will interest you," the officer tendered me a telegram from the Governor of Djibouti.

"*Now* I have no qualms about handing you over to the shore authorities," he remarked, accompanying the words with a smile that Dorset's confidences rendered less enigmatical than it might have been otherwise.

Later that morning, the governor's launch made another visit to the *Pinto*.

The gray official took me in charge, icily aloof as ever, looking over my head or past my ear each time his gaze risked meeting mine. Only once, he abandoned his taciturnity long enough to remark crisply as we reached shore:

"If you have requests or complaints to make you are to address them to me, in writing." Whereupon a squad of Somali askari, in blue shorts and turbans, installed me comfortably enough in a tent on the grounds of the Residence.

At noon, the governor sent to ask me, did I drink claret with my meals? On my reply in the affirmative, I received a bottle of Bordeaux, of respectable vintage. During the days that followed, I caught more glimpses of His Excellency, always at a distance and generally surrounded by a hedge of uniformed soldiers. Apparently he never made the rounds of his own garden without an armed escort. I found myself wondering whether the man had a personal existence. . . . If so, I saw no trace of it during my stay in Berbera.

Days dragged past; my stay gave signs of being indefinitely prolonged. Had my friends of the *Pinto* been there I would have questioned Dorset, but the day after my transfer, the yacht steamed out of the harbor.

When I had been a week in Berbera, I sent a letter to the governor, demanding the reasons for my detention. In reply came a note regretting that the lack of an interpreter made it impossible to answer my questions. A man-of-war was expected shortly with an interpreter on board. On its arrival, the courts-martial would "take up my case."

Meantime the lack of an interpreter did not prevent a lengthy exchange of correspondence with the gray official at the Residence. The crew of the *Fat el Rhaman* was, like myself, in prison, though undoubtedly in less comfortable quarters. As my boutre needed attention, I saw no reason why my men, during their inactivity at Berbera, should not set to work on the necessary repairs. At first, the governor objected. He refused to release the crew during the daytime to work on the boutre. However, he promised to procure me such material as I needed, and to supply workmen. In practice, his plan proved totally impracticable. To transmit orders third hand to a gang of unskilled natives entailed so considerable a correspondence that after four or five days of epistolary skirmishing, the governor relaxed his official rigidity sufficiently to allow my crew to work under guard on the boutre, beached on the sand before the Residence. He even permitted me to give oral instructions to Kassim in the presence of an askar.

Within ten days the repairs were finished and the *Fat el Rhaman* ready for sea. Of the promised man-of-war and the commission that was to decide my fate, there was still no sign. I began to find my captivity irksome, in spite of plentiful rations and the District Commissioner's claret. . . .

One afternoon as I scanned the hard blue line of the afternoon horizon, my eyes met with a welcome sight— the *Pinto* steaming in towards Berbera.

That evening I received a visit from Dorset.

"Guess where we've been?" he enjoined me when I had settled him on my one camp-stool with a glass of Bordeaux and a cigarette.

"Not Djibouti?" He shook his head.

"To Makalla, to hunt for your fellow-conspirators."

"Did you find them?"

"Unfortunately no. The gentleman over there," he nodded towards the Government House, "is going to be dreadfully grieved."

"Perhaps you didn't offer to pay enough," I suggested. Dorset grinned appreciatively.

"That's what I told Captain Crawford. But he has an idea that the only kind of testimony worth procuring can be got for nothing. It's the other kind that comes high. As a consequence, we have returned *bredouille* (with an empty bag)."

"Congratulations. Does the return of the *Pinto* mean that I shall soon be getting off?"

"Not so sure," Dorset discouraged. "The Commissioner may have something else up his sleeve. Besides, you must give him time for his dignity to cool. . . ."

"Or to melt."

"I should think anything would melt on this coast," Dorset agreed, rubbing a handkerchief over his damp forehead. "I see they have set you up here in style," he went on, taking in the details of my tent-quarters. "Probably you would not care to come back to the *Pinto?*"

"Wouldn't I? Just give me a chance," I warned him.

"It is Captain Crawford's idea," Dorset explained. "The old man misses your music. If you ask to be interned on the *Pinto*, I have a hunch your request may be granted. There is a chance, you know, that your jailer may be only too glad to get rid of you, under the circumstances. He had not counted on keeping you so long!"

Two days later, after an exchange of letters and the proper administrative delay, I returned to the *Pinto*, where I was welcomed like a brother-in-arms. I was still a prisoner, but only nominally—for, as the ever communicative Dorset confided, my release could only be a matter of days.

A week longer the *Pinto* lay off Berbera, making short trips up and down the coast, or out into the ocean for target-practice. Of the man-of-war and the courts-martial, no news whatsoever. In fact, to the best of my knowledge, that famous commission never sat. Nor did I ever heard a word concerning the four Somalis who had "helped" me unload machine guns *of German make* for Malmullah. I never saw the governor again; I never knew (aside from Dorset's indiscretions) what charges had been brought against me.

At the end of my week's internment, and after more than a month's captivity on shore and shipboard, I received a note from the District Commissioner—written in his own hand, cramped and as angular as the writer himself.

"Sir"—it read—"I am directed by His Majesty's Commission (my first and only intimation of the existence of that body) to inform you that you are at liberty to return to Djibouti with your dhow and crew. I am to inform you that the President of Aden has telegraphed that he forbids your landing at Makulla. I am also to acquaint you with the fact that His Majesty's Commission has issued an order that if you again enter the territorial waters of the Protectorate, you will be subject to arrest and prosecution. I have the honor to be, Sir, your most obedient servant."

Makalla, another door of the Empire slammed.

Three days later, the *Pinto* steamed into Djibouti harbor with the *Fat el Rhaman* in tow, all flags flying.

That night, before going ashore, my friends on the coast-guard offered me a farewell dinner followed by a concert. The lieutenant from Inverness repeated his brilliant performance of the Paderewski minuet (entirely by ear); Dorset, his struggle with *"Quand l'amour meurt"*; and when it came my turn to perform, the whole group demanded the song of the men of Morlaix. Over and over they joined in the chorus:

Et si Anglais te mord, mords-les!

For on the sea, as in France, even the most desperate situations often finish . . . with a song!

XVI

"Son-of-the-Sea"

I was a free man again, but with my dream unrealized. To be sure I owned the *Fat el Rhaman*, recalked and oiled, fitter than many a younger craft; but I had set my heart on a two-masted schooner.

What had occurred at Aden and Berbera only magnified my obsession. I set my teeth grimly. I would *build that boat*, though I owned neither teak nor iron; and I knew of no market where I could purchase them. It was almost as if I expected by sheer will-power to materialize my dream out of the sea itself; which in the end is practically what I did.

Back in 1875, a small sailing vessel had struck the reef of Obok and sunk in the bay. Ever since, its hull had lain there, half buried in sand and slime.

Working at low tide with a gang of Somali divers, I succeeded in running chains under the hulk, fastening them over the deck of the *Fat el Rhaman*.

The fifteen tons of the sturdy little boutre, lifting with the tide, dragged the wreck from its bed. Water-logged, it did not rise to the surface, but we succeeded in towing it under water to the beach.

The massive oak timbers of the wreck, hard as ivory, furnished the keel, the sternpost, and the stem of the new boat. Cheered by that result, I made a rapid trip to the Ethiopian plateau. A day's journey by mule above Addis Abeba, a Swiss had set up a sawmill. I spent a week in the woods selecting cedars to be felled; two months later I received a carload of planks. Wood for the ribs came from the Mabla. I sent a gang of Danakils into the bush with a lot of iron bars bent to the exact curve of each rib. When they found a tree that duplicated the curve of the bar, they cut it down and brought it to me at Obok.

I had to procure metal: iron for nails and rivets, and copper to sheathe the hull against attacks of the ship-worm. But where to find it? Europe was out of the question—Aden likewise. As before, I turned to the sea.

In the harbor of Djibouti lay, and still lies, another wreck, the old side-wheeler *Pingouin* sunk in 1890.

It was already partly dismantled; everything of value above the bed of slime in which it lay had been carried off by a generation of wreckers. But tunneling in the mud beneath the hull, my men salvaged six tons of copper and an equal amount of iron.

The sea, too, furnished me the coal for my forge. I located the spot where a coal barge had foundered thirty years before. From the sea bottom, my divers collected five tons of coal.

My "shipyard" at Obok worked full blast. Anvils and hammers rang busily from sunrise until dusk. In five months, the hull of the new boat was completed. It took 250 men to launch her, sidewise, in the fashion of the coast.

Then, while I racked my brains wondering where and how I was to procure the masts, the sea made me another gift. An 800-ton boutre loaded with hides and coffee, belonging to an Arab merchant of Aden, ran afoul of the reef at Obok. Working day and night with 300 Danakils, I succeeded in saving the cargo, which brought us 6,000 dollars of salvage money, but more precious still, to my way of thinking, I obtained the masts and yards of the wrecked vessel, which I adapted to my boutre.

Six months after my return from Berbera, the new boat stood ready—a 186-ton schooner, glistening with paint and fish oil, and bearing a name that recalled her origin: *Ibn el Bahar* (Son-of-the-Sea). I had wrested her (perhaps more accurately "him") from the sea itself. The affection which a sailor feels normally for his ship, was in my case doubled, tripled. She was my child; I knew every plank, every nail that had gone into her construction. From the first, I had worked with the Arab carpenters; had forged and hammered and calked and greased. As I stood before the finished ship, I knew the complete joy of the creator.

Her maiden trip, a journey to Massawa with a cargo of salt, passed off without accident. I returned to Djibouti in high spirits and within a few days had shipped another cargo—500 sacks of Abyssinian wheat for the Italian government at Massawa and 200 bales of hides, together with twenty-five passengers.

On the eve of our departure, Abdi came to me.

"Abd el Hai," he said soberly, "you have one sailor too many."

I stared at him in amazement. We had already agreed that a crew of fifteen represented a strict minimum.

"One too many," he repeated. "You had better leave Djebber on land."

Then I understood. Among the Danakils, Djebber—a Soudanese diver—bore the reputation of a "Jonah." He had been shipwrecked half a dozen times; and only a few months before had lost his fellow-diver, eaten by sharks in the Gulf of Tajura.

Members of the crew—(Soudanese right, Somali left)

Kassim goes aloft

"Djebber is a *Chakaba*," Abdi specified. "He brings bad luck to the boats on which he sails."

"But Djebber has shipped with us before," I pointed out. "So far I have seen no symptoms of his bringing us bad luck."

Abdi shook his head. "He was at Farsan and at Perim," he reminded. "This is a new boat, Abd el Hai. Neither you nor I know what its luck will be. . . ."

"Nor can we change what is written," I cut him short with the convenient Moslem phrase. However considerable my esteem for Abdi, I had no intention of parting with an expert seaman. Besides, I did not wish by dismissing the poor Soudanese to contribute to his sinister reputation. And so it was that Djebber-the-Chakaba shipped with the crew of the *Ibn el Bahar* on her second voyage.

On the outset, the trip began badly. As we neared the Sowaba Islands, the wind from the Red Sea caught us, blowing with a violence that promised a stiff gale before sunset. With a head wind and the current against us, it was folly to attempt Bab el Mandeb. I decided to run back for shelter to an anchorage in the lee of Ras Siyan, a precarious shelter as it proved; the current kept swinging our stern to the impact of the waves and threatened at any moment to drive us on the rocks. I resolved to beat our way across to Perim, in order to take advantage of the current that streams into the Red Sea with the rising tide.

That current, running against the wind, created a heavy sea. In the deep channel between the two main islands of the Sowaba group, it swirled with the speed of a mill race, piling up short, vertical waves higher than the mast. We had no more than entered the passage, when a big roller lifted the schooner high in the air and let it drop crashing to the bottom of a hollow that opened suddenly yards below. At the same instant, came one of those tearing cracks which a seaman perceives not with his ears but his entrails. (As if a fundamental part of his own skeleton had given way.) The foremast snapped fifteen feet above the deck. That meant returning to Obok. I hurried repairs, for the soaked grain had begun to ferment in the hold.

Four days later, we put to sea again. This time the monsoon held off. With a light breeze aiding us, we made good headway. Abdi held the tiller; I sat cross-legged beside him, sipping tea from a handleless cup. Suddenly, the mate lifted his fine nose, sniffing curiously.

"*Harek!* (something is burning)." I hurried forward to investigate. The smell came from the hold. It took me but a minute to discover its origin. The Soudanese boy, not wishing to build a fire on deck in the sun, had found it convenient to brew his tea over a charcoal burner in the hold. He had dropped hot embers on one of the extra sails. When I leaped down the hatch, they were burning a red nest in the folds of canvas. A pail of water sufficed to put out the blaze and the culprit received the cuffing he deserved. I delivered it perhaps with more than customary energy.

A few minutes later, a whining chant rose from the bow. Abdi listened a moment, then thrust the tiller into my hands.

"The death song," he muttered half to himself and galloped forward. The whining song rose to a shrill cry; a dark body shot through the air, disappeared. The boy had jumped overboard.

Abdi and Kassim leaped after him. It took several minutes to capture the would-be suicide who swam like an

eel, diving and swimming under water to escape his rescuers. They finally seized him, struggling and splashing,
while I brought the *Ibn el Bahar* alongside. We hauled
the boy aboard, still fighting like a mad thing. I had him
tied up securely and bundled into the hold to avoid further
accidents. Whereupon with native philosophy, he promptly
fell asleep.

The episode had taken over an hour of precious time.
Before we reached the Sowabo Islands, a dead calm caught
us. At sunset, the monsoon burst again. We shortened
the sails and for four hours tacked back and forth, gaining a hundred feet at each zigzag; at times, barely holding
our own in the wind. Ahead, the two horns of the main
island showed pale against the moonlit sky. Were we never
to pass beyond that wall? Little by little, we crept nearer.
At its base, the reef extending far into the sea beyond
the point of rock, glittered with phosphorescent fire. After
our recent experience in the channel, I counted on leaving
Sowaba to leeward.

When we were abreast of the island, the wind shifted
ever so little, but enough to swing the bow of the *Ibn el
Bahar* away from the open sea, towards the reef. Impossible to veer to windward in the heavy sea. There was not air
enough and we carried too little sail. Nor did I dare risk
veering away from the wind, the usual manœuvre with a
lateen sail; the reef lay too near. I let her run, headed
for the reef, hoping that close to shore I would find a
second eddy of wind to bring us back to our course again.
What I anticipated took place. Three cable-lengths off
the reef, the wind shifted abruptly twenty-five degrees,
sufficient to carry us in safety around that point of green
fire which held the attention of each one of us, staring
as if hypnotized. The *Ibn el Bahar* slid back into her

course; we skirted the outer edge of the reef on which the sea broke ever so slightly.

We approached the point; and there, when the moment of danger seemed safely past, by a phenomenon that I was powerless to explain, the wind scanted again. The sails hung flapping from the yards. We were within sixty feet of the rocks. I felt, though I did not take my gaze from the threatening line of green foam, the eyes of my men turned towards me, as if imploring, or, what is still more poignant for a ship's commander, as if *expecting* the miracle.

It did seem, at that moment, as if it would take a miracle to save us; but there was still a chance. . . . In that threatening line of green foam, I noticed a dark interval where the sea was not breaking. A passage between the rocks? No time to hesitate; a tug at the tiller and we bore down on the reef, the wind swelling our sails, straight for the dark gap in the phosphorescence. I could almost hear my men gasp and Abdi's (he stood beside me in stony immobility), muttered "Inchallah!"

And we passed through. On either beam, almost within arm's length, it seemed, pointed heads of rock showed above eddies of green foam. Like teeth of a submarine monster gaping to close again and crush us. But we slipped through its jaws and into black water beyond, while a chorus of *"Hamdullillah!"* went up from the deck. The reef lay behind us.

Leaving the islands astern, I headed for the Arab coast. The monsoon showed no signs of abating. Forty-eight hours later we reached Perim. By that time, I had grown weary of the battle against the daily onslaught of the wind. The condition of the grain in the hold decided me to resort to artificial means to get us through Bab el Mandeb.

I had discovered the fundamental defect of my new ship: for her size, *she carried too little canvas.* On our return from Massawa, I planned to lengthen the masts and add to the main- and foresails.

At Perim, I found a tug whose master agreed for the sum of 800 rupees to tow us through the Gate of Tears and as far north as the Djebbel Zukur Islands. He had already been commissioned to go to the relief of a liner which had gone aground on the rocks there the night before. North of Bab el Mandeb we found calm weather; the monsoon slackened to lamb-like docility. We reached Djebbel Zukur on a sea like glass. As we neared the islands, I sighted the wrecked liner, its foreward half from bow to midships, lifted high above the water. At full speed, sixteen knots or so, it had run afoul of a shoal barely submerged at high tide. A flock of boutres dotted the sea about its stern. I regretted that the state of our cargo prevented us from taking part in the salvage operations; a piece of luck of that sort was not to be met with every day. I am afraid I wasted little pity on the fate of the ship, copiously insured and belonging to a company that could well support the loss. . . . Had I foreseen what lay in store for me within the next few hours, I might have been less stony-hearted.

As the tug that had brought us from Perim steamed off in the direction of the wreck, we hoisted sail. Towards ten o'clock, the white band of the coming monsoon rushed towards us from the horizon. Dirty weather by nightfall, I predicted, and headed for Rakhamat, hoping to reach the anchorage on a single tack. But when we sighted the coast, I realized that we would fall several miles short of the point aimed for. When about six miles from shore in a region where the map indicated twenty-seven feet of water,

I attempted to tack about in the wind. My unruly boat
refused to obey. The wind was too feeble and our speed too
slight. But we had space enough to veer away. I swung
the *Ibn el Bahar* full about, forcing her inch by inch into
her course. All went well; I had succeeded in pointing her
northeast, when suddenly Djebber-the-Chakaba (it was
significant that it should have been he) gave a short cry.

"*Zema ari!*" (Ship aground!)

I had felt nothing, not even the slightest jar. Releasing
the helm, I caught up the lead and dashed forward to the
bow. A hurried sounding gave five fathoms. I hastened aft,
to sound again. But on the way, my ear caught an ominous
sound of splashing from the hatchway; water in the hold.
I threw a hasty look into my cabin. A tongue of black
liquid was spreading across the floor I understood. A
point of rock had opened our hull, like a knife-blade in an
orange skin. We were settling; the knife still in the wound.
A minute later the sea washed over the deck; only the
poop remained uncovered. There the terrified passengers
clambered, hugging their belongings. I tried vainly to get
them to help lighten the ship by throwing overboard the
bales of leather piled on deck. Failing in that—not one of
the huddled group could be dislodged from the dry little
island on which they had taken refuge—I ordered my
Somalis to launch the ship's boat.

As I gave the order—and only then—I felt a sharp
physical stab, as if that knife-edge of rock had pierced a
vital part of me, the captain. A cold little voice inside
spoke in hard monosyllables: "Your ship is lost—lost."
Until then, I had gone about like an automaton, as if the
accident—the schooner itself, with its cargo and passengers—belonged to a world in which I had no part. In that
instant of realization, the thin protecting crust collapsed.

Dizzy as from the impact of a blow, I threw an arm about the mainmast, that quivered like a live thing in the shock of the waves. The contact steadied me; with the serenity of despair, I promised myself that this time there would be no "to-morrow"; I and my boat would go back to the sea together. But first there was work to be done.

Night approached rapidly. It was five in the afternoon when we ran afoul of that fatal point of rock. The nearest land lay three miles away. The boat could carry only six passengers at a time, including the rowers. On the first trip, I sent the water barrels ashore, with an armed guard to keep watch over them. By eight o'clock, the last boat-load of passengers left the schooner: all the crew had landed but four Somalis who remained with me.

The sky had clouded over; the night was opaquely black, moonless and starless. The water about us shone phosphorescent as I have rarely seen it. After three hours soaking, the smell of the hides in the hold and those we had thrown overboard attracted all manner of flesh-eating monsters—sharks and other huge fish. All about us, the water boiled with serpents of green fire. In the swell that came with the rising tide, the schooner rocked and twisted lamentably on the dagger of rock, threatening at any moment to slide off into deep water. If that happened, it took no stretch of imagination to picture the fate that awaited the five of us among the creatures that swam and plunged in fiery circles all around us. As we huddled there in the dark, watching the great beasts spin their network of green flame, the instinct of self-preservation obliterated for the time being even the ache of despair. Go down with the ship, yes, but be torn to pieces at the surface by the teeth of the man-eaters—that was a fate no man could accept cold-bloodedly.

Feverishly we set to work building a raft, roping together all the available spars and planks. It was barely completed when a savage lurch of the wreck sent the two masts crashing to the deck, pinning down the fragile craft, our only hope of safety if the ship's boat did not return in time. Three hours had passed since it set off with Abdi in charge, on the last trip to shore.

The fallen masts rendered our situation doubly precarious. In the night, their silhouette afforded the only means of locating the schooner. We had nothing to light a fire with. It was tantalizing to picture Abdi and the others rowing about within a mile of us certainly, peering vainly through the night for a sight of the wrecked schooner; while we crouched helpless on that sloping square of water-washed planks, living bait for the waiting sharks.

Every few minutes we shouted in unison; and listened, every nerve tense, for an answer. None came. The only sound, the hideous groaning of the strained timbers (groans that seemed to come from the sea bottom) and the hollow shock and splash of water in the cabin, surf emprisoned in a box. The night dragged through. We grew hoarse with shouting; still no one came. Towards five o'clock, when a faint pallor showed along the eastern horizon, Kassim clutched my arm, pointing towards that pale strip of sky.

"*Zema!*" (The boat!) Vainly I strained my eyes in the direction he indicated; I could see nothing. We shouted again with all the despairing vigor of our five pairs of lungs. This time we got an answer—a faint cry across the water. We continued shouting to guide the rescuers. In another quarter of an hour, they reached us. They had been rowing about all night long; convinced that the schooner had gone down and we with it. Only Abdi had insisted on remaining on the water until daybreak; it was to him we owed our safety.

Kassim and the other three sailors climbed into the boat and stood waiting for me to follow. With the immediate danger past and rescue at hand, it was as if the will and the power to stir had abandoned me. As I look back on it, that moment when I crouched alone on the sloping afterdeck of my lost ship was one of the blackest and bitterest of my life.

Out of the dark came a voice, speaking my name— "Abd el Hai—*Ammi*." The voice was Abdi's. "*Ammi*," my master. It was the first, the only time I ever knew him to give me that title. It was a reminder—perhaps the shadow of a reproach. Like the sting of a lash, it brought life to my muscles. Swinging across the low rail, I joined the others. Yet as we rowed away through the night, I dared not risk a glance backwards towards the Son-of-the-Sea impaled on its rock, though its groans pursued us through the darkness as if proclaiming the shame of my abandon. Yet the *Ibn el Bahar* was not *my* child—though I had built it with my own hands. *Ibn el Bahar* belonged to the sea; I had taken it from the sea; and the sea had reclaimed its own. *Mektoub!*

On the beach I found shipwrecked passengers and crew bundled together like a band of drenched and disconsolate fowl. Why, I demanded indignantly, had no one built a fire?

"This is not yet the land," Abdi spoke quietly at my shoulder. "It is only a *sahel*, a sand bar. There is no wood anywhere—nor grass."

Five miles of marshland lay between us and the shore, impossible to cross on foot or by boat. With four of the crew, I set out again in the ship's boat working north along the tongue of sand towards the town of Rakhamat, which we reached at noon. There I found an Italian courier charged with one of the relays of the overland mail from Massawa to Assab. I gave him a message for the Italian Resident at Assab relating our disaster and asking for help in salvaging the cargo of the *Ibn el Bahar.* At Rakhamat I arranged with the *nakhoda* of a native boutre to carry my twenty-five passengers north to Massawa.

That done, we rowed back to the sand bank. Two Dankali shepherds had arrived in our absence, by a path known only to themselves. They brought wooden jars of camels' milk which the hungry castaways gulped greedily. Now camels' milk, which in taste differs little from cows' milk, has a very special effect on the average digestive tract when one is unaccustomed to drinking it. As a result, I preserve a particularly vivid recollection of the night that followed the shipwreck, nor can I disassociate the loss of the *Ibn el Bahar* from a nightmare memory of collective colic within the restricted limits of that all too fraternal strip of sand! Even tragedy has its ludicrous side. . . .

The next morning, a boutre arrived from Rakhamat to embark the twenty-five Arabs. With it, came two others—Arabs attracted by the hope of looting the wreck. I engaged the two *nakhodas* and their crews to help us bring the cargo of the *Ibn el Bahar* to shore; the bales of hides, in particular, since nearly all the sacks of grain had burst.

The *Ibn el Bahar* still clung to the rock covered by six feet of water at ebb tide. With Djebber-the-Chakhaba (an expert diver for all his sinister reputation) directing operations, my men set to work in the submerged hold, bringing up the bales of hides. They were bales no longer; the hides had burst their wrappings, taking on the consistence of huge, slimy pancakes.

When the divers had emptied the hold, I made a tragic discovery. Two of the men were missing. As I had spoken with both of them only a few minutes before, it was clear they had remained under water. One by one, their comrades dived through the dark hatchway. Djibber remained the longest below; at last he poked his head above water, croaked a hasty "I've found him," and disappeared once more, followed by two of the crew. In a moment, the head and shoulders of Djebber appeared again, bearing a body of which only the legs were visible, the trunk enveloped in a cowhide wrapped tight about it like a glove. The poor fellow had inserted head and shoulders in one of the slimy rolls and unable to free himself, had drowned, caught in a death trap. A few minutes later, the two others brought up a second body, coiffed like the first in a sinister hood of soaked leather.

We laid the bodies in the bottom of the boutre. I worked over one of the drowned men, while Abdi, copying my movements, busied himself with the other. The divers stood about watching our efforts with considerable skepticism.

"Khalass" (It is finished) they commented simply, accepting the phenomenon with Moslem philosophy. We succeeded in saving one of the victims, but his companion was indeed "finished." We buried the poor fellow on the strip of sand, marking the grave, Somali fashion, with a circle of stones.

For ten days, the crew and I camped on that desolate beach, living on camels' milk, which in time we had learned to digest, and now and then a handful of fermented grain. I sent off hides and grain (what was left of it) by boutre

to Rakhamat; and we dismantled the *Ibn el Bahar*, bringing to shore everything that could be transported. Only
the hull remained impaled on the submerged pinnacle of
rock.

I struck a bargain with the two *nakhodas*, who agreed
to carry what we had succeeded in saving to Obok, for the
sum of fifty rupees. But when we had loaded their boutres
with the salvaged material, the captains refused to hoist
sail. Instead of fifty rupees, they demanded five hundred
for each boatload, the sum to be paid in advance. As they
well knew, we had arms but no ammunition. At any show
of resistance on our part, they would have sailed away
with their plunder, leaving us abandoned on our sand
bank. Accordingly I manifested no surprise nor indignation. I stated quietly tht I would pay them half the sum
on the spot, and the rest as soon as we were at sea. I
called to Abdi to bring me the money-chest; while he made
a pretense of opening it, I gave orders in an undertone
for the crew, at a given signal, to fling themselves on the
two *nakhodas* and tie them fast. I rummaged in the chest
long enough to give Abdi time to mobilize his companions,
then having closed and locked the strong box, I crossed
the sand towards the spokesman of the Arabs who sat
crouched on his heels by the water's edge, waiting for the
promised rupees.

"Here is your pay," I told him, laying a hand on the
man's shoulder. At the signal, my Somalis rushed in. In
an instant, we had two Arabs face down on the sand,
trussed like a couple of astonished hens. At the sight, the
crews of the sambuks took to their heels. I divided my
men in two groups to man the abandoned boats and loading the two prisoners on board, we hoisted sail for the
south. It was my first intention, I told the Arabs, to carry

them to Assab and hand them over to police. The two bandits pleaded desperately, assuring me that the blame for their action belonged to the devil, that it was the *Chaëtan* himself who had tempted them.

"Remember, Abdel Hai, no man is above weakness," they insisted. I let myself be softened. (To tell the truth I had no intention of involving the poor devils with the authorities at Assab.) We removed their bonds and we continued our route, with the monsoon driving us forward, south to Obok. There, the *nakhodas* were forced to wait until their crews arrived overland from Rakhamat. Far from wresting a thousand rupees from a shipwrecked crew, they lost even the fifty rupees we had first agreed upon. The attempted piracy, I esteemed, merited no premium, however slight. A point of view which the Arabs themselves accepted as normal. Whatever his faults, the Arab—like the Somali—recognizes the law of cause and effect. . . .

All I had saved from the *Ibn el Bahar* (as I said, we left on the rocks of Rakhamat only the dismantled hull) represented the barest fraction of the schooner's value. The rest was a total loss, since the *Ibn el Bahar*, like practically all sailing-craft in those waters, carried no insurance. (To register my boat at Lloyd's would have necessitated taking her to Marseilles for a visit of inspection.) Once more, I was without a ship. What was even more tragic, I had no money with which to build a new one. To attempt another hashish venture with the *Fat el Rhaman* was out of the question. I had no wish to court shipwreck a second time. Her days of strenuous navigation were over.

I racked my brain to no effect. In my little shipyard at Obok, I still had timber left over from the wreck I had salvaged, suitable for the sternpost and stem of a new schooner. Wood for ribs, I could procure as before in the Dankali hills. But I lacked funds for purchasing planks and paying labor. Nor had I the slightest idea where such capital could be got. And here again, as always, the sea came to my aid. The *Altaïr*, my next schooner, like the unlucky *Ibn el Bahar*, was also born of the sea, though not so directly.

On day in Djibouti, I met an old school friend from Paris, the engineer in charge of the new molehead the government had agreed to build in Djibouti harbor. We spent an evening together talking over old times and commenting the odd chance that had brought us together, after so many years, on the Somali coast. As we spoke of the work to be done on the molehead, the engineer mentioned his difficulties with native workmen.

"The most daring swimmers in the world, no doubt. And yet we can't get one of them into a diver's suit," he complained.

"They regard it as an infernal apparatus and certain death," he went on. "And the trouble is, we need to have one man working under water all the time to place the blocks. A Greek offered his services, but it turned out he had never laid eyes on a diver's suit before. We nearly drowned him a couple of times. And now the whole job is held up until we can get a diver from Marseilles."

"How much do you pay a diver?" I inquired.

"Forty dollars a day."

"Forty dollars," I repeated. "Then don't bother to have any one sent down from Marseilles. Let me lay your blocks for you."

"You!" The engineer stared at me in round-eyed incredulity. "You don't mean to say that you . . ."

"Why not? I have followed a good many trades since we last met."

"I dare say." My former schoolmate laughed good-naturedly.

"Well, if you want the job, it is yours, and my gratitude along with it."

The next morning I tried out the apparatus in nine feet of water. If the truth were known, I too, like the unfortunate Greek, had never seen a diver's suit before, though perhaps I was better acquainted than the average layman with the theory of its working. The one unpleasant factor of the job, once I had learned to prevent an undignified bounce to the surface, seat foremost, by letting too much air into the suit—was the heat. During the day, the shallow water off the mole reached a temperature of 97° on an average. I sweated mightily within my metal helmet. But that was a minor matter.

Four hours daily I worked under water in the diver's suit—with the help of a gang of Somali divers, guiding the six-ton blocks as they were lowered into the water. In two months, we had finished the ground work of the mole-head, placing in all 250 blocks, 100 of them under water. With two thousand dollars in my pocket, I went back to Obok to build the new boat.

XVII

The Route to India

As I stepped out on the first-class deck from the purser's cabin of the weekly mail steamer, some one spoke my name.

"Abd el Hai . . . *quelle surprise!*" A lank figure rose from one of the wicker tables by the rail and came towards me, hand outstretched. For a moment I failed to place the man, then I remembered: Aden; the unlucky schooner requisitioned by the British; an accommodating ship's officer who had done me an occasional service in the matter of procuring building materials.

"Captain Turnwell. . . ."

"Captain no longer," the tall Englishman corrected. "I left the Anglo-India six months ago. No future. Gone in for business. Have a drink."

Judged by outward appearances, the change had been profitable. A first-class passenger on an Oriental liner, dressed in immaculate linens, a discreet brilliant on his little finger, it was not surprising that at first glance I had failed to recognize the former captain of the freighter *Mary Willard.* Yet Turnwell still preserved the same air of retarded adolescence: his bony frame, awkward in spite of the well-cut clothes; his round blue eyes with their expression of startled interrogation; the long chin, smooth not so much from close shaving as from lack of beard. His hair had grown thinner; a soft colorless fuzz covered his crown, like the down on a baby's head.

He squeezed my hand eagerly at parting, urging me to look him up if ever I came to Bombay.

"Don't forget," he called over the rail. "So glad to see you. If you have business in Bombay, always at your service. Remember."

"Poor Turnwell," I mused as I came off the liner, considerably skeptical as to the success of the brilliant schemes he had hinted at during our brief conversation. Fortunes in shark-fins, in sea slugs, in Kashmir leather, in seals, and salt, and heaven knows what else besides. He would have done better, I felt sure, to stick to the *Mary Willard* and honest freight, though Turnwell had qualities which might prove useful to some one. Honest, no doubt, with those eyes; would make a good subordinate, providing no chance was given to develop that dangerous initiative of his.

My interest in Turnwell, I may add, was not entirely disinterested. I should never have thought of him, had it not been for that chance meeting; but there were circumstances in view of which the reappearance of the former sea captain might be regarded as a happy coincidence. A seaman, an English citizen, living in Bombay, speaking French. . . . He could eventually be of use to me. And Turnwell needed money—if not just then, later on, certainly I could be useful to him.

And precisely at that time, I was contemplating a trip to Bombay. For weeks, my new boat rode in the harbor of Obok while I hesitated, undecided to what use to put her. Her construction had run me heavily in debt. I longed to free myself at a stroke; in addition I hankered after freight more inspiring and profitable than carrying coal oil to Doubaba or pilgrims to Mecca. The days of the blockade were over. I was restless. The stamp left by the smuggler's trade is, they say, indelible. I remember meeting an old gentleman at Sète, white haired and respectable, who confided (he had spent his youth in the alcohol contraband with Spain) that even to-day, when neither poverty nor the prospect of gain furnished a pretext (when the franc fell, Spanish liquors became higher-priced than French), occasionally he received a small shipment in contraband for the sheer joy of wading through the salt marshes on a moonless night with a keg of *anisette* on his shoulder! It may have been like that with me: trade with the Arab coast seemed singularly pale, once the blockade ceased. I thought of trying a hashish venture again, and made a flying trip to Alexandria to offer my services to Volikis. But he discouraged me. In Greece, the efforts of the League of Nations had all but stamped out hashish cultivation. Turkey, Roumania, and principally Syria, furnished practically all the hashish received in Egypt. And both Volikis and the Syndicate had agents and underground routes established, sufficient to control the hashish output of the three countries. I was already halfway down the marble stairway, when Volikis called me back.

"There might be a chance for you further East, now that I think of it. We get a drug which can be utilized to manufacture hashish, in small amounts, brought by sailors on the British liners. All I know about it is that they buy it on the open market in India. In Bombay, I believe. If you cared to look into the matter, it might be interesting for all of us. For my part, I would gladly put at your disposal a small sum for eventual purchases in case . . ."

I asked nothing better—India—it suited my purposes far better than Greece, since it meant crossing the Indian Ocean. I longed to sail in new waters. The *Altaïr*, I felt confident, could navigate in any sea. I had already prepared my new boat for her first long voyage, when chance had brought me face to face with Turnwell. I accepted the meeting as a good omen, and ten days later swung the *Altaïr* around the reef at Obok, headed east for India.

Aden—Bombay. We had the mountains of Arabia, ragged and black, on our left, a steep wall against which the swell of the Indian Ocean, piled high by the summer monsoon, crashed in immense breakers thirty to forty feet high. Two miles out, it rumbled like ceaseless thunder. For days, there was almost no wind, only the constant swell that set us wallowing madly, ripped the sails, and all but wrenched the yards from the masts and the masts from their sockets. We pounded ahead with the motor and the *fortune carré*, the only sail which resisted the terrific rolling.

Three days out from Aden, we touched at Bender Broom, a wind-swept bay with the town piled in a narrow cleft in the mountainside. Twenty boutres lay at anchor in the harbor, big fellows, four and five hundred tons, from Aden and the Persian Gulf, their masts horizontal, waiting for the monsoon to end. Most of them carried dates, making one trip a year with the wind astern: from Aden to the Persian Gulf in August, with the western monsoon; and back again in November with the monsoon from the east.

We halted only long enough to adjust a new glass to the compass which Abdi had smashed the first night out, flung over the tiller headforemost on the instrument, by a sudden dip of the boutre.

Then for a week we had calm, fitful winds, and fog; always the eternal seesaw of the swell, and on our left, the heavy thunder of surf. Once at midnight, as we lay in a dead calm in water too deep to permit anchoring, the shore currents sent us drifting in towards land. We made out the line of breakers in the moonlight, before the motor (it took an interminable time to heat it) began its reassuring thump-thump. I had planned to stop for water at Bender Hassik, fifteen miles farther along the coast, but that experience, combined with a fog that blew down from the mountains, encouraged me to abandon the Arab coast and steer for the islands of Kuria Muria.

We anchored in a narrow inlet at the eastern end of the largest island of the four; a cluster of ragged peaks, 1,500 feet high. The "well," indicated by the chart, proved to be a hole choked with gravel and sand on the edge of a little beach strewn with bales which I discovered to my astonishment contained cakes of rubber, still elastic. Debris from a freighter wrecked off the islands twenty years before. During the war, the same inlet served as shelter for a German submarine which in the space of four months torpedoed twenty-three British ships, one of which, a big liner, went down within three cable-lengths from the island. At low tide, we saw its two chimneys reaching just above the surface of the sea.

All this, I learned from the islanders: five Arab fishers and their families, who sold their catch salted and dried to boutres that came from Arabia several times a year. On the bare block of granite, cut by erosion in deep ravines, and honey-combed with caves, not an ounce of black earth, not a blade of grass. In one of the ravines, we found the "homes" of the fishers, each family installed in a rock-shelter like those of the prehistoric cave men. A heap of fish bones several feet high marked the entrance of each dwelling, like the nests of certain sea birds, visible at a distance because of the piles of detritus.

From the Archipelago of Kuria Muria, 960 miles of

open sea lay before us before reaching Bombay. We made the run in a week, rolling incessantly in the trough of the sea. On the afternoon of the seventh day, we sighted the Indian coast. Approaching nearer, I made out the red roofs of the city, and the harbor—a forest of cranes and masts sticking up through the fog. At five o'clock we rounded Prong Reef with its lighthouse; and cast anchor for the night behind the Sim Rock Light.

Early the next morning, I headed the *Altaïr* into the yellow waters of the harbor. To my surprise, a government launch darted towards us, dancing in the waves of the immense estuary. A voice called in English: "Are you the *Altaïr?*" My affirmative called forth other phases in English which I interpreted, more from the gestures that accompanied them than the words, as instructions telling us where to anchor. Though I failed utterly to understand, I followed my common sense, steering the *Altaïr* towards a part of the harbor where I saw other boutres lying at anchor.

Before noon, I received the visit of the port authorities, the quarantine and the customs. My lack of English prevented me from discovering how they had learned the name of my boutre. I took it for granted that the information had been furnished by the government of Aden. However, I encountered no difficulties. The customs inspectors politely offered their launch to take me ashore, and escorted me to a cab; my first step being to call on the French consul and secure the services of an interpreter.

A long drive along what seemed miles of docks, heaped with coal, scrap iron, and merchandise of all sorts, through streets of black mud encumbered with oxcarts. The European quarter: houses of black stone bristling with turrets and cupolas: the Victoria station like a ca-

thedral, and green gardens with thousands of crows wheeling and croaking above the trees. At last the consulate,
marked by a modest placard dangling askew in a window.
In the corridor, I collided smartly with a fat man in his
shirt-sleeves.

"Who-are-you-what-do-you-want? I suppose-you-are-
from-the-City-of-Paris?" he shouted over his shoulder, as
he made for a door at the end of the corridor.

"I would like to speak to the consul or . . ."

"*C'est moi le Consul*," he threw from the doorway, still
shouting. "I have no time. I am on my way to lunch. A
consul eats lunch, you know. Tell your story to my secretary."

The secretary, like all secretaries of all European con-
sulates in the countries of the Orient, was a native, a dignified Hindu of sixty or over, soft-voiced and suave. He
motioned me to a seat, listened absently as I talked, examining the while the nail of his little finger, incredibly
long. I had not finished before the consul bounced in again,
slamming the door behind him, still in his shirt-sleeves;
though for comfort, he had unbuttoned the belt of his
trousers.

"An interpreter? I have just the person for you. Our
Dubash will attend to everything, provisions, customs, insurance; you won't have to lift a finger." Without giving
me a chance to put in a word, the energetic representative
of France dashed from the office to return in a moment
with a little old man, in a black oilcloth hat and a long
frock coat, a Parsee, in speaking with whom, even the
consul had to lift his voice above its normal volume, for
he was deaf as a pot.

After a fruitless and fatiguing afternoon with my elderly interpreter (with whom I had more difficulty in com-

municating than with the Englishmen whose offices we visited), I dismissed the old gentleman with my blessing and a generous *baksheesh*, and decided to look up my friend Captain Turnwell.

The address he had given me—Remington Road—I found in a suburban quarter of ugly little bungalows, each with its pocket-handkerchief garden. In one of the bungalows, an exact duplicate of its neighbors except that it boasted a dooryard littered with all manner of broken pots and odds and ends of furniture, I found an old lady whose appearance coincided with what the dooryard had led me to expect. She answered my questions in creole French (Turnwell had told me his mother was a Maurician) regretting that her son had left Bombay for Goa several weeks before. I was about to take my departure when a neat old Englishman with eyeglasses, carrying a yellow valise, entered the room, looking distinctly out of place in the indescribable disorder of the little house. Mr. Turnwell, senior, was delighted, very, to make the acquaintance of any friend of his son the Captain (he stressed the word). He had just received word from him; within two weeks he would return to Bombay. In the meantime would I remain to dinner? Their poor house was at my disposal. I shamelessly admit that it was the poor house, infinitely less alluring than a Somali hut, which led me to refuse the hospitality so generously offered. Then I would take a cigar? Turnwell senior unlatched the valise, extracting a ragged cigar from an amazing welter of odds and ends— old newspapers, bits of brass, a china cup and a photograph—after which he shut the bag with care as if it contained a treasure. I accepted the cigar; with a handshake as cordial as I knew how to make it, I took my leave

of the strange couple, promising not to leave Bombay
without returning to see them.

It took ten days in the "City-without-a-soul," days
spent wandering through the mud of Prince's Docks,
through the mud of a labyrinth of streets, to all appearances nameless and numberless, and countless struggles
with a series of *dubash*, before I succeeded in discovering
a few general facts about the merchandise I had come to
buy.

In India, *charas* is eaten, not smoked. The native population consumes large quantities yearly, but the drug is
not produced locally. It is imported either as Charas, the
manufactured product, or Gangia, dried hemp leaves from
Chinese Turkestan. As in the case of opium, the imperial
government monopolizes the retail trade. Wholesale dealers import the drug from the north of the Himalayas,
selling it to the government which regulates its distribution throughout the empire. Charas like opium, I was told,
could be bought on the open market in quantities not ex-
ceeding ten grams. A larger amount, it appeared, would
have to be bought directly from the state.

While waiting for an export permit, which I had
charged the French consul to apply for in my name, I
decided to call on the Collector of Customs. For a wonder I found the gentleman in his office. I waited, my
dubash at my elbow, in an immense corridor, its walls
glistening with white tiles like an enormous bathroom,
while an impressive series of chevroned officers went in
and out through the swinging doors of the great man's
study, summoned and dismissed to the imperious buzzing
of a bell. Finally a turbaned Indian walked past, bearing
an empty tea tray; our turn had come to pass through

the swinging doors. Behind an immense desk, bare of all papers and glistening dark red like a pool at sunset, sat an immaculate gentleman, bald, blond and spectacled, who listened with an air of boredom to my explanations and after a long silence, his gaze vague behind his eyeglasses, remarked wearily that he had nothing to do with such matters; he referred me to the Excise Department. It was installed in a much less palatial structure, the former Customs House, a dingy eighteenth century structure, crowded with shoals of native clerks, banked behind inky desks like rows of schoolboys.

As usual, the English official was absent. In his place, we saw the invariable assistant, an impressive Hindu, very black, wearing a European business suit, with high starched collar and gold cuff buttons. I could only purchase charas, he told me, on payment of the retail consumer's tax, which raised the price of the drug six times above its original cost. I protested I saw no reason why I should pay a local consumer's tax on goods meant for exportation. The functionary favored me with a superior smile.

"That is the law, dear sir," he articulated precisely, and bowed me out of the office, having first presented me with a sample of charas from the state storehouses.

Back to the *Altaïr* through a pelting rain that transformed the streets leading to the dock into rivers of black mud, I found the crew shivering in the forecastle, huddled about a fire, as on the rare rainy days in their far-away desert. I shut myself in my cabin before a crackling flame of driftwood, I too regretting the dry *kamsin* and the flaming sun.

That night, I made my first and last experience with

charas. Curious as to the quality of the Indian drug, I bit off a piece of the sample I had just received. In Greece they had told me that only a dose of several grams (about the size of a hazelnut) produced any effect. I compromised on a morsel about the size of a lentil. An hour passed with no result whatsoever from the dose; I thought no more about it, and went to bed.

Towards three in the morning, I awoke with a nightmare sensation that I was dying. In the light of the swinging lamp, the cabin seemed distorted. I had the impression that the ceiling lay beneath my bunk and that all the objects in the room were piled in a pyramid before my eyes. I struggled to rise, but I was powerless to stir; my bones had melted into a jelly-like mass of muscles. Rapidly the objects about me lost their identity, resolved into geometric figures that tumbled and stretched rubber-like, ceaselessly changing in form and color. I felt as if my brain had split in two parts; one was going mad, and the other reduced to a rôle of spectator. I noted the progress of the intoxication, powerless to intervene. An icy chill crept gradually up my arms and legs. This, I thought, must be the end. At that moment, I felt rather than saw a vague movement in the cabin. It was Youssof, one of my sailors, come to put wood on the fire. I managed to articulate:

"Boon" (coffee).

The strangled tone alarmed the boy; he ran to bring Abdi. Between the two of them, they managed to pour down my throat a few spoonfuls of hot coffee. Instantly, in a violent spasm of nausea, I vomited the bit of charas I had swallowed. An hour later, I was myself again, though weak and dizzy from the experience.

That morning as I stepped out of my cabin into another day of black fog and rain, a motor boat sputtered around our stern.

"*Altaïr*, ahoy! Is the captain aboard?"

It was Turnwell, just in from Goa, jubilant with a boat of his own. "A schooner, formerly the yacht of the German Emperor. A little beauty and dirt cheap." Nothing would do but I should accompany him straightway to inspect the treasure.

She was a great lady and no mistake; dazzling with white paint and shining brasses. My *Altaïr* looked like a Somali girl from the bush in comparison. But that Somali girl had sinew and bone beneath her sunburnt hide; while the paint of Turnwell's "lady" masked, I suspected, a good many things that it was to some one's interest to ignore (which I suppose is the purpose of most of the paint that walks the world and the half-world). I felt astonished that Turnwell, who after all was not an amateur yachtsman, should set such store in the external trimness of his new craft, until all of a sudden I remembered that amazing home of his in the Bombay suburb.

He was all enthusiasm, poor fellow, so full of schemes and so confident in his chance of making a fortune overnight in sharks' fins, *nacre*, and transporting pilgrims to Goa, that I thought it well to keep my own plans in the background. I told him simply that I had been buying charas. He knew of it vaguely, "one of those things the natives eat." When I explained my difficulty in the matter of export tariffs, he manifested a friendly indignation.

That *was* a shame, he agreed, but he thought he might be able to fix things up for me. He had an old friend in the Excise Department, a Portuguese from Goa. They had been lieutenants in the Coast Guard together. It was de Souza who had taught him the salt game.

"The salt game? Oh, it is an old trick of the Coast Guard. You see, we got a premium every time we caught a native smuggling salt. They're a sly lot, those smugglers; slip through your fingers like butter, so premiums would run scarce, if you didn't help the business along."

"? ? ?"

"Oh, it was no trick at all. When you saw a boat beached with all the crew off fishing, you sent a sailor ashore with a bag of salt. And then you made a 'capture' in fine style. Lord, they were surprised, the devils, and mighty glad to get off with a fine of ten rupees!" Turnwell went off into peals of ungainly laughter. Something in my expression must have troubled him, however, for he ceased abruptly.

"They all smuggle salt, you know," he excused hastily, "so it really didn't matter. Besides, all the natives were on to the game. They knew it meant ten rupees; afterwards when you caught the same fellows with a *bona fide* load of salt, well, it didn't cost them any more." He eyed me uneasily.

"It *was* a rotten business, rather. But all the coast guards practiced it; every newcomer had to follow suit or they would have taken you for a prig. Though I felt the way you do about it, and in the end," Turnwell lied virtuously, "it was one of the reasons I left the service."

"And de Souza too?" I suggested.

"Oh, there is no one like de Souza. He is the man to help you out," Turnwell insisted, choosing to ignore my question.

I was not so sure. . . . The "salt game" had left me "dreamy," as the French say. But I saw no reason for refusing the offered aid, providing the intervention of the

Portuguese did not come too high. Accordingly the next morning we called on Turnwell's ex-comrade, a sleek little man whose manner did not suggest success, it screamed it.

"Delighted to be of service to a friend of Turnwell's," he assured me briskly. "A small matter of no importance, really, a mere formality."

In twenty-four hours the energetic young official had secured me a permit to buy and export 500 seers of charas.

"But you will have to go to the frontier to get it," he explained, "to the government storehouse at Hosherpour."

Before tendering me the permit, he wrote across one corner in red ink: "Duty paid."

"You will find that as good as the governor's signature," he remarked modestly, adding without transition, "You have undoubtedly planned to give Turnwell a commission." That, in a poor-devil-he-needs-it tone, adding without giving me a chance to assent or object, "Five hundred rupees, that is to say, one rupee per seer, seems to me a reasonable figure."

His solicitude for Turnwell was touching. I agreed to the reasonableness of the commission, but dropped casually that I would reserve payment until I had the merchandise on board ship for Djibouti.

That night I took the Punjab Mail for Hosherpour, a nightmare of heat and discomfort, despite the comfortable accommodations of the train. On my arrival, after a brief pause in an immaculate and spacious dak-bungalow, I lost no time in calling on Ram-Rai, an Indian merchant, one of the chief importers of charas.

He took me in his carriage to the Excise warehouse in which the drug is deposited as soon as it arrives by caravan. The "charas prison"—it had every appearance of a jail—was surrounded by high walls. A sentinel stood at the barred gate which he unlocked to let us pass and bolted again behind us. Within the court stood a massive building, windowless except for the customary "half-moons" of tropical prisons. A turnkey led us to a door closed with two padlocks. The owner of the charas possessed the key to one of these; the turnkey, that of the other.

The door opened on a cell, nine feet by twelve, aired by two half-moons placed on opposite walls. The imprisoned drug lay stocked on a row of shelves, wrapped in a double envelope of goatskin, blackened and greasy from the long journey over the mountains. The thickness of the two hides (the hairy sides turned inwards) served to isolate the charas from heat and dampness. That particular stock, Ram-Rai told me, represented three successive crops of hemp, an important factor for the Indian purchaser, as the state tax diminished with the increasing age of the drug.

We ripped open the bales, filled with what might have been taken for cakes of dried cow dung, and I made my selection: 500 seers which were weighed and repacked for shipment. Then came the question of taxes. I brought out de Souza's document, which somewhat to my surprise failed to produce the anticipated effect. The Indian inspector who presided over the weighing and packing of the drug, explained with elaborate precision that the permit authorized me to export 500 seers of charas, "duty paid." That meant, according to him, *when* the duty had been paid! I had merely to make over the sum to take possession of the merchandise. I expostulated, insisted that there must be some misunderstanding, and that I preferred to postpone the payment until my return to Bombay. The customs employee turned a deaf ear.

"Had I already paid the duty?" he inquired politely. "No."

"Then I had only to disburse the amount then and there, ten thousand rupees cash down. . . .

We seemed to have reached a deadlock, when a voice whispered in my ear: "Twenty rupees . . . and leave it to me. . . ." I returned to the dak-bungalow; a few minutes later, Ram-Rai rejoined me with a shipping-permit.

From then on, I had no more difficulties. I and my charas made the return journey to Bombay with the Punjab Mail, another matter easily arranged by the judicious distribution of a few rupees to the train crew. Here as elsewhere, the money was neither given nor accepted as bribery, merely a "just recompense" for additional effort on my behalf. . . .

In Bombay, my first object was to get the *Altaïr* out of the port as soon as possible. Procuring clearing papers, I discovered, was no simple matter; it necessitated the services of some one acquainted with the scribes and under-lings of half a dozen offices. Luckily for foreign captains, there exist specialists in such matters, the ever versatile *dubash*.

At the outset, the customs required me to furnish a ton-nage certificate. I possessed nothing of the sort; to pro-cure one would have taken two weeks of formalities. An impossible prospect.

"Pay what you have to, but get our clearing papers to-day," I admonished the *dubash*. I spoke in French, but evidently the Indian clerk divined the meaning. On the spot he proposed his services. He himself would accom-pany the *dubash* to take the necessary measures. I need have no anxiety whatsoever. . . . Leaving the two, I went on board the *Altaïr*; in a couple of hours, the *dubash* ar-

rived rubbing his hands with satisfaction. All difficulties
had been smoothed over: the *Altaïr* was free to leave for
Africa.

The port of Bombay, I learned later, has a very special
reputation among seamen. Perhaps it is no more corrupt
than other ports, but its ill name has received more publicity. I venture to state that you could pass an elephant
through the Bombay customs without leaving a trace anywhere! And at no great expense either; a dozen rupees, I
imagine, would suffice. The explanation, I believe, touches
a basic fault of the British administration in the East or
Near East. The titulary of an office (it may be consulate,
customs, railroads, or mails) is an Englishman—a distinguished gentleman, whose integrity is above all suspicion—who plays golf, or polo, attends teas, and is a
delightful host and a charming dinner guest. But he does
not know all that goes on in his office, in which the actual
routine is left to a native or a Levantine. A convenient
system from two angles. From the point of view of the
layman, the petty business operations which in the French
colonies, for instance, involve him in tangles of red tape,
in the British dominions he can expedite for an insignificant sum—a rupee or two or a few piasters. While from
the point of view of the high administration, in case of an
open scandal the native or the Levantine is pitilessly sacrificed and British prestige left unsullied. I have often wondered whether the rulers of India and the protectors of
Arabia and Egypt realize to what extent their administration is corrupt. Personally, I—as well as many others
—have found its corruption convenient. For that reason,
I ought to forbear to criticize.

The return journey of the *Altaïr* differed little from the
trip out. After five days in the trough of the sea, we made

the islands of Kuria Muria, shipping water like a sieve, for we were too heavily loaded. (I carried fifteen tons of coal oil on deck for a merchant of Djibouti.) From that point, skirting the Arab coast, we passed in view of Dihert, its sardine-fleet dotting the sea for miles around, and noisome with the stench of its fish oil trenches. We reached Makalla, our last stop before Djibouti, late one night after the moon had set. The bay lay calm and black beneath the barrier of mountains whose summits bit into the sky far overhead. Slowly the horizon grew pale; asses brayed; cocks crowed; the call to prayer sounded from a half a dozen mosques; and suddenly the town showed white, clinging to the cliff like the cells of a wasp's-nest. I started the motor and swung the *Altaïr* across the bay towards the wharf on which a crowd had gathered to see the boutre which advanced without a sail. Several greeted me by name, Arabs whom I had met during my journeys in the Red Sea or along the coast of Yemen. As I wore European dress, I heard them explain in discreet undertones, "*Hoowa Muslim*" (He is a Moslem). At that, the children ceased to run at my heels and the groups of men stepped aside with murmured *salaams* as I passed. Among them, I recognized a *nakhoda* from Djibouti.

"*Salaam alaicum*, Abou Khabil. *Kev al Khabar?*" (What news?)

"All is well with mine; and with yours likewise. All well, *Hamdullillah. Lakin* (only) . . . your three boutres are at the bottom of the sea."

I stared at him speechless. My three boutres, the *Sahala*, the *Fat el Rhaman*, and a third little sambuk I had recently purchased. All three. The news staggered me. Then suddenly I remembered. I had left Djebber-the-Chakaba in charge.

The sinking of the three boats, as I learned on reaching
Djibouti, had taken place in a most singular and un-
precedented fashion. As if some demon of the sea had
taken a malign joy in singling out precisely those three
to serve as scapegoats for the dozens of other boutres that
lay in the waters of Dahalak. I had the story from Kassim,
after Abdi, the most intelligent and trustworthy of my
Somali crew.

Shortly before leaving for Bombay, I had sent my little
fleet into the Red Sea to fish for pearls and *nacre* in the
Dahalak Islands. On the morning of the fifteenth of
August, the boats lay at anchor off Moghaida Island. The
crew had lowered the houris. One gang of divers was already overboard; the second group prepared to follow,
when the men noticed a dense black cloud gathered as if
by magic on the northern horizon. It mounted rapidly,
shot rapidly through and through with lightning; and in
a few minutes covered the entire heaven.

Every Somali understood that something serious was
about to take place. In that respect, the native, like the
animals, seems possessed of an instinct that warns him
when something threatens to upset the customary equilib-
rium of natural forces. The men hauled up the divers, put
down all the anchors and waited. Suddenly the wind
dropped. Not a breath of air. A strange twilight spread
over the water. Beneath the black sky, the sea began to
behave strangely—lifting and falling in cone-shaped waves
which the unearthly light streaked green and black. From
all the boutres anchored near the island rose a confusion
of cries.

Suddenly all saw, several miles away, a terrifying Something hung in the sky at a tremendous height. Like an
enormous canopy supported by a single gigantic pillar.

Divers at Work

The crew lunches

At each flash of lightning, it showed black against a livid ground. It neared with incredible swiftness. From the deck of the *Fat el Rhaman,* the terrified Somalis watched the column of water rush towards them with the roar of a winter flood; its base in a whirlpool sixty feet in diameter, bordered with foam.

When no doubt remained that the *Fat el Rhaman* lay in the path of the waterspout, the crew leaped overboard, swimming for their lives to the second boutre. A few moments later, the boat they had left disappeared in the whirlpool. As the spout continued its route towards the south, the terrified crews began to breathe freely again, when to their horror, they saw the great column describe a semicircle and turn towards them again, headed this time for the *Sahala.* "Like a living thing with eyes, hunting a prey," Kassim described the phenomenon. On the two boutres there was a moment of desperate panic. Screaming with terror, the men huddled on the deck as if hypnotized, incapable of making a movement. By that time, it had grown completely dark. As the spout approached, the crews heard in its roar the laughter of *chaëtans* and saw in the boiling whirlpool, apocalyptic monsters. One of the divers fainted; another gesticulated madly, shouting desperate exorcisms. In a moment the spout was upon them; tons of water crashed on the deck of the *Sahala,* and men and boat disappeared in the maelstrom. A few seconds later, the waterspout sank the remaining boutre, and swept on towards the south.

Little by little, it grew light again; at first a greenish submarine glow, and finally broad day. Of the three crews, only one man was missing; the diver who had fainted. The rest, though half-drowned, were otherwise unharmed. Of the three boats, no trace; their ballast had taken them to the bottom. With the aid of the three houris which they found floating on the surface, the crews reached the nearest pearl-boutres two miles distant. A *nakhoda* agreed to carry the men to Massawa, but all refused to help them salvage the sunken boutres. So that when the crews returned a week later to see what might be done to bring the wrecked boats to the surface (they had sunk in twelve to sixteen feet of water) they found only the stone ballast. The boutres themselves had completely disappeared. Had I returned sooner, it might have been possible to follow up the theft. As it was, I could devote no time to the quest of the stolen boutres. The *Altaïr's* precious cargo had still to be delivered. According to my men, the cyclone had done me one good turn. True, I had lost my pearl-fleet, but the waterspout had cost the life of Djebber-the-Chakhaba, the trouble-bringer. . . .

"Now you may leave in peace, Abd el Hai," Kassim assured me soberly. "You will have no more ill-luck."

XVIII

Fighting the Drug Ring: the Great Charas

Grow hemp myself. Why not?

During my trip to Greece, the idea first occurred to me. I came near suggesting it to Volikis when I learned that Greek hashish had vanished from the market. But the experiment with Indian charas drove the thought temporarily out of my head. Volikis, who expressed great satisfaction at the results of my Bombay trip, urged me to repeat the venture on a larger scale. I did not share his enthusiasm. The trip to Bombay, when I looked back on it, took on the proportions of a nightmare. The thought of returning, of traveling indefinitely shuttlewise from the Himalayas to Suez, the endless formalities, the shady interventions of de Souza, the journey itself—the battle with the monsoon and the tedious weeks of tossing in the swell of the Indian Ocean—all inspired a distinct aversion.

Not that I had grown weary of the sea. It was no doubt the fatigue that comes after a long period of effort. I longed for a respite—for an interval of peace. The instinct that years before had incited me to dream of a villa by the Mediterranean, made itself felt again. The old instinct to settle down somewhere in peace in prevision of a tranquil old age. . . .

Why not grow hemp myself? Not for Egypt necessarily. Better still for India; a vaster market. Compete with Chinese charas and have done with contraband. The idea did not appear preposterous.

The logical country for a hemp plantation, in view of
the ultimate market, was Abyssinia. The high plateau of
Harrar seemed well adapted for the experiment. I saw no
reason why Indian hemp-cultivaitng should not become a
source of wealth for the country. Hemp-fiber for local
rope manufacture and hemp leaves for export. Charas
itself would represent no danger for the native population.
The Abyssinian by nature has sober tastes; his religion
forbids all drugs, alcohol and tobacco included. The Galla
already has his narcotic, the tender shoots of *kat*. Besides,
I did not intend to manufacture charas but to export
gangia, the dried hemp leaves. But it would be several
years before I could count on my hemp plantations pro-
ducing a high-grade quality of gangia. To put Abyssinian
gangia on the market immediately, the best method, I felt,
was to mix with the dried hemp leaves a certain quantity
of powdered charas. That meant making one more purchase of Indian charas. To avoid the export tax, without
the assistance of de Souza and his kind, I resolved to buy
the drug in Chinese Turkestan and send it across India in
transit. If I succeeded in procuring a sufficient quantity of
charas, I would not be obliged to repeat the purchase. I
had no desire to spend several months yearly between
Bombay and Hosherpour steering charas through the
labyrinth of the Indian customs.

Volikis listened skeptically when I broached the plan.

"I have no doubt you would succeed, if you had only
yourself to count with. But people"—he emphasized the
word, his eyes tightening into slits—"have already begun
to know about you, my dear Abd el Hai. You have become
a serious competitor. And with your Abyssinian scheme,
my dear fellow," he dropped into an English drawl that
suited ill his Levantine elegance, "you have no idea what

antagonisms you are bound to arouse. Better stick to
Indian charas. Otherwise, take my word for it, you will
stir up a hornet's nest."

All of which implied that my principal customer, always
prudent, would risk no funds on that particular scheme.
I decided to say no more about it and go ahead with my
hemp plantations. I was willing to risk all I owned on the
venture, and the mysterious allusions to antagonisms and
hornets' nests merely added fuel to my enthusiasm.

I sent to France for selected hemp-seed of the Indian
species and went ahead with my plans. As a preliminary
measure, I arranged with one of my former associates in
Abyssinia to start an experiment station. Then I applied
to the Ethopian government for permission to import six
tons of charas, to be stored and employed on my plantations.

And so I embarked on my last and most important
charas venture. *The* charas adventure, I might well call it.
An affair that occupied and preoccupied nearly a year of
my life, that was to set the diplomatic agents of three
governments in action, keep the telegraph wires of half
the world humming for months, and bring me into a twilight region of intrigue whose existence I had not suspected
outside the world of movies and melodrama. It was as if I
had ripped off the lid from a seething underworld of greed
and envy. A hornet's nest—it was a miniature volcano I
set in action, and not so miniature at that! Volikis was
right, a thousand times more so than I had dreamed.

The story of the great charas began with a business letter addressed to Edwin Turnwell, captain of the schooner
Evelyn, Bombay. Would he be willing to act as my agent
in a new purchase of charas? Six tons to be bought in
Chinese Turkestan, if possible, and sent across India in

transit. Acting as my agent, would he make the preliminary investigations and obtain the necessary permits, *bona
fide* permits (I underscored) for its transport across the
British dominions. I could guarantee a large commission.

The answer arrived by telegraph. "*Accepte. Enchanté.*"
I could almost hear Turnwell jubilate over the wires. In
time came a letter. As I anticipated, he had been having
trouble with that boat of his. She had developed a mysterious ailment and was in dry dock; something had gone
wrong with the keel and the engines. "I am beginning to
think she wasn't as good a bargain as I first believed,"
her proprietor regretted naïvely. But that misfortune had
not blunted his enthusiasm. He had already thought up
another scheme for making a fortune, an affair of coco-
nuts in the Locadive Islands, a "sure thing," provided I
would furnish the necessary capital and the ship. "Though,
of course," Turnwell explained with characteristic caution, "the first trip, you understand, would be a risk; I
have no reason for doubting the information I had just
given you, but there is always a chance that the reality
may not turn out as brilliant as one hopes beforehand."
Poor Turnwell. I replied by cable, "Concentrate efforts
on charas."

That admonition produced the desired effect. Two
months later, Turnwell forwarded me a copy of a permit
obtained from the collector of Bombay, authorizing the
importation through Leh in Ladakh and the transport
from Srinagar to Bombay of 6,000 seers of charas.

Turnwell offered to undertake the trip to make the
purchase. I had no objection. With strict instructions, I
felt there would be little chance of his making many blun-
ders on the way. "I think I have foreseen all the obstacles
of the route," he wrote me. "The only detail that worries

me is this. If, when the charas reaches Bombay, there is
no ship in the port to receive it, it will have to be deposited
in the government warehouse; and that, you understand,
would be fatal." Fatal was perhaps exaggerated, but I
understood what Turnwell meant. Once the charas in the
grip of the customs, it would mean papers and somebody's
signature to get it out again. And given the very "special"
nature of the goods, undoubtedly there would be some
one—perhaps several "some ones"—to hold up the goods
in the hope of *baksheesh*.

That however would not constitute a serious danger;
what I feared more was that one underling's desire for
baksheesh might carry the matter into the upper regions
where blow winds of governmental policy. To be sure I
had a permit with all the official stamps and seals, but you
can neve.· tell when you raise a hare of that sort where it
is going to take you. There are so many ways of interpreting a law. . . . Turnwell's method of dodging the ob-
stacle was as usual; simple, direct and . . . transparent.
"The best plan, it seems to me, would be to buy the
schooner *Southern Cross* (a splendid little ship; I have
looked her over carefully), now for sale in the harbor. In
fact I am so sure that you will agree with me that I have
contracted to buy her at the end of the month."

That letter removed any doubts I might have felt concerning the advisability of a trip to Bombay. I had just
formulated an energetic message to send over the wires
when I received a cable:

"Your presence here imperative. Come immediately.
Urgent. Turnwell."

That night I left on the *Altaïr* for Aden, and four days
later, via a P. & O. liner, I landed in Bombay. Turnwell
was on the dock, waving his arms like a disjointed wind-

mill. His round eyes popped with excitement. I could see he was literally bursting with news.

"Well, Turnwell, what is the matter now?" The question seemed to startle him. He gripped my arm above the elbow and flinging a nervous glance to right and left, towards the groups of homecoming colonials proceeding imperturbably down the pier amid shoals of baggage, murmured through his teeth in a melodramatic tone, though scarcely audible:

"Not here, this is no place; wait, later."

As our cab bumped over the uneven pavement, he sat looking mysterious, his lips pressed together, like a small boy with a secret; as if fearing that if he opened them, it would spill over. We drew up at last before the little bungalow in the suburbs, with which I was already acquainted. Nothing had changed there since my previous visit, unless the dooryard was, if possible, even more littered and dirty. As he hurried me through a hall towards the rear of the house, I had a rapid vision of the old creole in an untidy wrapper, and the elderly gentleman in his shirt sleeves bent over a table on which lay spread what looked like a collection of doorknobs.

Turnwell's room stood like an oasis in that unspeakable cottage. I have no distinct recollection of it, except that it was quiet and in order. He shut the door carefully behind us, motioned me to a chair by the window and took a seat opposite me. He was beaming with importance.

"Man, that charas of yours. It is a fortune!" he burst out. "Do you know, you can sell it here in Bombay for ten pounds sterling a seer!" He leaned back in his chair to note the effect of the bomb. His joy in the discovery was so sincere, that I hesitated to dampen it. For in one sense he *had* made a discovery, which I was curious to fathom.

"You don't say!" I murmured, trying to look as astonished as possible before the question which interested me primarily. "Sell it . . . to whom?"

"Oh, that is a long story." Turnwell settled himself in his chair. "But to begin with, have you ever heard about hashish? They get it from charas, you know. In Egypt, they eat—smoke, I mean, tons of it. Smuggled into the country, it is worth its weight of gold!"

Something in the tone of that last remark of his, a certain excited glitter of his round eyes, affected me disagreeably. I began to regret not having taken Turnwell more fully into my confidence. But where had he acquired his information? "Who told you, and how—?" I started to question. He did not let me finish.

"As I said, it is quite a story," he broke in importantly. "A couple of weeks ago, a Greek came to see me. He said his name was Paleologus—or Logopoulos. Anyhow it doesn't matter. He wanted to know how to buy charas wholesale, by the ton. Explained that one of the retail dealers had sent him to me. Said he had plenty of capital and wanted to buy right away. I smelled a commission, so I made matters out as hard as possible. I played up the government monopoly, the difficulties of getting a permit, and the necessity of having some one with influence to take the matter in hand. I didn't propose myself outright, but intimated tactfully I was the man."

I could picture Turnwell's tactful hints.

"Did he give you a contract?"

"Our conversation didn't progress that far. But I was careful not to give him too much free information. He said he would think things over, and that I would hear from him again."

"And you did?"

"Not directly. Two or three days later, another stranger called at the house. This time it wasn't a Greek but an Arab. A handsome chap, very well dressed, with diamonds and a pearl tie-pin: he was staying at the 'Taj Mahal.' From him I learned about hashish. Though he didn't mention Egypt, he represented a group of capitalists, so he said. His idea was to buy an important stock of charas. He didn't know where nor how; he supposed that some one—me, for instance, could look after that end of the business and get it out of the country in contraband, so as to avoid the tax. He thought we might smuggle the charas aboard European liners; they stay in the port a week or two, you know. He said he had men on all the boats. But in case that scheme didn't prove practical, his group or corporation or whatever it was, could send one of their own boats here on purpose, or if need be, they could charter or buy a boat here in Bombay. At that point I began to take a special interest in the conversation. I told him he ought to buy the *Southern Cross* and I made him a proposition on the spot: me, as captain and agent, with a 'straw man' here in Bombay to represent us. Money meant nothing to that Arab. He talked commissions and bonuses until my head swam. He was willing, he stated, to sink a fortune in charas. He went away, saying he would put the matter up to his firm. That night, I don't think I slept at all. And then—"

Turnwell stopped impressively and puffed at a cigarette he had forgotten to light. Until that point he had scarcely paused for breath, stumbling over the words in his haste to reach the climax of the story. He looked even more boyish than usual, his cheeks stained dark red with excitement and his eyes between their colorless lashes opened so wide that a white ring showed all around the blue pupils.

It was clear he felt himself living an adventure such as he had never dreamed of. For my part I begun to discern a definite background to the story, and I waited for his conclusion with considerable impatience.

"And then," Turnwell took up the thread of the narrative, "I received a third visit. An Englishman. Oh, a gentleman. Here you have his name." He handed me the bit of cardboard, neatly engraved.

Leonard W. T. Ashby, Esq.

"He sent up his card one evening about seven," Turnwell went on. "Apologized for the hour, but said he had just arrived in Bombay and did not want to waste a minute before seeing me. Would I give him the pleasure of dining with him? Afterwards we could talk business. Though he didn't say so, I understood that it was charas again. Such a dinner!" Turnwell sighed beatifically at the recollection. "Later we came up here. And what do you think were the first words he said? 'Mr. Turnwell,' he remarked, offering me a Havana (he had a monogrammed case full of them), 'I hear you have just taken out a permit to export six tons of charas. Do you mind telling me what you are going to do with it?' That took me by surprise. But I kept my wits. 'Oh,' I answered carelessly, 'I am going to export it.' 'Do you mind telling me where?' I had no intention of telling him anything until I learned what he was driving at. 'I am sorry, but it is a business secret.' At that the Englishman thought a while, turning his cigar round and round in his fingers. Then he spoke crisply. 'Perhaps, Mr. Turnwell, I might make you a better offer than your present customer. What would you say to five pounds a seer?' At that I nearly fell off my chair, but I took care not to show my feelings. I told him I wasn't in a position to make any promises. But he evidently thought he hadn't offered enough. He said perhaps he could get six pounds a seer and maybe seven.

" 'You must understand, this is a serious proposition,' he went on. 'You may not have heard of me personally, but perhaps you know of my brother, Colonel Ashby of the Egyptian Civil Service. As for me, I represent an important group of Cairo financiers. . . .'

" 'There are Egyptians in your corporation? I thought there were only Greeks and Arabs.' I wanted to make him talk, and at the same time let him know that I understood perfectly the relationship of the three visits. He didn't turn a hair.

" 'You mean Salim Awad,' he said quietly. 'Yes, he is one of the group, one of the most influential members, in fact. But the majority are Greeks. As for me, since I see there is no need of hiding the truth: I have been sent here by Mr. Vaporidis, the head of the corporation. He sent me on purpose to communicate with you, and to make you a definite offer.' I told him I couldn't give him an answer immediately. I would have to consult my associate. 'Ah, you have an associate?' He said that in such an odd tone, I couldn't make out whether he was displeased or merely surprised. But, he added quickly, of course he understood. He would wait for an answer, and in the meantime I could always find him at his hotel. Well—and then I sent you the telegram."

"When was it you said Mr. Ashby came to Bombay?"

"Two weeks ago."

And Turnwell had seen him the day of his arrival. . . . That is to say he had telegraphed me nearly a week after their conversation. Why the delay, I reflected, or rather why had he telegraphed me at all? Was it loyalty—or discretion, I wondered, studying the rosy face before me, wreathed in cigarette smoke like an elderly cherub on a cloud.

". . . I wanted to get you here as soon as possible, for naturally I would rather work with you. (Was this meant for flattery?) I don't know any of that crowd. They may be a gang of bandits. And besides . . . the permit is in your name. . . ."

Naïve young man—so that was the key to the mystery. Had it not been for that detail, I might never have heard of my agent nor the charas he had agreed to purchase for me. Volikis, I realized, had spoken the truth. That charas shipment of ours had upset the Egyptian market. The "Ring" was out to eliminate the competition. But if I let them have that particular six tons of charas, it would be at my own terms, and when and where I chose. . . .

"I suppose the first thing is to see Ashby," I suggested. With that Turnwell agreed. We parted that evening planning to meet again as soon as he had arranged an interview. At ten the next morning, he was at my hotel.

"I have just seen him," he announced. "Ashby will meet us in an hour." It was astonishing how Turnwell's whole manner had changed. He had lost his diffidence, the boyish shyness I had always found appealing. He radiated energy and confidence. It was evident he felt he was dominating the situation, and that he held all the cards in his hand.

"On the boulevard?" I inquired as he gave an order to the cab-driver.

"Ashby will pick us up in his car. There we can talk freely. In a hotel, you never can tell who may be listening."

All this was very conspirative and mysterious, more so

than the circumstances justified; but the precaution, I imagined, was doubtless an invention of Turnwell's. Having reached the shore, we dismissed the cab and strolled leisurely along the parkway. The tide was full, it glowed like dull metal under the noon sun.

Promptly at eleven by Turnwell's wrist watch, a rented automobile, very vast with its one passenger lost in the wide back seat, drove slowly past and stopped a few rods ahead. Turnwell presented me to a little man of about fifty with sharp features over which a yellow skin lay in innumerable wrinkles. One would have said he had just issued from the hands of the laundress, so spotless he was from sun helmet to gaiters. He reached me a claw-like hand, with a smile that added additional creases to the waxy folds about his mouth.

"Charmed at this meeting, Monsieur Franqui," he chirped in excellent French. (I had charged Turnwell to withhold my true name, preferring for a variety of reasons to remain incognito.) "I am extremely confused at having caused you to take so long a trip at this season," the Englishman apologized, "but I trust we shall be able to make an arrangement that will be compensation for your trouble." I replied in a like tone, and the three of us took seats in the automobile—Mr. Ashby in the center, flanked by Turnwell and myself. As the car rolled over the smooth parkway between the grass plots and the sea, Ashby took the lead in the conversation, addressing his remarks to me.

First of all, it was only fair to explain who was behind the offer he proposed to make. Perhaps I was not aware that an important financial group, of which two Cairo bankers were influential members, held the monopoly of all hashish sales in the Near East.

"I may say that not a gram of hashish reaches the consumer that does not first pass through the hands of our organization," he affirmed. (A statement which I could have contradicted had I so chosen.) This group had become interested recently (and how recently I alone knew) in Indian charas. The merest hazard had brought him in contact with Turnwell, a most fortunate encounter, he was confident, for all concerned. It was true that the hashish trade was, well—to put it frankly, there was no reason to avoid the word—contraband. But I need have no hesitancy on that account. His group was accustomed to handling operations of the sort. There could be no possible accident. . . . Personally he had contacts of the closest sort in high quarters of the Egyptian administration—the charas being destined for the Egyptian market. Ashby remarked in passing that he had unlimited funds at his disposal and he was prepared to make an offer which Turnwell had let him understand was superior to what I was accustomed to receive from my usual customers. What would I say to a tentative figure of six or seven pounds a seer?

I replied that seven pounds seemed a fair basis for discussion. We finally agreed on ten, including Ashby's commission. He tried to get me to make over the charas to him in Bombay; but I explained that I had obtained the permit for exporting the drug with the understanding that it was to be shipped to Djibouti. If it were to become known that I had disposed of the charas in Bombay to the Egyptian hashish syndicate, it would undoubtedly compromise the success of any further purchases I might desire to make in India. Ashby had no difficulty in grasping my point of view; he expressed the hope that in the future we might continue our coöperation. We ended our conversation with the understanding that I was to inform him at his Cairo address when the charas might be expected at Djibouti. In the meantime he would make all the necessary arrangements for its delivery.

I was not over-pleased to enter in contact with the Egyptian hashish syndicate, which Volikis had always characterized as a "den of bandits." If I let them have the charas it would mean postponing my Abyssinian project, perhaps indefinitely, since I was now convinced that I could not rely to any great extent on the services of Turnwell in the future. Sooner or later, the syndicate would get him; I could not hope to compete with that powerful group when it came to a question of funds. In fact, if I pretended to accept the Englishman's offer, it was chiefly because I saw no other way out of the situation. Had I refused, there was a strong possibility that I would never lay eyes on my 6,000 seers of charas. I did not mean intentionally to misjudge Turnwell, but I knew he was not remarkable for strength of character, and he had just shown me to what extent he could be dazzled by the display of money in large quantities.

The agreement with Ashby, which privately I had no intention of keeping, removed the danger from that quarter, particularly since instead of the initial commission I had promised my "agent," I now agreed to split with him the entire profits.

I had a boat leaving for Aden within two days. Turnwell was to leave within twenty-four hours for Kashmir to purchase the drug. Ashby too was eager to return to Cairo, but he felt that it was imprudent to travel on the same boat as I; he would wait over for the next one. Besides he had a little affair to finish up in Bombay—for in addition to his connection with the hashish syndicate, he attended to matters of publicity on the side—and he was making engagements with a troupe of Indian dancers for music-halls of Cairo and Alexandria. An odd little man, Ashby, in appearance stiff and reserved as a Protestant pastor. He had a finger in a good many odd operations, among which the hashish trade, I suspected, was perhaps the most reputable. . . .

In my last conversation with Turnwell, I learned that my irrepressible agent had still another scheme up his sleeve.

"How soon do you suppose it will be before I can count on my commission?" he inquired as we sat over our coffee after dinner that evening. "As soon as your friend Ashby makes the first payment. Why?" I inqu red, wondering what lay back of the question.

Turnwell hesitated and grew red.

"It . . . that . . . I have found another steamer for sale. The *Caiman*, a former Chinese coast-guard. A much better bargain than the *Southern Cross;* it can be bought for a song."

Turnwell and his boats. It was almost pathetic, that insistence of his, as if every instinct pushed him to navigate again. Boats had become an obsession; after his unlucky experience with elegant sailing-craft, he had gone back to steam. Where I suspect he belonged. . . .

But I was in no mood for philanthropy. Nor did I intend to let my sensibilities be moved by the pathos of the situation. As I remember, I quashed his enthusiasm with brutal directness, telling him that once he had fulfilled his obligations towards me, he could buy a fleet of steamers if he chose. That was his affair. Personally I had no need of a steamer. The *Altaïr* answered all my purposes, far more adequately than any worn-out tramp freighter. It was for him, as my agent, to see that the charas arrived in Bombay at a time when it could be loaded immediately on a boat for Aden. If he felt incapable of assuring me that, I would remain in Bombay myself to handle the affair.

Turnwell muttered sullenly he supposed I was right; at any rate, I could count on him to do his part as we had agreed. He did not mention the *Caiman* again and that night I saw him off on the Punjab Mail for Kashmir. The idea of leaving Ashby in Bombay disturbed me somewhat. But with Turnwell out of the way, and the Englishman due to leave on the next boat for Suez (I had met him in the offices of the Company, purchasing his ticket), I saw no reason for prolonging my stay in the Indian port. I was eager to start putting my scheme for hemp-cultivating into execution. The more I thought about it, the more I grew determined not to concede the six tons of charas to the hashish syndicate. What guarantee had I that I might secure a second shipment? I could not count eternally on the coöperation of the Indian officials. Of that I felt positive. And I needed that charas to launch the hemp plantations in Abyssinia. In any event the first step was to get it in safety to Djibouti.

That alone, it developed, represented something of a feat. Two weeks after my return to the African coast, I received a telegram from Turnwell, announcing the purchase of the charas and his own arrival in Bombay. Owing to certain difficulties of transport, he explained, he had been obliged to abandon the drug in the north, to follow after him, he assured me, within a few days. That news gave me a fresh opportunity to regret my choice of Turnwell as a business agent. Had our situations been reversed, I would have traveled with the precious shipment day and night, not leaving it for an instant until I saw it aboard ship for Aden. I could not help wondering what pressing business had demanded Turnwell's presence in Bombay, while my charas wandered over the railroads of India, unattended.

However I refused to let myself worry over that aspect of the matter. I even forced myself to remain tranquilly in Djibouti when an obscure instinct warned me I ought to take the next boat for Bombay. Why have an "associate" in India, I argued, if at every step I intervened in the business I had entrusted him to handle? Not that I felt any too sure of Turnwell in general, but I had promised him money enough to insure his loyalty with respect to that one particular affair. Afterwards I would have no further need of him. When it came to putting Abyssinian hemp on the market, I meant to assure myself of a more level-headed collaborator.

After that first telegram I received no further news from Bombay for fully two weeks. Then in reply to a letter and a cable of my own, demanding news of the traveling charas, a letter came, crammed with excuses. The shipment had been held up at Srinagar because the Maharajah had mobilized all the motor-trucks for his personal use; in consequence Turnwell had sent the charas to Rawalpindi in horse-carts—a nine days' journey. At Rawalpindi, another delay: first, because of local holidays; then the Simla Secretary of Finances (Turnwell was very precise about the details) had given orders to detain the charas until further notice, or to put it concretely, until Turnwell by dint of great energy had secured an additional permit. When he wrote, he was about to make a flying trip to Rawalpindi with the papers. He urged me to be patient, assuring me that such delays could not be avoided, and promised to put the drug aboard a steamer leaving a week later or at most within ten days.

A week passed, two weeks, and no further news came from Bombay. I cabled again. In reply, I received a re-assuring message.

"Merchandise leaving end of week on steamer *Canossa* after difficulty with Excise Office."

I drew a breath of relief, reproaching myself with having nourished unjust suspicions. Such delays, as Turnwell had said, were not extraordinary under the circumstances, as I knew from personal experience with the Indian administration. I made the *Altaïr* ready for sea; several days later, we hoisted sail for Aden. We reached port on the eve of the day scheduled for the arrival of the *Canossa*. I went ashore to spend the night at a little hotel in which I had put up many times before, in fact where I had lived for eight months while I built the schooner which the British confiscated. The proprietor greeted me like an old friend.

"Well? Abd el Hai, on your way to India again?"

I explained that this time I had merely come for goods the *Canossa* was bringing from Bombay. In the course of our conversation, I mentioned Turnwell, whom the hotel-keeper remembered from the days when the young Englishman was captain of the freighter *Mary Willard*.

"Odd you should speak of him. Only the other day I had news of Turnwell from one of our guests. I had not thought of the man for months. It seems he is going back to the sea again."

"? ?"

"On an old Chinese freighter, I believe. Belongs now to an Englishman who bought it in Bombay. It was the

owner himself who told me. He engaged Turnwell to bring
it to Europe."

"Do you remember the owner's name?"

"Fellow by the name of Ashby. Though what he could
want of an old Chinese tramp, I can't . . ."

"You don't recollect what he called the steamer?" I
broke in hastily.

"He told me, but I have forgotten. Some Chinese name,
I suppose. He bragged a lot about his purchase, that Mr.
Ashby. I took it he had never owned a boat before."

The news, I confess, staggered me. Ashby, Turnwell, and
presumably, the *Caiman*. . . . The situation seemed all
too clear. The *Caiman* on the way to Europe with Turnwell and doubtless my six tons of charas on board. The
hashish syndicate had carried the day; I could imagine
no other explanation. At any rate, the arrival of the
Canossa would remove any doubts I still might cherish in
the matter. While awaiting that certainty, I cabled the
Port Commissioner of Bombay asking for the owner's
name and the port of destination of the steamer *Caiman*.

Early next morning, the *Canossa* dropped anchor in
the port. I hurried on board, but as I had feared, the ship
brought no freight for me. The captain said yes, he remembered. Captain Turnwell had arranged to ship a load
of charas with him, but at the last minute he had changed
his mind and put it aboard a little steamer—he did not
recall the name; it had a yellow funnel.

When I came off the *Canossa*, I found a reply to my
Bombay cable awaiting me at the hotel. "Owner and master steamer *Caiman*: Captain Turnwell. Destination, Abyssinia, via Perim." My charas had been stolen. It was on
the way to Egypt. But by what route? The declared port,
Perim, was manifestly a blind. Turnwell, Ashby as well,

knew better than to touch at an English port, as dangerous for a vessel carrying stolen goods as a French one, under the circumstances. Remember, in so far as I was concerned, the charas could not be interpreted as contraband: purchased and paid for on the open market, shipped from a British port with the consent of the French consul and the local authorities, for a *bona fide* destination (by that time I had received permission from the Ethiopians to bring the charas into Abyssinia). I had the right to appeal both to English and French authorities to protect my interests—a right I intended to utilize to the utmost.

On the other hand, the men who had appropriated the charas had committed an act of piracy; there was no other name for it. They had loaded it on a ship which left Bombay with false papers, to be smuggled into Egypt in contraband. For once, I had the powers of the law on my side!

Then began the battle of telegrams. A one-sided battle, at the beginning. I cabled the Collector of Customs at Bombay, the French consul, the Governor of Djibouti, the Governor of Perim, explaining the situation and asking for support in running down the fugitive *Caiman*. I interested the telegraph-operators in the hunt; they gave me priority over the wires. I sent dispatches to all the ports of the Red Sea, all the ports of the Indian Ocean, even to Maurice Island and the Rodriguez Archipelago (the birthplace, I remembered, of Turnwell's parents), and to Madagascar, in case the *Caiman* should attempt the journey round the Cape. And I cabled the Customs at Suez. "Steamer *Caiman,* bringing six tons charas for Egypt. Seize at Canal."

That done, I returned to Obok to await developments. During a week or more, answers to my cables poured in from all directions. No news of the *Caiman* anywhere. As if it had disappeared into thin air. Then one morning, I received a dispatch from Alexandria. It was signed Vaporidis (the name of a Cairo banker whom I had already heard mentioned in connection with the activities of the hashish syndicate), and read:

"Cease action. Goods in our hands. Come Alexandria for understanding."

The first concrete result. Five days later, I climbed a dark stairway of an old house in Alexandria, and was received in a dusty office, much less luxurious than I had anticipated, by an Egyptian clerk who opened his eyes wide as I handed him my card. The banker was absent; he would not return to his office before five in the afternoon. Promptly at five, I repeated my visit. In the dingy office, I found only the solitary clerk. He bade me be seated and went back to his desk, sifting and sorting papers with a great appearance of energy. Several times I caught him studying me out of the corner of his eye; on each occasion he dived into his papers, sneezing and snuffling in the dust of his own activity.

When I had sat there for nearly an hour, a bell buzzed somewhere overhead. Getting instantly to his feet, the clerk with an air of mystery, swung aside a row of bookshelves that masked a door in the wall. A door which, even without the protecting shelves, was all but invisible, as the chocolate-colored wall paper of the room lay smooth across the panels. I heard the clink of a bolt on the other side, and the door opened inward on well-oiled hinges.

Beyond, in a vast room containing massive office furniture, had assembled what looked like a Board of Directors' meeting. Ten men sat about a mahogany table at the end of which a gray-bearded Greek presided with the dignity of a Cabinet Minister. He waved me to a chair facing him and during the conversation that followed, acted as spokesman.

"We are glad of the chance to talk with you," he began as I took my place in the circle. "By the publicity you have given to—ahem—certain matters, you threaten to compromise your own interests and ours."

"Publicity?" I repeated stiffly. "I fail to grasp your point of view. There is nothing illicit about the merchandise you refer to. I shipped it to Djibouti through the regular channels. . . ."

"You *were* to have shipped it . . ." the speaker corrected with a dry smile. "Come now, Abd el Hai," he went on with a change of tone. "We are men of business and this is a business matter. How much do you want?"

"Not a *piastre*. When the charas reaches Djibouti we will talk business if you so choose. Not before."

"That sort of stubbornness is not going to advance matters," the Greek remarked, tapping the mahogany board with a manicured finger nail. "Besides you seem to forget. . . . Under the circumstances, it is not for you to dictate terms. On the contrary. But as we are not thieves, we offer you, in all loyalty, a fair payment for the goods."

"Will you or will you not, give me back the six tons of charas?"

My interlocutor bit his lips with impatience.

"There is no question of returning you anything," he returned coldly. "We offer to make you a fair payment, nothing more. If you do not choose to accept it, that is your affair. We are seated here, comfortably," he went on. "Keep on running about; make all the noise you want to; we can afford to wait." At the words, a discreet smile went the rounds of the table. I got to my feet.

"Stay in your armchairs, gentlemen. Take your rest while you may; you may have plenty of sleepless nights ahead. . . ." I took my leave, flaunting an air of confidence which in no way expressed the true state of my feelings. From their attitude, it was clear that the members of the Ring felt their position secure. I deducted that the charas had already been stored in a place of safety.

Before turning south again, I thought of running across to Cairo, to tell my troubles to Volikis who might be able to give me useful advice. I planned to leave Alexandria that night, but as I passed before the Hotel Claridge on my way to the station, I caught sight of a familiar figure in the lighted hallway. Ashby himself. A sudden impulse carried me through the door. The Englishman had disappeared.

"Mr. Ashby?" I inquired at the desk. The clerk consulted the register.

"The gentleman is not in." I came near protesting he was mistaken, but thought better of it and walked away. Half an hour later I again demanded Ashby. He was still invisible. From the way in which the clerk replied to my question I suspected that the gentleman—who undoubtedly knew of my presence in Alexandria—had given orders to that effect. . . . But I did not intend to be disposed of so easily.

I waited on the terrace until the day clerk of the hotel went off duty. As soon as he left the building, I presented myself at the desk, carrying a bag, and asked for a room. On the register I signed, "Captain Turnwell, Bombay," and walked off to the room assigned me, wondering how long it would take before the fish rose to the bait. . . . I did not have long to wait. Barely an hour later, a call came from the desk. Could I receive Mr. Ashby?

"With pleasure."

I switched off the electricity, leaving the room in semi-darkness, lighted only from street-lamps beyond the window. At Ashby's knock, I admitted my visitor, closed the door behind him, and turned on the lights again. The Englishman tottered as if he had received a blow. His waxy features went dead white. Visibly he was frightened. My back against the door, I spoke with utmost affability.

"Forgive the stratagem. It was my only hope of seeing you. All I want is a few minutes' conversation." Ashby, still thoroughly stunned, let himself be led to a chair; though his gaze traveled constantly from my hands to the door . . . measuring the distance which lay between him and the threshold. I plunged rapidly into the heart of the matter.

"See here, Ashby," I stated frankly. "You have been working for a group of bandits. It may mean serious trouble for you in the near future. Don't you think it might be more to your interest to swing over to my way of thinking? I could make it worth your while. . . ."

"No doubt, no doubt." Again the nervous glance towards the door. Manifestly the man was thoroughly scared.

"I make no threats of any sort," I reassured him. "You have only to tell me what became of the *Caiman.* . . ."

"I . . . I have no idea where your charas is," Ashby muttered. His face had not yet resumed a normal color and his fingers twitched as he spoke.

"And there is no convenient means of reviving your memory?" I glanced casually towards a check book which lay on the table between us.

"I tell you, I don't know what has become of your charas," he repeated unsteadily. Then without transition, he broke into a hysterical tirade. Some one had played him false. He had done all the work; and now he had been shoved aside. He didn't know why. He had no inkling of their plans. He was not even sure of getting his commission. He had been a fool to pay over all the money to Turnwell; he ought first to have looked after his own interests. He continued for several minutes in the same strain, almost on the point of tears. Was the man lying? In any case, it seemed clear that he could or would furnish me with no information. I put the check book back in my pocket and rose to my feet, signifying that my visitor was free to leave. At the door, he turned to me with a word of entreaty.

"Don't show yourself much in the hotel, I beg you. If they learn that the two of us are staying here, no knowing what might happen. They already accuse me of having warned you. . . ."

I closed the door on the worthy servant of the drug ring. Perhaps the scene had been carefully played; but something told me the man had spoken the truth.

Volikis, whom I saw in Cairo the following day, shared the opinion.

"That is the way they work, Vaporidis and his crowd," he assured me. "They use a fellow like Ashby to put through a shady deal; and once the operation is finished, they drop him. Probably his police record is black enough so he won't dare risk making a fuss. . . . You were right not to make an arrangement with the Ring. Don't give in an inch; chances are you may end by getting back your charas. They won't be able to land it anywhere on the Red Sea coast. I have all the Bedouins in hand. If the *Caiman* touches anywhere on the east shore, the Syndicate will never see an ounce of the drug!"

According to Volikis, the cargo was still on the high seas.

"My advice is to keep your eyes fixed on the south of the Indian Ocean. They may try to send the *Caiman* around the Cape."

The idea seemed plausible. In that case, Turnweli's steamer would have to put in somewhere to take on coal. I found the optimism of the Greek most consoling. Though as I thought it over later, the south of the Indian Ocean seemed rather too large a region for one man to survey . . . by telegraph.

XIX

The Great Charas (concluded)

During that trip to Egypt, I acquired another ally besides Volikis. A young French pearl merchant established in Cairo, with whom I had done considerable business, offered to help me in the quest for the lost charas. Pelletier viewed the whole matter with romantic enthusiasm; he knew several members of the hashish syndicate personally; and he felt convinced that he would have little difficulty in ferreting out information. I counted little on the aid that might be furnished by the amateur detective . . . but I considered it useful to possess a partisan in no way connected with the drug trade and who, if need be, could act as a disinterested intermediary, on neutral ground.

Pelletier took his rôle seriously. I had scarcely returned to Djibouti when I received a telegram.

"Discovered whereabouts *Caiman*. At Socotra. Will transfer cargo to ship for Zanzibar."

I experienced a moment of emotion, until I realized that none of the ports of Socotra Island offered a safe anchorage for a steamer. Besides, within twenty-four hours, a second cable from Pelletier arrived, contradicting the first.

"*Caiman* hiding Red Sea. Information sure." Six hours later, the pearl merchant telegraphed again.

"News confirmed. Steamer *Elsa* passing Canal to meet *Caiman*."

That was an eventuality I had not foreseen. The Ring had decided to risk no encounter with the Bedouins of the Red Sea coast. They were sending the charas through the Canal on another ship, to land it somewhere on the north shore of Egypt. But that I meant to prevent at any cost. Assured of the presence of the *Caiman* in the Red Sea, I could begin to act. In the Red Sea, I felt at home; I knew its two shores by heart. There was not a group of islands I had not visited. And I could think of few spots where a steamer might lurk unnoticed while waiting for the *Elsa* to arrive from the north.

The *Caiman*, I had ascertained, had not been equipped to send messages by wireless. That meant it had to preserve a contact with a telegraph station on shore. Turnwell would avoid African ports, all of which I had warned. The Arab coast was safer; Moka, in particular, provided a good anchorage little frequented by other than native craft. To be sure, he could not telegraph to Egypt from Moka, but he might easily send some one in a boutre to Assab to send or receive messages. As I studied the map, the conviction grew that the *Caiman* could only be stationed at Moka or somewhere in the neighborhood of Assab.

After that decision, I wasted no time. Preparing the *Altaïr* for sea, I mounted a toy cannon in the bow; provided the crew with rifles or revolvers; and manufactured several hand-grenades—a capsule of dynamite and a handful of buckshot in a pickle bottle. Nor did we lack the customary classic equipment for such expeditions; each man wore a curved *gembia*, belted at the waist. When we met with the *Caiman*, I planned to send a shot into the engines, and in case of resistance to recover my property by force of arms, if necessary. However, knowing Turn-

well as I did, I little feared that matters would progress
as far as that. A mere show of force would suffice.

Two days after the receipt of Pelletier's last telegram,
we got under weigh. As we passed before Perim, we crossed
an Arab boutre traveling south. Approaching within hailing distance, I called to the *nakhoda* to ask whether he had
seen a small steamer with three masts and a yellow funnel.

"Two days ago," came the answer. "Fifteen miles north
of Moka, close to the land." My suspicions seemed confirmed."

We reached Moka the next morning. No trace of the
Caiman in the harbor. The usual crowd had gathered on
the beach—askari with guns and silver dagger-hilts;
Bedouins shining with butter, black-skinned coolies, and
Soudanese slaves, splendid of torso, but invariably bow-
legged or knock-kneed. An askar offered to conduct me to
the house of the Sheik—for I had brought with me a letter
from a former Arab customer of mine, requesting the dignitary to furnish me all coöperation in getting back my
stolen charas.

My guide left me at the door of the Sheik's house, an
ancient building four stories high, with a spiral stair, built
doubtless for strategic reasons, narrow and steep, lighted
only by occasional slits in the wall. A slave to whom I
surrendered my letter, led me into a dark little room in
which twenty Arabs sat about, chewing the green shoots
of *kat*. In a few words, I related the story of the stolen
cargo and my quest of *Caiman*, the fugitive. But no such
steamer had entered the port of Moka. In case it should,
the Sheik promised me to lure the captain on land and to
hold him prisoner till my return. For my part, I guaranteed a reward of 1,000 francs payable when the prisoner
was turned over to me. Inquiries made in town and along

the beach brought no further information. Absolutely no one had seen the *Caiman* nor any ship like it. The steamer had evidently avoided the port; perhaps it lay at anchor among the Hanish Islands, the only possible hiding place for a boat of its dimensions.

Accordingly at midnight, we hoisted sail for Djebbel Hanish. Morning came as we rounded its southern tip. Not a boat in sight; not even a boutre of fishers for us to question. We headed for Little Hanish Island, a rock three miles long, which at the north encloses a little bay affording excellent shelter.

As we rounded the northern end of the island, I made out between the two capes that mark the limits of the bay, the vertical lines of three masts against the sky. A single cry went up from the deck: the *Caiman!* Starting the motor for greater speed, I swung the *Altaïr* to starboard and steered straight for the anchorage. To my surprise, as we changed our direction, I saw the three masts shift their position against the sky and disappear. Had we been seen? In thirty minutes we rounded the cape into the bay. It was empty. Far out at sea, a big freighter was making for the horizon.

The *Caiman*, I decided, must have slipped around the southern end of Little Hanish as we approached, and from that point, hidden from us, had headed for the east coast of Djebbel Hanish. The wind had risen in the meantime and the sea was running high. I dared not risk the *Altaïr* on the eastern side of Great Hanish; it took us nearly three hours to beat our way across to a little anchorage at its southwestern tip. There I left the boutre, and accompanied by Abdi, climbed painfully up a steep slope of crumbling lava-rock to the summit of the island. From that point we could view the entire sea. Not a boat anywhere. Even the big freighter had disappeared. I had been duped by an optical illusion. What I had taken for the *Caiman* lying at anchor, had evidently been the freighter passing between the two islands. When I changed our direction, its speed became apparent as it continued its route towards the north.

Fully discomfited by that discovery, I started down to the beach again, Abdi following behind, by a longer but easier path than the one by which we had come. As we crossed the dried bed of a lagoon, Abdi halted, bending down with a sharp exclamation:

"*Shoof*, Abd el Hai, white men's tracks!"

On the sand, hardened with salt crystals, showed the print of European shoes. What European could have landed so recently on the deserted island of Djebbel Hanish? Turnwell, he and no other! That night we crossed to Assab. I cabled to Aden, signaling the presence of the *Caiman* in the Hanish Islands and requesting the aid of a gunboat to aid in its capture. Questioning the crews of the boutres at anchor in the port, I found two zarougs of *zaramigi* who assured us they had seen a little steamer several days before, close to the Arab coast and directly across from Great Hanish Island. They had taken it for a coast guard. As the *Caiman* was painted white, with a yellow funnel, they might easily have confused it with an English patrol.

The statements of the two crews differed in one respect —the number of masts on the steamer they had seen. One *nakhoda* affirmed it carried only one; his colleague insisted he had counted two. I promised the men a prize if they succeeded in capturing the captain and agreed to make them a present of the ship! We drew up a paper to that effect, which the *zaramigi* were to transmit to their chief, the Sheik at Khor Gouleifa, who ruled over these professional pirates.

At Assab, I learned also that a boutre of pearl divers had been stationed for weeks near the island of Djebil, close to the Hanish group. I resolved to pay the men a visit, confident that if the *Caiman* had cruised in those waters, it could not have escaped their notice. The following morning I returned to Great Hanish Island, and leaving the *Altaïr* in the anchorage, I took three Somalis with me in the ship's boat and we struck across towards Djebil. If the *Caiman* lay near the island, our approach in so insignificant a craft would not alarm the crew. We might even succeed in boarding the steamer by surprise.

At high noon we reached the west coast of Djebil. As we worked towards the north, skirting the shore, I observed bands of gazelles lying in the shade of the rocks along the sea, as unconcerned at our presence as a flock of goats. Generations of them lived there undisturbed, the sole inhabitants of the island. By three o'clock we made the shelter at the northern end of Djebil. No trace of the *Caiman;* only a boutre, beached on the sand. It belonged to the pearl divers who for two months had fished in the waters about the island. Not one of them had seen a vessel that resembled the *Caiman.* The only vessel to anchor off the islands, they said, was a British gunboat which had recently spent several days at target-practice, cruising about Great and Little Hanish.

"Did the officers land?" I inquired.

"They went ashore on all the islands to shoot gazelles."

I had the explanation of the mysterious footprints on the sand. As for the *Caiman,* I began to doubt whether it had ever entered the Red Sea at all!

Feeling it useless to play hide-and-seek with our own shadows, I resolved to return straightway to Djibouti, in the hope that during our absence fresh news of the fugitives might have come. Instead of the anticipated telegrams, I found only a letter from Pelletier, explaining with pride how he had happened on the news of the *Caiman*. It appeared that while waiting in an anteroom at the house of Vaporidis, he had "discovered" an open telegram lying on a table. As if by accident. . . . The amateur detective had led me on a pretty chase. The Drug Ring must have hugged themselves with delight at Pelletier's gullibility . . . and mine. How nicely I had fallen into their trap.

Where was the *Caiman?* As if in answer to the unspoken question, a pair of bare feet thudded across the room behind me. A Somali, carrying a blue envelope. I tore it open; read it once, read it twice.

"Steamer *Caiman* at Seychelles Islands." Signed: French Consulate, Bombay.

"Nothing yet, Abdi?"

"No bottom, Abd el Hai."

My mate drew in the lead, in wet, even coils. The metal clinked on the deck. All about us, black waves rose and sank with clock-like regularity. The seventh sounding since sunset, and still no sign of the submerged plateau that rises, a vast submarine mountain, sheer out of 9,000 feet of water.

Two weeks earlier we had left Aden. A six-day battle with contrary winds brought us to Cape Gardafui. Ever since we had driven steadily south, reaching that morning the parallel of Mahé, largest of the Seychelles group, 4° 30′ south. At that point, I swung the *Altaïr* eastwards. My second voyage in the Indian Ocean without a chronometer. Had my calculations gone astray? Evening should have brought us to the submerged plateau, 120 miles in diameter, which bears on its surface the Seychelles Islands. At midnight, the lead still gave no sign. Two miles of water lay between the *Altaïr's* keel and the ocean floor.

"No bottom, Abdi?"

"Not yet, Abd el Hai."

A month had passed since I received from Bombay the news of the *Caiman's* presence in the Seychelles Islands. For days the wires hummed with messages. Telegram to the Governor of Seychelles: "Seize the cargo of the *Caiman*." Telegram from Seychelles: "Regret, impossible under local laws." More cables to Bombay; the cumbersome machine of the law put in motion. The voice—telegraphic—of governmental authority: "Seize the cargo of the *Caiman*." A silence, of consternation no doubt, followed the command; then a reply came from the distant islands: "Seizure effective Monday providing owner of cargo transmits 30,000 rupees bond." At the same time I received an urgent dispatch from the attorney whose services I had engaged at Mahé—also by cable. "Send bond sure. Dutch ship in harbor will load cargo *Caiman* Monday if seizure not made."

I received the two telegrams on a Saturday afternoon. The banks of Aden were closed. I had until Monday morning at nine o'clock to deliver the sum at Mahé; otherwise, once more the fugitive charas would slip through my fingers. On the face of it, it seemed obvious that others beside Turnwell had an interest in preventing the seizure of the *Caiman's* cargo. It scarcely seemed probable that Turnwell would have put in to Mahé harbor without assurance in advance of certain protection. . . .

But for once I had the Empire on my side. It alone could dominate the situation. I climbed the hill above the port of Aden to call upon the Resident. The official was not at home. He had left to play golf that afternoon and would dine in town. Undiscouraged—by this time, I had been given many a lesson in Oriental patience—I sat down by the roadside at the gate of the villa, to wait for the dinner-guest's return.

A midnight interview, courteous and brief.

"Deposit the sum with the trading-house of Cowadjee," the Resident told me. "Bring me the receipt and I will guarantee the transaction."

Sunday morning an official cable went over the wires to Seychelles: "Bond deposited here. Seize the *Caiman's* cargo." Twenty-four hours later the reply came announcing the seizure. I had scored my first victory.

But immediately another difficulty arose. The seizure had a time-limit, it appeared. The owner of the *Caiman's* cargo must appear in Mahé within three weeks to claim his property; otherwise the embargo would be lifted. And the Dutch ship remained in the harbor. . . .

I consulted the sailing-lists. The only boats for Seychelles left via Bombay or Dar es Salam on the African coast. No sailing was scheduled for a month. Odd coincidence. . . .

There remained the *Altaïr*. It had made the crossing to Bombay; it could also attempt Seychelles. I equipped the boutre, selected a crew with care, and we headed south into the Indian Ocean.

"What does the lead say, Abdi?"

"Nothing as yet, Abd el Hai."

Morning broke over the sea whipped at the surface by a fine rain. Were the currents carrying us east and north?

Had we left the Seychelles behind us? If so, we might plow on indefinitely. . . . And time pressed. Only three days of the allotted weeks were left! That plateau, over a hundred miles square, shrank to a grain of sand when you thought of it lost in the immensity of the ocean.

The day dragged through and brought no change. At each sounding, the lead spun out endlessly. . . . Night came; I resolved to keep on until noon next day, before putting about. At midnight, a sharp cry forward—echoed joyfully by a dozen voices:

"Bottom, Abd el Hai. Twelve fathoms."

The currents had not carried the *Altaïr* out of her course. They had merely held us back.

When morning came, the Seychelles lay before us, granite peaks, their summits wrapped with rain clouds and streaked by torrents; their base green with coconut palms. By noon we reached the channel of Mahé, above which the town lay piled in a succession of terraces, gleaming white through a heavy curtain of leaves. But more welcome still, sight of a ship moored to the wharf—a steamer painted white, carrying three masts and a yellow funnel. The *Caiman*. . . . My quest had ended!

That afternoon I saw Turnwell, a Turnwell crushed and lamentable, a schoolboy caught cheating, a child before a collapsed house of cards, a pricked balloon. I almost found myself pitying him—but not quite. He had cost me too much time, money, and worry. However, I did abandon the legal action I had started against him. Once I recovered my property, it was immaterial to me what became of my former agent.

When I came to take over the stock of charas, I made a surprising and agreeable discovery. Its quantity had multiplied. From six tons, it had grown to twelve! Turnwell, aided no doubt by the accommodating de Souza, had made use of my purchase-and-export permit not once but twice. Their attempt at piracy was costing the Hashish Syndicate a pretty sum. Aside from the expenses of their various missions to Bombay, they had "purchased" Turnwell (for no mean sum, I fancy); bought a freighter; bought six tons of charas . . . and all to provide me with a rich compensation for my twelve months of hunting the *Caiman.* Twelve tons of charas, bought in my name and set down as my legal, rightful property. The great charas adventure was turning out better than I dreamed.

"I hope you bear me no ill will," Turnwell mumbled as we parted, offering me a hand that trembled slightly.

"*Au contraire,*" I assured him. I shook the limp hand vigorously as I left him, solitary, round-eyed, and pathetic, helpless as a lost dog in the pelting tropical rain. I never saw him again.

But the charas adventure was not over.

In two weeks' time, the *Altaïr* with its precious cargo, put into Djibouti, and unloaded on the Customs' docks. There it could not long remain; goods of that nature deteriorate in the heat, and it was to my interest to transport it as rapidly as possible to the Abyssinian plateau, to my future hemp plantations.

The night of our arrival in Djibouti, I received a visitor. A gentleman preferring not to give his name, but who presented himself as an old friend. "Old friend" was scarcely the title I myself should have given him—I had last seen the gentleman comfortably seated in an armchair in Alexandria, as he said, to await my return. Vaporidis himself.

He came towards me, very man-of-the-world, his hand outstretched.

"I congratulate you sincerely. You have given my former associates the lesson they deserved."

I rose to the bait obligingly.

"Your *former* associates?"

"I have broken with them completely. Disapprove heartily of their methods. The affair of the *Caiman* proved the last straw. . . ." He paused with a virtuous sigh. "And now, if you have time, we can talk business."

"Business," I repeated innocently. "But if you have severed connections with the Syndicate?"

"From now on I plan to work independently. Like your friend Volikis. I am sure we can coöperate. . . . Tell me, how much do you want for your charas?"

"No price you can pay," I told him bluntly. "I am keeping it for myself."

"Come, come," the Greek retorted with impatience. "This is a business proposition. I have told you I condemn the attitude of the Syndicate."

"You took a different view when you held the upper hand," I reminded.

"You are not the man to nourish a grudge," he flattered. "I am ready to pay any price. . . ."

"And I tell you I do not intend to sell."

"But you are taking the charas out of the country," Vaporidis objected.

"Merely to get it out of the heat."

"You can sell it to us from Abyssinia as well as Djibouti," he suggested slyly. "We have a man up there who can arrange matters. A European who—"

"I am not going to sell," I cut in briefly, "to you, nor to any one else."

"Not even six tons?"

"Not even six."

"If that is the case," the smooth features of the Greek grew sharp with restrained anger, "look for trouble ahead. Only, don't come to me to help you out!"

With that, the "old friend" departed after telling me with suspicious casualness that he had not made the trip to Djibouti to see me. Not he. He had merely happened to be passing; had heard by accident of my arrival; and thought I might like to sell some superfluous stock. A personal favor, his intervention. More important to me than to him. He had plenty of opportunities to get all the charas he could sell. . . .

"Trouble ahead. . . ." I wondered what the Greek had meant. I had purchased the goods legally; the forces of international law, of two governments, had aided me in recovering it. I had been authorized, legally, to import it into Abyssinia. Before my hemp plantations furnished their first crop, I would have ample time to work out a careful plan for putting my gangia on the market—on the Indian market, that being my first goal. I saw no obstacles in that quarter; hemp-growing was no monopoly of the Hashish Syndicate. My recent quest of the stolen charas, the assistance which had been furnished me, made me confident that the same coöperation which had been accorded the buyer, would not be refused the producer.

I was still naïve. . . . Ten days after this interview, I found myself in a situation fully as serious as the affair of the fugitive *Caiman*, though less spectacular. As I lingered on the coast, making preparations for a prolonged absence from the sea, a telegram informed me that the charas which I had shipped to Harrar in Abyssinia and which lay in deposit at the Customs, had been seized by order of the Ethiopian government and transported to the capital, Addis Abeba.

The measure, I was told, followed on vigorous intervention by the British representative in Abyssinia, who demanded immediate destruction of the goods on the grounds that the charas was a public menace. . . . While yielding to the pressure, the Ethiopian government (from first to last irreproachable in its dealings with myself) refused to take further action until my arrival, arguing with its habitual common sense that since no one in Abyssinia consumed the drug in any form, it could not be an immediate danger to the people.

At the news that my charas had been seized, I took the next train for Addis Abeba to plead my case. At the British legation, I learned from a slim young Levantine, a Greek naturalized citizen of the Empire, to whom the new charas offensive had been entrusted, that it was indeed true that his government had decided to interfere; in fact no stone was to be left unturned until the charas was destroyed.

A sad blow to my dream of hemp-cultivation. Even in free Ethiopia I might not expect to withstand successfully so imposing an opposition. My Ethiopian friends could ill afford to offend so powerful a neighbor. The most I could hope was to prevent the destruction of the merchandise I had spent so much time, money, and effort in procuring. Was it just, I argued, to destroy goods which I had been authorized to import? That argument, I observed, made a serious impression on the Ethiopian authorities. With the matter still pending, I lost no time in calling on the chief of the local Customs, a Syrian who, I may add, was subsequently dismissed from office. That

The *Fat el Rhaman* an-
chored near Rakhamat

Carrying planks for the
Ibn el Bahar

The *Ibn el Bahar* under
construction

Typical street scene

Abysinnian Merchants

Arab shops—Assab

Caught by a Nomad's Camera

elegant young man received me in silk pajamas, having just risen from his bed at eleven in the morning.

He motioned me to a chair, yawning copiously, ordered coffee for the two of us, and remarked with a smile of disdainful compassion:

"You are making a desperate struggle, but I warn you in advance you will not succeed. The odds are staked against you. What do you plan to do? Fight the Union Jack alone?"

I replied hotly that I did not see what the British Empire had to do with it; and that I still was confident the Ethiopian government would restore the charas, even if it obliged me to take the drug out of the country. The official shook his head.

"The government is going to burn your charas," he stated definitely. "Only," he paused with an enigmatic smile, "as you know, charas is a poor combustible. It might be—hem—more practical to burn something else in its place! That is, if you are interested in getting your merchandise back again."

"If I am interested . . . ?" I repeated with considerable astonishment. "What do you mean? Is it a question . . . of price?"

The Syrian yawned ostentatiously.

"Of course. What did you think I meant? Suppose you recover a part of the charas; a ton, say; will you be content to let the matter rest?"

For an instant I experienced an hallucination: the shade of Vaporidis standing by the speaker's elbow. Yield to them my charas? Far better destroy it! I had been ruined before. Rather than lose the battle to the Greek and his associates (I had not believed for a moment that he had broken with the group) I would burn the shipment myself, and stand over the bonfire until the last gram of charas was consumed!

"I want all my merchandise or none at all," I told the Syrian firmly. "What is more, I have no intention of paying for it twice." With that, I took leave of the official, leaving his coffee untouched.

Ten minutes later I reported the conversation to a friend at the French consulate. It was clear, the diplomat assured me, that the Syrian had acted entirely outside his official capacity. The Ethiopian government had no inkling of the matter. Were it to learn of the proposed bargain, the Syrian would not remain five minutes in office. . . .

"But tell me," the speaker continued, eyeing me quizzically. "If the Ethiopians do give you back the charas and order you to take it out of the country (which they are perfectly justified in doing), once you have the shipment in Djibouti, what do you plan to do with it?"

"Ship it to Germany and sell it to manufacturers of chemicals," I told him. "And what is more, I will send it from Aden in a British ship!"

The Frenchman opened round eyes of astonishment.

"But, my dear man, it will be like putting your hand into the jaws of the lion!"

I shook my head.

"Take into account the sporting spirit of the race," I disagreed. "If I entrust the charas to the English, they will watch over it like a babe in arms."

Subsequent events proved me right. My decision to hand over the drug to British protection facilitated everything. The Ethiopian government sent me forthwith a notification stating that the charas would be returned to me . . . in Djibouti; and that all expenses incurred, transport and storage, would be refunded. I was present when the charas received careful inspection from the Anglo-Levantine, who pronounced the drug authentic; after which an armed guard conveyed it to the station and locked it in a freight-car, sealed with the arms of three nations: Ethiopia, England, France. Whereupon the charas and I in the same train began the long descent to the coast.

Until Diré Daoua all went well. There, as is the custom, the train stopped for the night. The following morning, when I arrived at the station, I discovered that the car containing the charas was no longer attached to the train.

"A hot-box," some one explained. "The inspector gave orders to have the car uncoupled."

"A hot-box . . . during the night?" I remarked incredulously. "Call the inspector."

He came straightway, a Greek employee of the road. The man explained that an axle had heated. He had taken off the car because of the value of the goods it contained.

"It can continue, of course," he admitted dubiously, "though at your own risk."

I replied that I was willing to assume the entire responsibility; the car was brought from a far corner—a particularly discreet corner—of the yards; coupled to the end of the train, and we got under weigh at last, one hour after the scheduled time of leaving.

I decided now not to take my eyes off the precious shipment until our arrival in Djibouti. I installed myself in a third-class compartment crowded with natives, separated from the charas by two freight-cars and a third filled with baggage. As the train pulled out of the station, a section-boss—also a Greek—ran down the track and jumped aboard. He traveled with us until Adagala. I confess I remarked his departure with relief. I had begun to view every Greek, however humble and innocent in appearance, with suspicion.

During the halt at Adagala, I walked up and down the platform surveying the car of charas and chuckling inwardly at the myth of the hot-box. For myth it was undoubtedly; I had examined the axle at every station— it showed no signs of heating. On leaving Adagala, the road climbs a steep grade for six miles or more to a tunnel, beyond which the roadbed becomes level again. I remained at the window, leaning out from time to time to assure myself that the car of charas still followed docilely at the rear of the train.

Straining and puffing, the locomotive attacked the grade. When we had covered over five miles of the distance between Adagala and the tunnel, my diligence received its reward. A dark form slipped through the doorway of the baggage car, felt its way cautiously along the rail and disappeared between the baggage car and the car of charas. In one bound I reached the platform. No means of passing around the two freight cars; I hoisted myself to the roof and ran towards the end of the train—no great feat in view of the slow speed we were making up the grade. I leaned over the rim of the baggage car. Below me, a Somali was working at the coupling.

"*Esh te savvi?* (What are you doing?)" I shouted. His start of surprise almost threw the Somali on the tracks. I clambered down beside him.

He mumbled something about the guard having sent him to repair the coupling (he had been trying obviously to knock out the coupling-pin!) The plan was clear. The car, uncoupled in the tunnel, would have rolled down the grade, carried by its own weight. By the time the "accident" was discovered, or I had time to notify the station or return to Adagala, the trick would have been played. I would have found the seals broken, the car empty, and the charas vanished beyond recovery.

I rode beside the Somali on the couplings, to the next station. There I confronted the man with the train-guard, an Abyssinian whom I knew personally. As I suspected, he had given no orders whatsoever to the Somali, who did not belong to the train-crew. He was a section-hand, it appeared, who had boarded the train at Diré Daoua. I let the fellow off without punishment. I held no grudge against him; he had merely done what he had been told.

At Djibouti, where I and my charas arrived that evening, I saw the drug deposited at the Customs and straightway set about obtaining a permit for its transport to Aden. My countrymen seemed to think I had gone temporarily mad. The officials humored my folly to the extent of granting me the permit on the receipt of which I paid down 50,000 francs in bond, to be refunded when I brought word from the authorities in Aden stating that the charas had been delivered into their hands.

The next day, a squad of askari loaded the charas on the *Altaïr*. A government launch accompanied us to the limit of French waters, and twenty-four hours later we arrived in the Bay of Aden. At the Customs, to which I went to inquire where I might unload the charas, I was ordered none too courteously to return to my boutre. A tug lay alongside the *Altaïr*, manned by soldiers in uniform.

"Keep your hands off the cargo. My men will attend to the unloading," an officer commanded.

Obediently the crew and I stood aside while the askari emptied the hold, conveying the charas between two rows

of bayonets to the Customs. The assistant director, an
Indian, received the merchandise and delivered me a receipt—so many tons of charas, to be shipped to Hamburg. For the first time in months, I breathed a long sigh
of relief. The shipment was at last in safe-keeping . . . in
the hands of the English.

In Djibouti, I presented the receipt and had the bond
refunded. It was evident that the Europeans of the port,
my countrymen in particular, viewed my content with
considerable amazement. They took pleasure in painting
for my benefit the jubilation of the British legation at my
lack of elementary foresightedness. I let them talk; my
responsibility had ended. The merchandise was on the
way to Hamburg. That part of the transaction, I felt
assured, would be carried out with scrupulous exactitude.
Once the shipment arrived in Hamburg . . . well, we would
see. . . .

And we did. Not being possessed of second sight, I could
not follow from afar the details of its reception. But all
in due time the story came to me.

In Hamburg the charas received a welcome generally
reserved for traveling diplomats. The representatives of
three nations, the Customs, and the police, stood waiting
on the pier to receive it. The British agent was particularly in evidence, for once again the influence of the Empire had been at work persuading the local authorities
that within the heavy cases lurked a grave menace, only
to be avoided by seizure and destruction.

A procession formed, the merchandise carried in the
lead like a catafalque, and diplomatic agents, customs
men, and police following behind. Escorted to a private
room and in the presence of two chemists, the cases were
ripped open and the first of the sacks opened to the light.

The chemists bent over the contents, which gave off a slight musty odor. One of the scientists dipped his fingers in the dark mass, lifting a fragment to his nose. He wrinkled his brows in a puzzled frown.

"I have never seen any charas like this," he muttered.

He turned to his colleague, who also was busy examining a dark powder in the palm of his hand. The two men conferred together in undertones. Then they turned to the representatives of the three nations who stood looking on against a background of uniforms.

"Gentlemen," the spokesman began. He said "Gentlemen," but his remarks were addressed to the English in particular. "This is not—ahem—precisely charas. In fact —ahem—it is not charas at all."

"Not charas? Then what is it?"

The chemist tossed aside the sample, dusting his fingers.

"*Erde*," he said shortly. "Humus, or, if you will, top-soil."

Hastily the other cases were hammered open, the sacks torn apart and their contents dumped on the cement floor. All contained the same dark powdery substance. *Erde* . . . as the chemist had said. And while less interesting, no doubt, than the charas it had replaced, it offered a certain rarity to the group that crowded about the heap of earth to finger and comment . . . for it was authentic—the rusty-red soil of the African desert.

IN CONCLUSION

"—And there the story ends."

Abd el Hai set down the *keshir* cup he had been turning in his fingers as he talked, and looked out over the water, his eyes reminiscent, his lips pressed together as if to check a smile.

"But the charas?" I persisted.

"What more is there to tell? The Drug Syndicate checkmated; the Intelligence as well. . . ."

"And you?"

The smile of my companion grew more definite.

"I told you once, that like the rat of the fable, I have left a good many tails on the battlefield. But not on that particular occasion."

With that, I had to be content.

He finished the story of the Great Charas one evening as we sat overlooking the harbor of Obok from the terrace of the house by the water's edge. As he told on, the sun slipped down behind the Mabla; the tide had come in— its long waves rippled against the wall below. Along the beach, white figures crouched or stood with arms lifted, attitudes of ablution or of prayer. A dozen boutres lay near shore or beached on the sand. Out near the light-buoy, the rigging of the *Altaïr* showed black against the sky. A flame flickered at the bow; Abdi and Kassim were preparing tea. Still beyond, the flash of Ras Bir swept the sea at clock-like intervals. . . .

Beside me, Abd el Hai tilted the heavy water jar on its

ring of palm fiber. A thin cloudy stream trickled from the mouth.

"Oudini-o!" he called.

The Dankali, ever watchful, stepped forward from the shadow of the door.

"No need to replenish this. We leave for Djibouti at moonrise."

Joining me at the parapet, he followed my gaze towards the darkening horizon, his eyes melancholy.

"All this belongs to yesterday," he murmured with a touch of bitterness. "Here at Obok and on the coasts we have visited together I am like a ghost among dead things. To-day when I make the *Altaïr* ready for sea, it is only to make a pleasure trip, to take a friend on a sight-seeing excursion into the past. This afternoon I spent hours forging a new ring for the sail-yard. To what end? Sometimes I am tempted to bury myself up there in the mountains, to sell my boat, and forget the sea. Only I know I never will. . . ."

It had grown quite dark. The flame on the deck of the *Altaïr* flickered up and vanished. But the spark of the light-buoy remained and the sweeping flash of the Ras Bir.

"All that is a part of yesterday," Abd el Hai repeated. "Ended and over with, like your book. For adventure belongs to youth. And besides, there are other reasons . . . which you cannot put into your story."

The note of bitterness had left his voice.

"Listen," he said, lifting a hand.

Down in the court, some one was singing—the gay little voice of Abou Nochta, the boy of the *Altaïr*, grinding *durra* for the morning. The words of the song floated up to us, distinct in the soft night air:

Abd el Hai has a daughter
She is not black nor white
But red like the sun
Strangers think her a boy
A young girl, red like the sun . . .
Give us your daughter, Abd el Hai
She will bring us your luck.

Obok, French Somali Coast,

November, 1929.

THE END

CPSIA information can be obtained at www.ICGtesting.com
Printed in the USA
BVOW02s0226250116

434128BV00038B/585/P